Modernism and the
Architecture of Private Life

Gender and Culture

Gender and Culture   A series of Columbia University Press
Carolyn G. Heilbrun (1926–2003) and Nancy K. Miller, Founding Editors

In Dora's Case: Freud, Hysteria, Feminism
Edited by Charles Bernheimer and Claire Kahane
Breaking the Chain: Women, Theory, and French Realist Fiction
Naomi Schor
Between Men: English Literature and Male Homosocial Desire
Eve Kosofsky Sedgwick
Romantic Imprisonment: Women and Other Glorified Outcasts
Nina Auerbach
The Poetics of Gender
Edited by Nancy K. Miller
Reading Woman: Essays in Feminist Criticism
Mary Jacobus
Honey-Mad Women: Emancipatory Strategies in Women's Writing
Patricia Yaeger
Subject to Change: Reading Feminist Writing
Nancy K. Miller
Thinking Through the Body
Jane Gallop
Gender and the Politics of History
Joan Wallach Scott
The Dialogic and Difference: "An/Other Woman" in Virginia Woolf and Christa Wolf
Anne Herrmann
Plotting Women: Gender and Representation in Mexico
Jean Franco
Inspiriting Influences: Tradition, Revision, and Afro-American Women's Novels
Michael Awkward
Hamlet's Mother and Other Women
Carolyn G. Heilbrun
Rape and Representation
Edited by Lynn A. Higgins and Brenda R. Silver
Shifting Scenes: Interviews on Women, Writing, and Politics in Post-68 France
Edited by Alice A. Jardine and Anne M. Menke
Tender Geographies: Women and the Origins of the Novel in France
Joan DeJean
Unbecoming Women: British Women Writers and the Novel of Development
Susan Fraiman
The Apparitional Lesbian: Female Homosexuality and Modern Culture
Terry Castle
George Sand and Idealism
Naomi Schor

Becoming a Heroine: Reading About Women in Novels
Rachel M. Brownstein
Nomadic Subjects: Embodiment and Sexual Difference in Contemporary Feminist Theory
Rosi Braidotti
Engaging with Irigaray: Feminist Philosophy and Modern European Thought
Edited by Carolyn Burke, Naomi Schor, and Margaret Whitford
Second Skins: The Body Narratives of Transsexuality
Jay Prosser
A Certain Age: Reflecting on Menopause
Edited by Joanna Goldsworthy
Mothers in Law: Feminist Theory and the Legal Regulation of Motherhood
Edited by Martha Albertson Fineman and Isabelle Karpin
Critical Condition: Feminism at the Turn of the Century
Susan Gubar
Feminist Consequences: Theory for the New Century
Edited by Elisabeth Bronfen and Misha Kavka
Simone de Beauvoir, Philosophy, and Feminism
Nancy Bauer
Pursuing Privacy in Cold War America
Deborah Nelson
But Enough About Me: Why We Read Other People's Lives
Nancy K. Miller
Palatable Poison: Critical Perspectives on The Well of Loneliness
Edited by Laura Doan and Jay Prosser
Cool Men and the Second Sex
Susan Fraiman
Virginia Woolf and the Bloomsbury Avant-Garde: War, Civilization, Modernity
Christine Froula

Gender and Culture Readers

Modern Feminisms: Political, Literary, Cultural
Edited by Maggie Humm
Feminism and Sexuality: A Reader
Edited by Stevi Jackson and Sue Scott
Writing on the Body: Female Embodiment and Feminist Theory
Edited by Katie Conboy, Nadia Medina, and Sarah Stanbury

Modernism and the
Architecture of Private Life

Victoria Rosner

 Columbia University Press   New York

Columbia University Press
Publishers Since 1893
New York   Chichester, West Sussex
Copyright © 2005 Columbia University Press
All rights reserved

Library of Congress Cataloging-in-Publication Data

Rosner, Victoria.
    Modernism and the architecture of private life / Victoria Rosner.
        p. cm. — (Gender and culture)
    Includes bibliographical references and index.
    ISBN 0–231–13304–9 (acid-free paper) — ISBN 0–231–50787–9 (electronic)
    1. English fiction—20th century—History and criticism. 2. Architecture,
Domestic, in literature. 3. Woolf, Virginia, 1882–1941—Knowledge—
Architecture. 4. Modernism (Literature—Great Britain. 5. Space (Architec-
ture) in literature. 6. Personal space in literature. 7. Dwellings in literature.
8. Sex role in literature. 9. Privacy in literature. 10. Home in literature.
I. Title. II. Series.
    PR888.A7R67   2004
    823'.9109357—dc22   2004058289

Columbia University Press books are printed on permanent and durable
acid-free paper.
Printed in the United States of America
c 10 9 8 7 6 5 4 3 2 1

For NKM

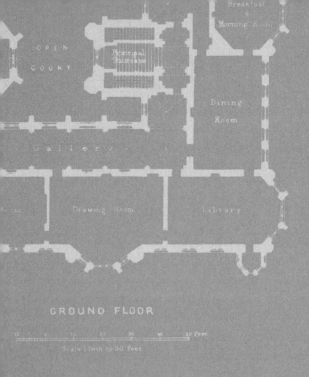

Contents

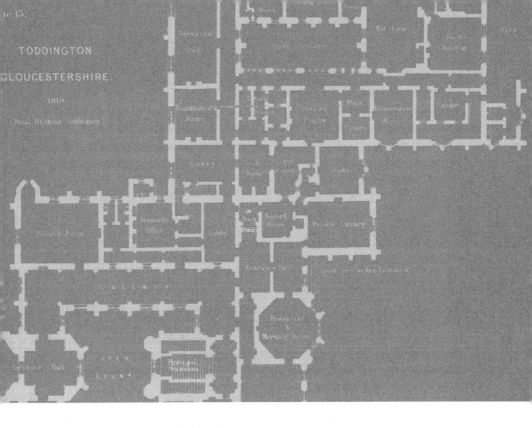

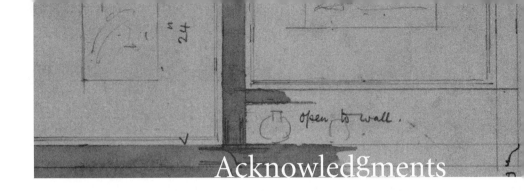

Acknowledgments

An interdisciplinary book depends even more than is usual on the collaboration of willing and talented individuals. I have benefited tremendously from the guidance and benevolence of a number of colleagues, mentors, experts, and assorted playmates: Siraj Ahmed, Tony Bradshaw, Anna Brickhouse, Kimberly Brown, Anke Finger, Richard and Susanna Finnell, Susan Stanford Friedman, Judith Kegan Gardiner, David Kastan, Mick Kidd, Jerome Loving, Carla Mazzio, D. A. Miller, Elizabeth Moore, Rob Nixon, Mary Ann O'Farrell, Jay Prosser, Teri Reynolds, Sally Robinson, Miranda Sherwin, Richard Shone, Susan Weber Soros, and Tom Staley. Personal as well as intellectual support made my work possible. I am grateful to my parents, Claire and Felix Pflaster, and Karen and Bill Rosner, and my brothers, Eric Birnbaum and David Rosner, for their patience ("isn't it done yet?"), for their encouragement ("you would make a great TV newscaster"), for sometimes taking me away from my work so I could return to it renewed ("come to New York!"), and most of all, for their boundless love.

Several individuals read large sections of the manuscript and, unbelievably enough, in many cases the entire work. The conversations I shared with them were rewards in themselves, providing the intellectual exchange that sustains my work—and sometimes the hand-holding that makes it feasible. They gave abundantly of their time and their extraordinary talents, and this book was immeasurably enriched by their good counsel. Sarah Cole offered astute suggestions that helped reshape the entire project, and she understood that some-times it helps to be a little drunk when you talk about your book. Laura Frost was there every step of the way, contributing her characteristic intelligence, rigor, and wit to every page, as well as the dirty pleasures of instant feedback. Martin Hutner brought me into the world of Whistler studies with generosity, grace, and tremendous learning and did his best not to blush at my ignorance. Since this project's inception I have called upon Mary McLeod's rich and extensive knowledge of nineteenth- and twentieth-century architecture and design, and she invariably responds with limitless intellectual largesse and a thousand new references. Deborah Nelson's capacious mind and ability to see the big picture made her an invaluable interlocutor—along with the stamina that allows her to talk on the phone for over two hours without fainting.

I wish to thank all the museums, libraries, and archives that welcomed me and enabled my research: Avery Library at Columbia University, the Berg Col-lection of the New York Public Library, The British Library, Charleston Farm-house, Courtauld Institute and Galleries, Freer Gallery of Art, Harry Ransom Humanities Research Center, The Huntington Library, Kensington Central Library, King's College Archives, Princeton Rare Books Library, RIBA Library, Tate Gallery Archives, University of Sussex Archives, and the Victoria and Albert Museum. Certain individuals at these institutions went far out of their way to share their knowledge with me, to tutor me in art and design history, and to lead me along the path of discovery. Special thanks to Gabriel Austin, Sally Brown, Sorrel Hershberg, Kenneth Myers, Charles Newton, and Susan Scott. Thanks to Henrietta Garnett for her kind permission to reprint certain images. I am very grateful to Jennifer Crewe, Liz Cosgrove, and all the others at Columbia University Press who helped produce this book. The anonymous readers supplied by the press made many valuable suggestions.

I wish to acknowledge the institutions that provided financial support for this project: the Graham Foundation for Advanced Studies in the Fine Arts, and the Harry Ransom Humanities Research Center. At Texas A&M University, I ben-efited from the support of the Department of English, the College of Liberal Arts, the Glasscock Center for Humanities Research, and the Women's Studies Program. My department head, J. Lawrence Mitchell, provided sage advice about the profession and unstinting support. I am further indebted to the stu-dents who provided assistance with research: Paige Brundidge, Erin Fleming, Seung-a Ji, and Amanda Reed.

I first began to study modernism in earnest in the late Carolyn G. Heilbrun's classroom, the best place imaginable. I still hear her voice in my head when I write, probing, questioning, and clarifying, and I hope I always will. Her bottomless knowledge of Bloomsbury fed my own on many occasions and her healthy cynicism kept my eyes open.

Douglas Brooks read every word of this manuscript several times, and his patience and enthusiasm never failed. Further, he provided gourmet home cooking that sustained the author when the voice of the muse was faint. Our collaboration renews my spirit on a daily basis.

This book is dedicated to Nancy K. Miller. For more than ten years, it has been my great good fortune to have her as my intellectual hero, my inspiring mentor, and my remarkable friend. She has taught me to be ambitious about what academic writing can achieve, to write in my own voice, and to get out of my own way. Her acuity, humor, insight, and judgment have enriched this work at every stage.

Modernism and the
Architecture of Private Life

1. Kitchen Table Modernism

"Quite like old times," the room says. "Yes? No?"
There are two beds, a big one for madame and a smaller one on the opposite side for monsieur. The wash-basin is shut off by a curtain. It is a large
room, the smell of cheap hotels faint, almost imperceptible. The street
outside is narrow, cobble-stoned, going sharply uphill and ending in a
flight of steps. What they call an impasse.
—Jean Rhys, *Good Morning, Midnight* (1939)

"Yes? No?" No. The opening lines of *Good Morning, Midnight* (1939) capture what seemed so wrong with the forms of private life in the first part of the twentieth century. Rootless and solitary, protagonist Sasha Jensen passes her time in a fruitless search for rooms. Rooms speak to her, tell her in suggestive tones what they're about. This particular room, like so many, is all about "old times." It keeps male and female as far apart as possible, defining them through opposition. The room recommends marriage to its occupants, dubbed "madame" and "monsieur." Madame's larger bed, presumably intended to accommodate monsieur should he choose to pay a nocturnal visit, announces the sexual ground rules of this space. The sanitary facilities have yet to migrate to a separate room and are cordoned off by a curtain, a divider that invokes the impropriety of the body by hiding away its ablutions even in the intimate environs of the bedroom.[1]

For Sasha Jensen, the verdict on this kind of room is mutely upheld by the street outside, a narrow alley that arcs and cuts off in a dead end. Sasha warns the reader later of the latent power in the rooms she inspects: "Never tell the truth about this business of rooms, because it would bust the roof off everything and undermine the whole social system."[2] An anonymous room may wield more influence than appearances suggest. Like many texts of its time, *Good Morning, Midnight* reflects a deep understanding of the values and hierarchies implicit in the design of living spaces. Sasha cannot alter the rooms that present themselves; all she can do is continue the house hunt. Rhys's talking room is as droll as Sasha is earnest. The room mocks her, attesting to the vigor of a tradition Sasha seems able to refuse but not remake. Yet she keeps up this disappointing dialogue with rooms throughout the novel. Rooms won't give her anything but old times, so why does she keep asking for something new? Maybe because she wants it so badly, or maybe because she hopes against hope that her desire can bring its fantasized object to life.

Many British modernist writers focused their attention on the structure and function of domestic spaces and found little to praise. "My house is a decayed house," complains the speaker in T. S. Eliot's "Gerontion," charging the Victorian home of lingering past its time. In modernist texts whatever smacks of the radical—transgressive sexuality, feminism, or the spirit of the avant-garde—is either accommodated with difficulty by the domestic or simply shunted outdoors. Influenced by new trends in British design, many writers sought to undermine and even reconstruct the form of the home in order to redefine its purpose and meaning. Yet as Sasha's example demonstrates, though old-fashioned rooms are unsatisfying, they can be hard to think beyond and hard to leave behind. The talking room she encounters offers a representative display of the powerful or magical qualities that attach to domestic spaces, qualities that can alter or derail plans for renovation or redesign.

This book proposes that the spaces of private life are a generative site for literary modernism. These spaces compose a kind of grid of social relations that shifts and slips, often upending the individuals who traverse it. Modernist spatial poetics are attuned to architectural dynamics of privacy and exposure, spatial hierarchies demarcating class, the locations and routines surrounding the care of the body, and the gendering of space. But if literary modernism is explicitly preoccupied with the structure of private life, it is also shaped by the discourse of space in more subtle ways. The modernist novel draws a conceptual vocabulary from the lexicons of domestic architecture and interior design, elaborating a notion of psychic interiority, to take one example, that rests on specific ideas about architectural interiors. Uncovering such discursive connections makes possible a kind of material genealogy of some of literary modernism's apparently autonomous elements. It acknowledges the role of literature in the work of imagining a post-Victorian reorganization of private life to accord with changing social customs. Further, and perhaps most unsettling, it exposes the fundamental role of the built environment in creating the categories we use to organize and understand who we are. In *Good*

Morning, Midnight, it might be said, Sasha searches for a room of her own, never fully realizing that she is already owned by the rooms she encounters.

◤ ◤ ◤

"On or about December 1910 human character changed," wrote Virginia Woolf. Surely not. Yet something inward, something personal, something significant did seem to be altering in the early years of the twentieth century. "All human relations have shifted," Woolf continued. She laid her emphasis on relations specific to private life: those "between masters and servants, husbands and wives, parents and children."[3] Woolf felt that the organization and customs of daily life were changing, if not in a fashion readily ascribed to any given individual then certainly in one measurable in its impact on the home. The peace and stability of the Victorian household deteriorated, deformed by the pressure of changing social, sexual, and cultural mores. What took its place was a far more provisional, more embodied, more unstructured kind of private life—the kind of life we still call "modern." The story of this metamorphosis is my subject. It is a story that can only be told through a dual focus on human relations and the intimate spaces that contain them.

Woolf might have based her claim for the signal importance of 1910 on numerous public artistic, social, and political events: the publication of E. M. Forster's *Howards End*, unrest in Ireland, the controversial second Post-Impressionist exhibition, the renewed clamor for women's suffrage, and more.[4] But rather than ground her claim in any of these events, she pointed to the kitchen table:

> In life one can see the change, if I may use a homely illustration, in the character of one's cook. The Victorian cook lived like a leviathan in the lower depths, formidable, silent, obscure, inscrutable; the Georgian cook is a creature of sunshine and fresh air; in and out of the drawing room, now to borrow the *Daily Herald*, now to ask advice about a hat. Do you ask for more solemn instances of the power of the human race to change?[5]

Woolf's class-bound assumption—that her readers would all have cooks and that none of her readers might *be* cooks—is irritating. Less retrograde and more surprising is her decision to locate the origins of modernism in the kitchen's homely environs. Many critics do seem to ask for "more solemn instances," and when tracing the impact of modernity they bypass the kitchen table in favor of other locations more traditionally sanctified by the avant-garde: the street, the café, and the gallery, among others. Yet Woolf hews to her choice, for the next piece of evidence she provides remains on the same homely terrain: "Consider the married life of the Carlyles, and bewail the waste, the futility, for him and for her, of the horrible domestic tradition which made it seemly for a woman of genius to spend her time chasing beetles, scouring saucepans, instead of writing books."[6]

If Victorian society dictated that Jane Carlyle commit herself to kitchen duties, by about 1910 she might have respectably abandoned that sphere in favor of a writer's study. After 1910 human beings were different, says Woolf, and modernist literature both responds to and produces that difference. But what has that to do with kitchen tables?

Take another Woolfian kitchen table, this one imaginary and found in her novel *To the Lighthouse*. The novel concerns the Ramsays, a British family vacationing in the Hebrides and their guests, one of whom is Lily Briscoe, an unmarried woman artist. Mr. Ramsay is a philosopher and Lily seeks an explanation of his work, which one of the sons provides: "Think of a kitchen table . . . when you're not there."[7] Lily is indeed not there; she is not at the kitchen table because she has neither a husband nor children. The novel stresses that her decision to pursue her creative work entails abandoning domestic responsibilities. If Mr. Ramsay's phenomenological credo stands for the solidity and independence of things apart from persons, Lily's aesthetic program is somewhat different.[8] Her technique is abstract, though she works from life; in her painting, the reality of objects dissolves into the vision the artist imposes on the model. As she puts it, "A mother and child might be reduced to a shadow without irreverence."[9] The sacred center of the Victorian household can be dislodged by the modernist artist, converted into a formalist statement. Lily's painting stands in for Woolf's novel, itself a modernist work that tells the story of the displacement of traditional family structures like the Ramsays'. For Woolf, the kitchen table represents not what the modernist artist must discard but what she must transform into the basis of her work. Christopher Reed writes that the "standard of modern art [has been] a heroic odyssey on the high seas of consciousness, with no time to spare for the mundane details of home life and housekeeping."[10] If modernism and the domestic have often seemed like antithetical categories, Woolf weaves them together as she locates modernism's origins squarely in the spaces of private life.

Private life is an amorphous category that changes over time. Antoine Prost notes: "The boundaries of private life are not laid down for once and for all; the division of human activity between public and private spheres is subject to change."[11] I use the term "private life" broadly and flexibly in this book, as I think it must be used, encompassing issues such as the physical setting of the home, the social network of family relations, the routines of the household, and the habits of the body. My focus will be on the domestic sphere, the physical location that Hannah Arendt describes as central to private life: "the four walls of one's private property offer the only reliable hiding place from the common public world, not only from everything that goes on in it but also from its very publicity, from being seen and being heard."[12] The walls of the home proffer an umbrella of privacy, an apparent ability to retreat from the general gaze, but as we shall see, the home does not proffer its protection equally to all household members, nor does its protection invariably extend autonomy to those who dwell within its doors. The home is not often conceived as a progressive site. Yet for Woolf, as for many others, the home was seen as a kind of laboratory for social experimentation. Woolf was also joined by many of her contemporaries in her view of how literary modernism could participate in key changes in the conduct and organization of British private life. The anecdotal history of modernism is strewn with evidence of this involvement, from Lytton Strachey uttering the word "semen" aloud in the drawing room, seemingly for the first time in English history; to James Joyce's representation of Bloom on the toilet; to Natalie Barney's lesbian expatriate salon in her own home on Paris's Left Bank; to Woolf's famous claim to a room of her own on behalf of all women writers. All these moments are flavored with bravura. They are flourishes designed to call attention, provoke controversy, and signal an unwillingness to carry on with things as usual. They are rebellions located in that most sacred and custom-bound site, the home.

Vanessa Bell's granddaughter Virginia Nicholson has recently described the writers and artists of pre–World War II England as "Bohemians," a "tiny, avant-garde minority . . . set . . . apart from the vast mass of conventional British people."[13] Such a characterization overlooks the broader influence sought by British writers and artists who proselytized directly and indirectly to the general public on the need to reform the home. In his widely publicized 1882 lecture tour of America, Oscar Wilde addressed remarks on the reform of home decoration to a variety of audiences, including Colorado coal miners. Wyndham Lewis's short-lived Rebel Art Centre produced fiercely avant-garde applied arts to sell to the public, and Lewis himself undertook commissions in interior design. Roger Fry published widely on the need for British design reform.

Though much of the British public had neither the desire nor the resources to make dramatic alterations in their domestic arrangements, by the end of the nineteenth century the Victorian home was being subjected to a critical examination. The drive for domestic reform had an origin in the design agendas of William Morris and John Ruskin, but it is also possible to trace a literary genealogy of domestic reform with roots in the early feminism of the New Woman novel. Beginning in the 1880s and 1890s, novelists asserted the New Woman's incompatibility with Victorian domesticity and often refused the form of the marriage plot.[14] The heroines of these novels sought to create unconventional households, and they disdained traditional marriages. For example, in Thomas Hardy's novel *A Laodicean* (1881), the aptly named Paula Power is the orphaned daughter of an industrialist, "a personification of the modern spirit, who had been dropped, like a seed from the bill of a bird, into a chink of mediaevalism."[15] When the story opens, she has inherited an ancient and crumbling castle where she installs telegraph wires and a gymnasium to accommodate her modern needs.[16] The impoverished aristocrat whose family sold the castle seeks an alliance with Paula, but she ends up with the architect who renovates the castle, a task he accomplishes by annexing the old ruins "as a curiousity" and building a modern house by their side. If a conventional happy ending would have used a marriage to ally the new industrial wealth with the old landed aristocracy, Paula's interest in an architect who is neither her social nor her financial equal turns her away from convention and toward modernity. Paula does marry, but she marries a man whose only qualification is his ability to build, as Paula puts it on the last page, "a new house . . . [to] show the modern spirit for evermore!"[17]

A Laodicean was not the only novel to represent the home as a problem the New Woman had to resolve. Paula Power marries an architect who will help her build a future, but others lacked either her pluck or her resources. In George Gissing's *The Odd Women* (1893), Monica Widdowson flees the home of her doltish husband and attempts unsuccessfully to gain the scandalous protection of her lover's flat: "She knocked at her lover's door, and stood longing, praying, that it might open. But it did not."[18] Unable to gain admission, she returns to her husband, becomes pregnant, and dies shortly after giving birth. Similarly, in Hardy's later *Jude the Obscure* (1895), Sue Bridehead wanders from one rooming house to another, unable to find accommodation because of the unconventional nature of her family. And in Grant Allen's 1895 best-seller *The Woman Who Did*, Herminia Barton is finally driven to suicide by her inability to provide an acceptable home from which to marry off her illegitimate daughter. Like New Woman writers, female aesthetes sought to reshape the home to better accord with women's changing sense of self. Rosamund Marriott Watson's work on interior design, *The Art of the House* (1897), writes Talia Schaffer, represents the home as a place that "must be redefined as women's identity changes."[19]

These stories intimate the kind of pressures on conventional British domesticity during the late nineteenth century.[20] The basic constitution of the household community was revised: over the course of a few decades the birth rate among married couples was cut almost in half; at the same time the servant class declined rapidly. A middle-class family employed one or two servants, not more.[21] Household guides and etiquette books proliferated and advised women about how to cope with these changes. Design reformers, inspired by Ruskin, criticized—though not always with popular agreement—the heaviness and excessive eclecticism of the Victorian interior and promoted more unified designs with less ornament and more emphasis on craftsmanship. The gradual introduction of indoor plumbing wrought important changes in housekeeping and personal hygiene; eventually electricity started to find its way into the home, powering not only brighter lights but labor-saving devices like vacuum cleaners and washing machines.[22] Woolf was thrilled when the royalties from *Mrs. Dalloway* allowed her to provide her Sussex home, Monk's House, with its first indoor facilities in the form of two lavatories and a bathroom. Mr. Ramsay's kitchen table might have looked more or less the same, but many things around it had changed.[23]

For all the ambition of reformers like William Morris to change the look of the average British home, movements like the Arts and Crafts never penetrated far beyond the provinces of the avant-garde. Given the distance that Woolf and her fellow writers claimed to have traveled from their Victorian predecessors, it is perhaps surprising that the British home in some ways changed so little in appearance and organization in the early years of the twentieth century. It is not easy to tell the history of something that did not happen, but looking around America and Europe, where designers like Frank Lloyd Wright and Le Corbusier and groups like the Bauhaus and the Wiener Werkstatte were dedicated to a total restatement of the problem of the house, England offers very little by way of comparison. Richard Weston notes: "Nowhere offered a more daunting challenge to Modernism than Great Britain. In the 1920s 'taste' was still thought to have ended in the late eighteenth century, and 'modern' meant a contemporary reproduction of antique furniture."[24] Unlike the Victorians, whose country house architecture represented a physical embodiment of "proper" social organization, modern British middle- and upper-class private life lacked an architecture to house and give shape to its values and hierarchies. The novel offered a space for the reinvention of private life, dramatizing the defects of the Victorian domestic sphere and sometimes articulating fantasized alternatives.

From the late nineteenth century on, many novels portray how Victorian spaces could limit personal ambition and dramatize how individuals were constrained by hierarchical and compartmentalized Victorian spaces. Birkin, a character in D. H. Lawrence's *Women in Love* (1920), despises the oppressive life of Breadalby, a Georgian country house, and is so beset by the behavior of its mistress, Hermione, that he runs out of the house into the woods, tears off his clothes, and rolls in the leaves and nettles. Aldous Huxley's *Crome Yellow* (1921) is set in a country house built to put into practice its owner's conviction that the "base and brutish" functions of the body should be housed as close to heaven as possible to obviate their degrading nature.[25] In Radclyffe Hall's *The Well of Loneliness* (1928), the main character is evicted from her family's ancestral country house because her ambiguous gender identity does not fit with the home's strict division between male and female zones.[26] In Mervyn Peake's *Titus Groan* (1946), the first part of his Gormenghast trilogy, the house is by far the most important character in the work, directing the fates of all the characters. And in Doris Lessing's first novel, *The Grass Is Singing* (1950), the main character develops a disabling claustrophobia as a result of her confinement to the home.[27] These works and others evince an involvement with the social and architectural history of the home that straddles the intersection of domestic space and gender boundaries.[28]

Spatial arrangements are influential in many modernist texts, yet the confluences between architectural history and modernist literature have gone largely unremarked by critics. Recently, however, scholars of British literature have begun to take an interest in the relationship between architecture and literature in the nineteenth century.[29] Judith Chase and Michael Levenson's work has provided a suggestive account of how architecture underwrote Victorian notions of privacy and family life; as they argue, "The ambitions of the midcentury family, its longing for privacy and its fear of exposure, were not only enacted through image, idea, and emotion; they were performed in rooms, among objects, near streets. . . . Victorian domesticity was as much a spatial as an affective obsession."[30] Similarly, Sharon Marcus has observed that nineteenth-century stories of haunted houses gesture to a failed domesticity, transmuting into myth anxieties that could not be aired in a more realistic tale.[31] The sacralization and safeguarding of idealized Victorian homes underscores the protected status enjoyed by these domestic spaces. The hallowed aura around the nineteenth-century home may help to explain why it was so slow to change, and highlights the irreverence of the modern writers and artists who denounced it.

Although International Style modernism was slow to emerge in England, the problem of interior design was more fully addressed. As Raymond Williams notes, the early nineteenth century produced the idea that "aesthetic, moral and social judgments are closely interrelated."[32] This idea is closely associated in its early form with the architect A. W. Pugin, who saw a strong connection between the art of a society and its values. Following the Great Exhibition in 1851 and the subsequent foundation of the Victoria and Albert Museum the following year, more artists took an interest in the question of design and worked to educate the taste of the public. Designer William Morris styled himself as a social reformer guiding the populace toward a better way of life through good design. British design of the early twentieth century eschewed the International Style (or, as architect John Gloag dubbed it, "robot modernism") in favor of a crafts-based aesthetic with a simplified use of line, stress on individuality, and maverick experimentalism. It was interior design—and not architecture—that articulated a visual and spatial vocabulary for describing the changing nature of private life. As the canons of morality and behavior shifted, the designed environment of the home both reflected and helped give shape to what Woolf describes as the new tone of "human relations"—"between masters and servants, husbands and wives, parents and children." British design reform constituted a spatial counterpart to the human reforms identified by Woolf.

The decorative arts represent a self-contained specialization today, but it is striking to consider how many well-known visual artists in late-nineteenth- and early-twentieth-century England also worked in design, seeing in it a natural extension of their aesthetic goals. Many artists trained in the fine arts moved into different aspects of design—including well-known figures such as Vanessa Bell, Edward Burne-Jones, Frederick Etchells, Roger Fry, Eric Gill, Duncan Grant, Nina Hamnett, Wyndham Lewis, Paul Nash, and Edward Wadsworth. Nash predicted in 1932 that "the professional artist of the future would be a professional designer" because it was the duty of the artist to help remake the home.[33] The notion that artists had a responsibility to shape the taste of the middle class and bring the traditional British home into the modern era was surprisingly widespread. It was also hardly limited to England. In Germany, Walter Gropius charged the Bauhaus school, which he founded in 1919, with the fusion of "art and technics." Belgian artist Henry Van de Velde, one of the originators of the Art Nouveau style, had given up painting entirely by 1892, preferring to work at fusing the aesthetic with the practical.[34] As nearby as Scotland, at the Glasgow School, Charles Rennie Mackintosh and the Mac-Donald sisters were combining art and design in creative ways. Fry, the preeminent British art critic, taught himself textile, furniture, and pottery design and believed artists could work "with the object of allowing free play to the delight in creation in the making of objects for common life."[35] Fry was one of the founders of the Omega Workshops, a design collective active between 1913 and 1919 that translated the Post-Impressionist style into home furnishings. Artists at the Omega painted large-scale murals, made and decorated pottery and furniture, designed rugs and other textiles, and scandalized the British press, which found their work threatening and borderline obscene. Nor was the Omega unique in its quest for an interarts aesthetic that would transform the objects of everyday life and redound on the nature of private life itself. The Omega, following the example of the Arts and Crafts, as well as Art Nouveau, was one of many societies of architects, designers, and fine artists interested in pursuing the cause of good design. This confluence of interarts dialogue, interior design, and social reform was characteristic of a number of design societies active in England from the fin-de-siècle through World War II, including the Art Workers' Guild (founded 1884), the Arts and Crafts Exhibition Society (1888), the Rebel Arts Centre (1914), the Design and Industries Association (1915), and the Society of Industrial Artists (1930).[36]

The membership of these societies comprised both artists and designers; in addition, many prominent British writers had ties to one or more of these groups. So many of the writers who now make up the canon of British literary modernism were connected with groups of artists and designers who were seeking to reimagine the British home. Besides Woolf, a partial list would include Cecil Beaton, Clive Bell, Noel Coward, Ford Madox Ford, E. M. Forster, David Garnett, Thomas Hardy, Aldous Huxley, Wyndham Lewis, Mina Loy, Bernard Shaw, Lytton Strachey, H. G. Wells, and Oscar Wilde and would also include American expatriates such as Natalie Barney, Henry James, and Ezra Pound. A number of these writers dabbled in design themselves: Loy designed lampshades, Lewis designed furniture, Hardy worked as an architect. Other writers materially supported avant-garde designers: Shaw was a patron of the Omega, Leonard and Virginia Woolf's homes were liberally furnished with the Omega's output, and even Arnold Bennett, who came to such grief in "Mr. Bennett and Mrs. Brown," placed orders with the Omega. Others, including Huxley and Evelyn Waugh, wrote architectural journalism. Still others were exposed to recent design innovations by spending time at homes like Charleston, the Sussex home of Bell and Grant, who were co-founders of the

Omega and who slowly covered every available surface in their home with colorful Post-Impressionist designs. Lewis worked at the Omega when it first
opened and then went on to form the Rebel Arts Centre, undertaking the
design of Vorticist interiors, including the redecoration of Ford Madox Ford's
study. Sometimes, the connections point in many directions at once. Fredrick
Etchells, a painter who worked at both the Omega Workshops and the Rebel
Art Centre, also translated Le Corbusier's books into English.

As these examples suggest, the story of the aesthetic links between British
modernist writers and avant-garde interior designers is a rich and ongoing tale
that I can only partially tell here.[37] This book is also, in part, an influence study,
an examination of how modernist writers found inspiration in avant-garde
design. But neither of these projects constitutes my chief focus. Rather, I am
primarily interested in drawing on the history of personal, professional, and
thematic relationships between designers and writers as a way of calling attention to the interarts foundation of modernist literary aesthetics. Doing so, I
argue, yields a new understanding of what interiority means for modernist
writers. By "interiority" I refer to a cluster of interdependent concepts that
extend from the representation of consciousness to the reorganization of home
life; revised definitions of personal privacy, intimacy, and space; and new
assessments of the sexualized and gendered body. These categories not only
influence each other but also construe each other, holding modernist interiority in a tension between abstraction and materiality, between metaphor and literality. This definition is far broader and more permeable than the generally
accepted critical view of modernist interiority, which emphasizes the mind's
ability to craft an individual reality, to live in a world exclusively populated by
personal associations and memories. Astradur Eysteinsson more fully summa-
rizes this tendency among the moderns: "It seems that modernism is built on
highly subjectivist premises: by directing its attention so predominantly toward
individual or subjective experience, it elevates the ego in proportion to a dimin-
ishing awareness of objective or coherent outside reality."[38]

In some sense, then, this book seeks to dismantle a myth that literary modernism tells about itself: that consciousness is the writer's exclusive subject, that
reality is merely the phantasmagoric projection of interior life onto the outside
world. "Look within," Woolf urges the modernist writer in "Modern Fiction."
Marcel Proust avers that "it is only a clumsy and erroneous form of perception
which places everything in the object, when really everything is in the mind."[39]
It might be said that the imperial modernist mind seeks to live in a world
entirely of its own making. As critics, we can understand the modernist excess

of consciousness in many ways—as a reaction against realism, as an expression of hyper-individuality, as the basis for a new formalism, as a strategic retreat from the shock of reality, as symptom, as aestheticism, as play—but we cannot see it as literal or accurate. In order to fully understand the psychology of the modernist subject it must be allowed that interiority has spatial as well as cognitive dimensions. Recent work in modernist studies that places material culture and history in dialogue with aesthetic philosophy is already moving in this direction.[40]

In the chapters that follow, I trace the migration of certain ideas, motifs, and techniques among different art forms in late-nineteenth- and early-twentieth-century England and show how they find different but related expression in the fields of literature, art, interior design, and architecture. In the cases I describe, these fields share an aesthetic vocabulary, cross-referencing each other as they work out what it means to be modern and to live in an unstable but exciting era of violence and rapid social change. Thus I examine, for instance, how the modernist literary notion of interiority is rooted in the design of the domestic interior, or how the history of the picture frame is told through Wilde's *The Picture of Dorian Gray*, or how the figure of the woman writer is authorized by Victorian architectural precepts. This study proposes that British modernist writers, together with artists, architects, and designers, were collectively engaged in a far-reaching and multilayered project to redefine the forms and meanings of middle-class private life.

With so much creative energy marshaled in the service of transforming the look of the British home, it should not be surprising that many writers identified this transformation as indispensable to the creation of a modern way of life. The changing nature of middle-class private life could be said to have found material expression in a radicalized program of interior design. This connection between design and domestic relations is staged repeatedly in modern British literature. Time and again in the modernist novel, the home undergoes a mysterious transformation that is material as well as spiritual and which yields new codes for behavior among families and intimate friends. In Henry James's *The Spoils of Poynton* (1897), also known as *The Old Things*, a houseful of precious antiques are fought over across the generations and finally destroyed, unable to survive the passage to modernity. In Forster's *Howards End* (1910), two sisters must redecorate a traditional English farmhouse in order to accommodate a very unconventional family. In Woolf's *To the Lighthouse* (1927), as a family is torn apart by the changing times, their home goes into concomitant decline.

If gender is now understood to be integral to modernist studies, domesticity remains, for many critics, the antithesis of modernism.[41] Christopher Reed has written that in art and architecture, "in the eyes of the avant-garde, being undomestic came to serve as a guarantee of being art."[42] With its origins thought to lie in urban culture and flânerie, modernism is widely considered an art of the public sphere. But like Reed, literary critics have recently begun to think through modernism's relationship to the domestic. Jessica Feldman characterizes domesticity as "an important artistic accomplishment" of both Victorian and modernist writers, whose work she sees as continuous.[43] Thomas Foster argues that works by modernist women writers "should be read as a transitional moment between nineteenth-century domestic ideologies and postmodern concepts of space."[44] For these critics, domesticity is central to modernism in terms of ideology, aesthetics, materiality, and gender.[45]

Certainly, the home has long possessed strong symbolic value in literature. But for many modernist writers the home had a richer significance: more than a backdrop or a symbol for family, the home departs from its Victorian identity as a repository of tradition to become a kind of workshop for interior design and social change. The writers included in this study sought to bring the spirit of the avant-garde into the staid environs of the home, to erode the physical and social divisions that structured the Victorian domestic sphere, and to find new artistic forms for representing intimacy and daily life. They criticized the gender- and class-based hierarchies of Victorian domesticity and the doctrine of separate spheres, and they offered proposals for a new domesticity—new both in its systematic reconfiguration of domestic space and in its redefinition of the nature and composition of a family. This work demonstrates that the spaces of private life were revitalized during the modern period and that modernist literature is broadly informed by—and indeed contributes to—the project of reconstructing the form, function, and meaning of the home to meet the demands of modernity. It might be said that at the very moments when modernist literature depicts itself as autonomous and sealed within psychological interiority, it is most reliant on the built environment of things, rooms, and spaces.

In *The Poetics of Space*, Gaston Bachelard made us aware that rooms, houses, and other intimate spaces are amenable to literary interpretation. But if for Bachelard spaces had archetypal significance, the writers I discuss depict space as a heterogeneous and differentiated category. To put it plainly, although Virginia Woolf grew up in the same house as Ellen Eldridge, Woolf, who was a daughter of the homeowners, and Eldridge, who was a housemaid, were affected by it in very different ways. Both were taught certain formative lessons about femininity, propriety, class, and duty. The question of how different spaces cast individuals in particular roles is one that critics have taken up with new force in recent years, a question that has been asked with particular urgency from the standpoint of gender. Indeed, over the last decade a substantial body of scholarship has looked at how space organizes gender and sexuality; this work, which has come from fields including architecture, design, geography, and urban planning, has made my study possible by offering bold and perceptive lessons in how to read the relationships among gender, sexuality, and architecture.[46] Two architectural critics have exerted an especially guiding influence on this project: Alice T. Friedman and Anthony Vidler. Friedman's *Women and the Making of the Modern House: A Social and Architectural History* sets out to probe the significance of the fact that many of the homes now considered the greatest achievements of the masculinist enterprise of modernist architecture were built for women clients, women who were the heads of their households. Friedman discerns a certain strategic alliance between a group of wealthy, adventurous women looking for new ways to live and a group of (mostly) male architects looking to revolutionize domestic architecture. She writes:

> The conviction shared by modern architects and their women clients [was] that the essence of modernity was the complete alteration of the home—its construction, materials, and interior spaces. . . . Not only did women commission avant-garde architects to provide them with houses in which to live out their visions of a new life, but these visions rested on a redefinition of domesticity that was fundamentally spatial and physical. A powerful fusion of feminism with the forces of change in architecture thus propelled these projects.[47]

No social institution is more closely tied to the construction and reproduction of gender and sexual identity than the home. Domestic architecture is thus key to understanding the history of gender and sexuality in the early twentieth century. Like Friedman, I see the dismantling of the traditional home as a modernist gesture that ineluctably and materially links feminism to modernism. I also hope to show how the dismantling of Victorian domesticity undid conventions of both femininity and masculinity as well as helped to bring to light sexual identities that deviated from the standard of the married couple.

If Friedman's vision is almost utopian, energized by the spirits of social and aesthetic reform, Vidler's view of modernist space is far more pathologized, invested in the phobias and neuroses that defined the modern condition.

Vidler weaves architecture together with psychoanalysis in order to better understand how subjects create and are created by space; he articulates a dynamic that is composed of "the complex exercise of projection and introjection in the process of inventing a paradigm of representation, an 'imago' of architecture, so to speak, that reverberates with all the problematics of a subject's own condition."[48] Architecture is startlingly personal in Vidler's account; space warps and twists to body forth the subject's interior life. This is not so different from Woolf's account of architecture as a kind of case study, a historical narrative that offers insight into an individual's mental processes. In her autobiographical text "A Sketch of the Past," Woolf reflects on her childhood bedroom and wonders what current visitors to the room (a boardinghouse at the time of her writing) might make of it and, by extension, of her and her work: "I suppose that, if one of them had read *To the Lighthouse*, or *A Room of One's Own*, or *The Common Reader*, he or she might say: "This room explains a great deal."[49] In a sense, this book fuses the methods of Woolf and Vidler, for I frequently read spaces and objects as symptoms, overdetermined in their meanings and painful to experience. Like the symptoms of hysteria, they sometimes substitute for inarticulable narratives: Woolf's childhood room mutely offers a story her memoir cannot tell. Literary modernism, in this way of thinking, seeks a means of representation that is determined by the need to repudiate its connection to the past, and modernist spaces become the key to retrieving that submerged connection even as they deny their own history.

Woolf is the guiding spirit of this study. No other major novelist of the period was so preoccupied with the critique of Victorian domesticity or so explicit about the relationship of literary modernism to the changing nature of private life. For this reason she stands at the center of any account of modernist literature that is organized around the radicalization of the domestic sphere. Woolf's interest in the domestic interior is evident to even a casual reader of her work, from the emphasis on personal space in *Jacob's Room* (1922) to the many-roomed ancestral estate at the center of *Orlando* (1928) to the detailed re-creation of her childhood home in *Moments of Being* (1985). But her interest was of a particular kind—she felt that the spaces of private life had a determining effect on their occupants and that, inversely, individuals could create new ways of living by making changes to those spaces. These beliefs were, of course, also at the heart of British design reform movements. For Woolf, the commitment to changing domestic interiors had particular importance for women, since women were socially identified with the home, responsible for its smooth functioning, and for all practical purposes largely confined to its environs. "Women," she writes in *A Room of One's Own*, "have sat indoors all these millions of years, so that by this time the very walls are permeated by their creative force."[50] And women, in Woolf's view, had the most to gain from a strategic redesign of the built environment. Thus, writing to an imaginary correspondent in *Three Guineas* who sought to build a college for women, she offered this advice:

> Let it be built on lines of its own. It must be built not of carved stone and stained glass, but of some cheap, easily combustible material which does not hoard dust and perpetrate traditions. Do not have chapels. Do not have museums and libraries with chained books and first editions under glass cases. Let the pictures and the books be new and always changing. Let it be decorated afresh by each generation with their own hands cheaply.[51]

In place of the Gothic style of the traditional university, which looks ancient the day it is built, Woolf proposes an institution which is counter-institutional in its willingness to see itself replaced and renovated by each succeeding generation of entering students. In place of respect for the past, she proposes excitement about the future. In place of tradition, she asks for originality. Flexibility, innovation, freshness, and a do-it-yourself spirit: these, together with an expressive use of color, were the values espoused by Woolf's peers, such as those who founded the Omega Workshops.

Looking back and forth between Woolf and the Omega requires a kind of exotropic vision—an interest in looking in several directions at once. Such a split interpretive practice must at once be alert to the differences between media such as painting and writing and also attuned to the synergies between these forms. The chapters of this study are organized according to such an exotropic scheme, each designated by a term that contains two histories, one a history of design and the other a history of modernist literary aesthetics. My intent is to accrete meaning around the title term of each chapter as it unfolds, to show how the two histories intertwine with each other, and, in particular, to expose the material basis of the putatively autonomous aesthetics of the modernist novel. The relationship of design to literature is, in my account, generally the relationship of abstract form to lived experience, a relationship activated by an energized conception of space that tears down walls and sets furniture flying.

I begin in the next chapter with the influential figure of Oscar Wilde, who throughout his career was associated with designers and artists seeking to bring beauty, taste, and simplicity to the Victorian home. The chapter "Frames" takes as its subject the frame that surrounds the eponymous picture in Oscar Wilde's *The Picture of Dorian Gray*. For the artists affiliated with aestheticism, the frame was the exemplary decorative object, the all-important link between the fine and applied arts, between the realm of art and that of ordinary existence. In the hands of Wilde and his friends, frame design changed more profoundly than ever before in its history. Frames are critical in *Dorian Gray*, creating and dissolving the borders between aesthetics and ethics, private and public, art and design. This chapter examines Wilde's role in British design reform and shows how he brought his theories of design to bear in his only novel, where changing notions about picture framing determine the shape and structure of the story.

Chapter 3, "Thresholds," is concerned with the writers and artists of the Bloomsbury Group. I examine memoirs by Lytton Strachey and Virginia Woolf in which these writers carefully anatomize the London homes of their childhoods. For both writers, home was a place of restriction, censorship, and physical filth, a place ineluctably linked to what they considered the equally antipathetic conventions of Victorian life-writing. Their "household memoirs," as I term them, reveal writers who work against the conventions of life-writing in the same way they resist the confinements physically imposed upon them by their surroundings. I argue that resistance to Victorian domestic practices and resistance to Victorian life-writing practices intertwine in these memoirs and that the threshold—the transition between rooms—is the ground of such resistance. By textually rebuilding and critiquing their childhood homes, Woolf and Strachey negatively delineate the contours of an alternative domesticity which forms the basis of their life-writing practice.

Chapter 4, "Studies," narrows the argument to a single room in the private house. Studies have been found in homes for hundreds of years, with a range of uses and users, but in late-nineteenth-century England the study came to be defined specifically as a private room devoted to the master of the house. The study offered a space for sanctioned professional work within the domestic sphere, a space that—were it not for its thoroughly masculine character—might seem tantalizingly proximate to the aspiring woman writer. In this chapter I trace the history of this space and, through readings of texts by Arthur Conan Doyle, Radclyffe Hall, and Woolf, ask what role the study plays in the construction of modernist female authorship. The texts I examine depict the study as the crucible of a masculinity that is linked to secrecy and authorship, even as they show how women attempt to usurp the study's privileges by prying masculinity away from biological maleness.

One defining feature of modernist narrative is its preoccupation with interiority. Rather than emphasize the well-described psychological aspects of modernist literary interiority, in the fifth chapter, "Interiors," I show how the genealogy of this term lies in the aesthetics of modernist art and design. Focusing again on the Bloomsbury Group, I trace commonalities between the fiction of Forster and Woolf and the designs of Roger Fry, Vanessa Bell, and Duncan Grant. I read domestic novels by Forster and Woolf in conjunction with designs by the artists of the Omega Workshop to show the symbiosis between these two forms and demonstrate how Bloomsbury's radical domesticity participated in the broad reassessment of interiority that is central to British literary modernism.

By way of excursus, let us consider the model nursery on view at the Omega Workshops and executed by a number of Omega artists but based on a room Vanessa Bell created for her children in her London home. The nursery, which is no longer extant, was simple but gay and lively, clearly inspired by the needs and preferences of real children. Its colorful murals were cut-out paper collages that anticipated a technique Henri Matisse would adapt years later (fig. 1).

Bell translated painterly practices into everyday life, aestheticizing the domestic. Yet the toy animals were not for display only, being fully jointed and posable. Bell's color scheme was lurid if not practical; yellow felt, for instance, was the floor covering. Richard Cork calls this mural an "unrepentant fantasy where children would immediately feel happy to let their imaginations roam at will."[52] Indeed, the abstract animals depicted in the mural seemed to invert the widespread criticism of Post-Impressionism that it resembled the artwork of children by giving these forms to children as an inspiration to their creativity. The notion of a child-centered nursery was a dubious proposition for reviewer P. G. Konody, who wrote in the *Observer*: "The whole room is gaudy with an effect like a piano-organ. These things are bound to delight the infant who can scribble on the wall in perfect harmony with the design. But is it ungrateful to suggest that to the weary adult who goes home after work and finds the children noisy enough without the encouragement of roofs and walls, they might, in time, become rather boring?"[53] The domestic interior, Konody implies, should subdue children, not encourage them. Under the influence of Post-Impressionism, the writer seems to fear, the home will become not a sphere dedicated to the needs of the male breadwinner ("the weary adult who goes home after work") but rather one that encourages self-expression among all family members. The *Daily Sketch* affirmed Konody's concern with its skeptical caption, "Would you let your child play in this nursery?"[54] More than just a

Figure 1. Vanessa Bell, Nursery, Omega Workshops, 1913. © 1961 Estate of Vanessa Bell, courtesy Henrietta Garnett and the Courtauld Institute of Art, University of London.

new kind of interior design—though it surely was that—Bell's room seemed to suggest a new way of thinking about the hierarchy of household life.

A literary companion to the "Post-Impressionist Nursery" can be found in Virginia Woolf's "Nurse Lugton's Curtain," a children's story written for Woolf's niece.[55] This short magical tale tells of a homely children's nurse sitting over her sewing. The curtain she sews seems to have been taken from the "Post-Impressionist Nursery," for it is covered with jungle animals. When the nurse dozes off over her work, the figures on the curtain come to life: "The animals with which [the curtain] was covered did not move till Nurse Lugton snored for the fifth time. . . . The antelope nodded to the zebra; the giraffe bit through the leaf on the tree top; all the animals began to toss and prance."[56] The scene is one of license and joy in contrast to the nursery's discipline. Nurse Lugton's usual strictness makes her brief nod an interlude of exultation in which the animals can express their natures: "The elephants drank; and the giraffes snipped off the leaves on the highest tulip trees; and the people who crossed the bridges threw bananas at them, and tossed pineapples up into the air. . . . Nobody harmed the lovely beasts; many pitied them. . . . For a great ogress had them in her toils, the people knew; and the great ogress was called Lugton."[57]

Like Bell's nursery, "Nurse Lugton's Curtain" imagines household objects as animate and possessed of narrative capacity. Just as the nursery seems like a room a child might design, "Nurse Lugton's Curtain" gives voice to the common childish fantasy that household objects can come to life. Just as the nursery's design suggests an overturning of domestic authority, "Nurse Lugton's Curtain" converts the room's décor into a tool to challenge the powers that govern the space. The very curtain that Nurse Lugton sews is plotting against her. This story prompts us to trace the themes of anarchy and rebellion in Bell's work. We can also read back in the other direction, from Bell's room to Woolf's story, for the nursery makes a dramatic case for the agency of the seemingly impassive material apparatus of domestic life and guides the reader to attend more closely to the dynamics of space in Woolf's writing.[58] The dour Nurse Lugton is a kind of model for the bad critic, whose oversight drains the life from aesthetic objects. Instead, in the pages that follow, I would like to emulate the sleeping nurse, whose nap sets the objects free to express their natures. My plan is to secretly keep one eye open in order to watch as rooms come alive and their contents begin to toss and prance.

2. Frames

Every artwork brings forth its own frame.
—Friedrich Schlegel

The picture of Dorian Gray changes throughout Oscar Wilde's famous novel, steadily deformed by Dorian's displaced career of sin and scandal. The picture appears in identical form only twice: at the beginning when it is newly finished and on the last page of the text, when Dorian is dead. It is similarly described on each occasion, first as "a wonderful work of art, and a wonderful likeness" and then as "a splendid portrait of [Dorian] . . . in all the wonder of his exquisite youth and beauty."[1] Yet there is a difference between the portrait we see first and the one we see at the last: the picture in the artist's studio is a plain canvas, while the one that witnesses Dorian's death is elaborately framed. Thus, while Dorian's portrait frames the novel, it also establishes an arc for the narrative, which moves from unframed to framed. This frame-work seems particularly significant in a novel that is not only about an artwork but also dramatizes the philosophy of aestheticism, that is, the conversion of life to art.

Though the frame is easily overlooked, and is sometimes designed to be overlooked, it is an important element of the work of art. In fact, the frame was at its most prominent in Wilde's time, when frame design changed more than it had in any era since frames were used for the first time by the ancient Egyptians. In the latter part of the nineteenth century, as Eva Mendgen writes, "the artist-framed work was a symbol for the rejuvenation of the arts as a whole."[2] Many painters designed their own frames, and the frame was an important area

21

for experimentation and change in the decorative arts. For the aesthetes, the picture frame was an exemplary decorative object, but it was more than that. It was a tangible link between the fine arts and the applied arts. The frame functions in both artistic registers, connecting the painting to the larger context of the house, even as the frame also divides the image it contains from that context. In the epigraph to this chapter, Friedrich Schlegel asserts that "Every artwork brings forth its own frame." It is also true that the frame brings forth the picture, both by calling attention to it and by helping to assign it to the sphere of art. The new frame designs prominent in Wilde's time were part of a larger design philosophy that minimized the boundary between the frame and the work of art and, more broadly, between art and decoration.

What exactly happens to a painting when it acquires a frame? To begin with, it becomes a decorative object as well as an artwork, ready to be integrated into a decorated interior. Though today we may esteem the artistic more than the decorative, for Wilde's circle the integration of the fine and applied arts was a central plank in the aesthetic platform. Decorative art had an elevated status in late-nineteenth-century England, in part because of proselytizing by Wilde and his contemporaries. The title of his novel describes a work of art, but when Wilde defended his story against charges of immorality leveled by the press, he did so with an appeal to the decorative. In a letter to the editor of the *Daily Chronicle*, Wilde wrote: "My story is an essay on decorative art. . . . It is poisonous if you like, but you cannot deny that it is also perfect, and perfection is what we artists aim at."[3] *The Picture of Dorian Gray* is filled with objects that are both poisonous and perfect, and the picture, entire with its frame, is one of them. Despite his many impressive collections, the ultimate decorative object in Dorian's home is his portrait, which expresses its owner's personality to an appalling extent, recording Dorian's increasing age and decrepitude while Dorian, more portrait-like than his portrait, remains unchanged from the moment the painting is completed. Far from wishing to diminish the significance of his novel by equating it with interior decoration, Wilde hoped thereby to elevate and transform it. To call it "an essay on decorative art" takes the novel out of the realm of morality and into that of aesthetics. In the same gesture, it takes decorative art out of the realm of mere ornament and makes it matter.

Reading *Dorian Gray* as an essay on decorative art means attending to the profound changes in the theory and practice of interior design under way in England in the latter part of the nineteenth century. Wilde was deeply involved in the design reform movement, which he described in "The Soul of Man Under Socialism."

Beautiful things began to be made, beautiful colours came from the dyer's hand, beautiful patterns from the artist's brain, and the use of beautiful things and their value and importance were set forth. The public was really very indignant. They lost their temper. They said silly things. No one minded. No one was a whit the worse. No one accepted the authority of public opinion. And now it is almost impossible to enter any modern house without seeing some recognition of good taste, some recognition of the value of lovely surroundings, some sign of appreciation of beauty. In fact, people's houses are, as a rule, quite charming nowadays. People have been to a very great extent civilised.[4]

The transformations Wilde describes were not ubiquitous, but they were appreciable. The major figures of design reform were both designers and writers—many of them personally known to Wilde. Though Wilde was no designer and few of the new reforms in interior decoration originated with him, he was widely identified with design reform, especially its aesthetic arm, and did much to disseminate the new ideas to the public. He was a figurehead for the aesthetic movement; more than anyone else, his dress, his opinions, and his personal style affected the public perception of the aesthetes and colored the movement's legacy. For the aesthetes, the house produced its owner as a work of art in his own right, a philosophy Wilde carried into his own home. The same can be said of Dorian Gray's relationship to his home, the décor of which plays an active part in the novel.

Charlotte Gere's recent work, *The House Beautiful: Oscar Wilde and the Aesthetic Interior* is the first to broach the topic of Wilde's relationship to the decorative arts and the great changes that took place in the English domestic interior during Wilde's lifetime. She characterizes Wilde as an "opportunist" and a "consummate propagandist" who "sensed the artistic climate and was quick to exploit areas outside his immediate literary horizons."[5] Wilde was pleased to encourage the cult of personality that sprang up around him even before most of his literary works were published, and many of the ideas he carried to America in his famous 1882 lecture tour that introduced America to the aesthetic movement were drawn from the work of the artists, writers, designers and architects who were part of his London circle. But he also made more substantive contributions. A principle tenet of design reform lay in the unity of the arts. By weaving together poetry, handicraft, painting, and philosophy in his lectures, Wilde helped build this unity. Another core concept was the idea that the home, rather than modeling the latest fashion, should express the distinct personality of its occupant. With his idiosyncratic dress, affectations, and wit, Wilde embodied this celebration of individuality. To get at the meaning of the objects in *Dorian Gray*—to read the novel as an essay on decorative art—it is perhaps most useful to see Wilde both as an influential tastemaker and a disciple of the leading architects and designers of his time.

This chapter focuses on a moment in English history when interior design carries associations of social change, when it begins to partake of the spirit of reform. It is not by chance that Wilde creates a protagonist for whom design becomes an entire philosophy of life. Dorian has all the trappings of a gentleman on the *qui vive*—he is a dandy and an aesthete with a widely imitated sense of style. But in truth, he is a throwback whose atavism lies in his refusal to fully integrate his public life as a society figure with his private life, whose history is chronicled only in his secret portrait. Dorian's two lives, as I argue below, are continuous in reality. But he cherishes a fantasy that they are distinct, and he creates this distinction by sequestering the portrait in a locked room. Many aspects of the contemporary design scene find their way into Wilde's novel, but none is more consequential than a seemingly trivial change in the nature of picture frames, a change that in Wilde's novel sabotages Dorian's fantasy of leading two lives. Dorian relies on the picture frame to contain his private life, and though it fails to do so that failure can also be seen as a triumph of design. In the chapters that follow this one, the desire to expose hitherto concealed aspects of private life is seen as a staple of both modern literature and modern design. In *The Picture of Dorian Gray*, this exposure exacts a painful price on the protagonist, who, despite his up-to-date tastes in design, is not yet prepared to expose his private affairs to public scrutiny. Dorian is caught between two worlds, and the increasingly unwilling guardian of the portal between those worlds is the picture frame. This, then, is a paradox to rival any of Wilde's: as the frame collapses, its importance expands until, finally, dissolved into the picture it contains and the wall that contains it, the frame helps rewrite the relationship between aesthetics and morality at the fin-de-siècle.

"An essay on decorative art"

Political radicalism and interior design have a long history of interconnection in Britain, one that began in the mid-nineteenth century during the age of reform. The idea of a connection between good design and social and moral health found a strong exponent in the influential writings of John Ruskin, who offered a vision of a new medievalism in place of the corrupting influence of industrialization. In an 1859 lecture, Ruskin urged a deepened respect for the

workman, whom he felt had been starved out of all creativity by modern man-
ufacturing techniques:

> If you want to give [the workman] the power [to design], you must give
> him the materials, and put him in the circumstances for it. . . . Without
> observation and experience, no design; without peace and pleasurable-
> ness in occupation, no design; and all the lecturings, and teachings, and
> prizes, and principles of art in the world are of no use as long as you don't
> surround your men with happy influences and beautiful things.[6]

Workmen could hardly be expected to design beautiful objects for everyday use
if they had not been educated about the beauty of good design. But creating the
opportunity for such exposure required nothing less than the redistribution of
social resources, a radical project that went unfulfilled. Wilde echoed Ruskin's
sentiments many years later in his American lectures, when he argued for the
integration of art and design education into the American school curriculum.

For Victorian reformers like Ruskin, as well as for his student William Morris, design had to embody a social mission and contain social value. It had to
enrich the lives of those who lived with it. Design could include ornament, but
it was more than ornamental; it was a means to promote civil virtues and a
more just state, where all parts of society could live surrounded by beautiful
objects.[7] The movement's aesthetic reforms were interconnected with its moral
ones. As a bulwark against mass production, Morris urged a simpler, plainer
style of decoration and a return to an artisanal culture of craftsmanship. He
sought a strengthened relationship between form and function as an antidote
to the excesses of Victorian overdecoration: simple designs for a simple life.
Many Arts and Crafts designers looked for inspiration in the rhythms, details,
and values of the English countryside and the local materials found there. Morris's well-known textiles and wallpapers used botanical patterns to celebrate the
inherent simplicity and beauty of nature and the dignity of rural tradition. Arts
and Crafts was more than a style; it was a way of life.

Such ideals may well sound out of keeping with Wilde's urban sophistica-
tion and upper-class tastes. Though aestheticism was related to Arts and Crafts,
it eschewed the latter's social commitments. Each group sought reform, but for
different ends and by different means. As Sheridan Ford explained in 1889,
"There are in England to-day two new and in their origin distinct methods of
interior decoration. . . . These two methods may be termed the *Whistlerian*, and
the *English* or *Pre-Raphaelite*; the one spontaneous, fresh, simple—the other, a
revival, complex, reformatory."[8] Wilde favored the Whistlerian. His aestheti-

cism drew on familiar Arts and Crafts precepts, but with an unexpected twist. In his lecture on "The Decorative Arts," first delivered in Chicago in 1882, Wilde informed his audience that "the art I speak of will be a democratic art made by the hands of the people and for the benefit of the people," but he went on to label "the most practical advance in art in the last five years in England" the designs of his fellow students at Oxford—"men of position, taste, and high mental culture."[9] While Arts and Crafts advocated the use of simple, country materials, in "The House Beautiful" (itself a Paterian formulation), Wilde suggested, "there can be no nobler influence in a room than a marble Venus of Milo."[10] In the introduction to a book by Rennell Rodd published the same year Wilde gave his lectures, he was explicit about his divergence from Ruskin: "to us the rule of art is not the rule of morals."[11] Not art for the people's sake but art for art's sake was the aesthetic credo. And for the sake of art, Wilde advised his audiences, drawing on Morris, everything in the home should be useful or beautiful. As he predicted in his 1882 lecture on "The English Renaissance of Art," "in years to come there will be nothing in any man's house which has not given delight to its maker and does not give delight to its user. The children, like the children of Plato's perfect city, will grow up 'in a simple atmosphere of all fair things.' "[12]

This was a fairly eccentric proposition for some of Wilde's more rusticated listeners, and one of the interesting aspects of the message was its male messenger. Interior decoration and the care of the domestic were women's sphere in the nineteenth century, but the aesthetes as a group sought to claim this area of expertise for men. As Arts and Crafts designers argued for the value of craftsmanship and the domestic arts, men sought an expanded role in traditionally feminine areas. According to their design philosophy, the home could and should express the virility and taste of its owner. In *The Importance of Being Earnest*, Gwendolen opines, "The home seems to me to be the proper sphere for the man. And certainly once a man begins to neglect his domestic duties he becomes painfully effeminate, does he not? And I don't like that. It makes men so very attractive."[13] Gwendolen's spirited paradoxes turn British home life on its head and speak to the reversal of traditional gender roles that formed an important subtext for Wilde's design agenda. As Talia Schaffer argues:

> One of the most controversial aspects of male aestheticism was its appropriation of the female sphere, as male aesthetes increasingly claimed to be the authorities on home decoration, fashion design, cookery, and flowers. These male aesthetes insisted that women's work was an important

realm that deserved the intellectual effort, specialized training, and artistic skills that they could bring to the field. It was profoundly significant and possibly unprecedented in Western culture to exalt everyday female duties to high art.[14]

Dorian Gray is a fictional incarnation of the new male homemaker. While he has a full complement of servants to do the housework, his London home is very much Dorian's own creation. Like the best hostesses, he is renowned among London society for his skill in entertaining. His house is a showplace: he devotes himself to enlarging his various collections of beautiful objects. As his collections grow, Dorian's house becomes the record of all he has studied and experienced. The house becomes the fullest expression of his taste, and his taste the fullest expression of his personality. And yet, like that of Virginia Woolf's Clarissa Dalloway, another famous hostess, Dorian's public hospitality is enabled by the possession of a private room at the top of the house where he can expose his real identity. There he displays the decorative object that most fully reflects who he is. In Dorian's mind, however, this division between public and private is not secure—hence the many bars and locks he places on the room to keep it apart.

The things in Dorian's collections are not empty objects to him. More than merely beautiful, they incarnate Dorian's system of values; they are connections to the past and tokens of the many modes of life he has sampled.[15] If Wilde advised his public audiences to seek the beautiful, he gives his protagonist a far more complex and compensatory theory of interior design: "For these treasures, and everything that [Dorian] collected in his lovely house, were to be to him means of forgetfulness, modes by which he could escape, for a season, from the fear that seemed to him at times to be almost too great to be borne" (109). In these lines lie the clearest explanation for why Wilde termed his novel "an essay on decorative art." Everything in Dorian's collection is a displaced version of the one that he will never consent to display: the portrait by Basil Hallward that records the deterioration of body and soul even as Dorian's physical form remains unmarked and unchanged. Drawn into the minutiae of decoration and collecting, he can forget the most powerful and important object he owns. But imagine the frustration of a collector who cannot display his most important piece, the piece that ties together everything in his collection. Dorian's artful display of his objects is designed to compensate him for the one he believes cannot be displayed.

In fact, Dorian's collections are all closely related to his portrait. The anomalous chapter of the novel in which the narrative ceases and Dorian details the objects in his collections is unusual but not, as some readers have thought, digressive; it represents a careful anatomization of the portrait itself. In this chapter, Dorian does to the reader what he does to the guests who visit him at home: he shows us everything except what we would most like to see—the portrait. But the items he does show us are intimately related to the portrait. In fact, they are so similar that the collections should be seen as domesticated, sanitized versions of the portrait they resemble in a variety of ways. As such, the objects offer an implicit argument for Dorian's exoneration, an argument bound up with Dorian's claim that he is outside the realm of moral judgment since his life has become a work of art.

If *Dorian Gray* is an essay on decorative art, the argument of the essay is that the arts offer a self-contained ethical system that can compete with more typical ethics organized around family, morality, or religion. According to this shaky logic, this essay on décor has only an aesthetic, not an ethical, story to tell; thus Dorian is not open to accusations of immorality (as most contemporary reviewers charged) but only to critiques of his taste. If Dorian's things are substitutes for his portrait, and Dorian's portrait is a substitute for Dorian himself, then all Dorian's things are also facsimiles of Dorian. They are, in effect, role models for Dorian, who tries to follow their example by remaining unmarked by history. Beautiful, deadly, compelling, Dorian's things are all that Dorian has made himself and would like to remain. The subject of Wilde's essay on decorative art is a man who would like to escape from the world of conventional morality by becoming a decorative thing himself. In fact, his very name, a reference to the Doric architectural order, suggests that Dorian is another decorative element in his home. Dorian's association with ancient Greece can be read as a coded reference to homosexuality, but the Greek references in the text also invoke the world of ancient Greek art: Dorian has "beauty such as old Greek marbles" (33–34); he defines an artistic style that contains "all the perfection of the spirit that is Greek" (14).

Certainly Dorian's things contribute a good deal to the general atmosphere of the novel. Scattered throughout the text, they convey an air of opulence, decadence, and deadly attraction. If Dorian's fantastic sins cannot be named in the novel, his possessions suggest the tenor of his appalling deeds. All of his things are beautiful, but like the portrait, they are as noticeable (and of most interest to Dorian) for their histories of depravity or temptation. Like the hidden portrait always draped with a funeral pall, many of Dorian's objects are *memento mori*, like his flutes made out of human bones (104) or the pearls that have been placed in the mouths of the dead (106). Just as the portrait can only be looked upon by Dorian, its subject collects objects that must not be looked at or are horrible to look at— "things of bestial shape" (105) or the "*juruparis* of the Rio Negro Indians, that women are not allowed to look at, and that even youths may not see" (104). Dorian's portrait is a form of protection, concealing the evidence of his misdeeds, and thus he collects other artifacts with protective powers: a stone that cures the plague and another that is an antidote to poison (107). The portrait's protection is what corrupts Dorian, keeping his crimes secret from the world of society. Likewise, many of his pieces have a history of corrupting their owners, including artifacts of the church and the poisonous novel given to him by Lord Henry, which Dorian collects in multiple editions and bindings (113). In spite of their powers of corruption, no one questions Dorian's taste in displaying these objects—and might not the portrait also someday be considered fit for the public gaze?

Of all Dorian's collections, none correlate more closely to the hidden painting than his family portraits. These works manage to convey both the intense beauty and the propensity for evil that Dorian's picture contains and that Dorian embodies. There is the portrait of George Willoughby, whose "sensual lips seemed to be twisted with disdain," and that of the second Lord Beckenham, "with his chestnut curls and insolent pose," whom "the world had looked upon . . . as infamous" (112). The portrait of Lady Elizabeth Devereux, with its lovely, placid surface, evokes in Dorian the same rumors that Dorian's presence evokes in others: "He knew her life, and the strange stories that were told about her lovers" (112). These portraits, which Dorian displays in his country house, have in part been sanitized by death and by history: hanging in the "gaunt cold picture-gallery," they have the appearance of a record of a proud ancestry, not a rogue's gallery of shame. Formally framed and ceremoniously hung, the pictures are primarily aesthetic objects, not moral statements. Though they seem to reveal their subjects' dubious characters, the paintings are not considered the less beautiful for that. But Dorian's portrait (at least during its subject's lifetime) cannot be added to the gallery, for unlike the others this portrait confirms what the others only hint at. The paintings in Dorian's gallery, like all his objects, are "means of forgetfulness" because they distract him from his secret but also because they seem to expunge it, to deny its consequences. If Dorian's things, with their often dreadful pasts, can be cleansed of moral opprobrium by the passage of time and the processes of collection and exchange, might not Dorian's portrait find the same fate? Might it conceivably hang in the picture gallery in years to come, after its owner's death?

Dorian acknowledges that even if his portrait were to be exposed to public view his secret life would not be revealed; alone, the portrait would be inadequate to expose him: "He would laugh at any one who tried to taunt him. He had not painted it. What was it to him how vile and full of shame it looked?" (110). Yet he cannot rid himself of the idea that the discovery of the portrait would also expose his secret, and as a result he becomes more and more consumed with guarding the painting, placing bars across the room where it is kept, remaining in London to watch over it, and forbidding the room to members of his household staff. Dorian's best hope of finding peace lies in the discovery of a "means of forgetfulness," either by distracting his attention from the portrait, or by finding a way to understand the portrait in the way he experiences the things in his collections, as the realizations of an amoral artistic vision.

Of course, that's impossible. For part of what makes Dorian's portrait so exceptional is that it refuses to abide by the rules of design that Dorian struggles to establish in his house: that the arts are one, that art is separate from ethical considerations, and that beauty can defeat death, evil, and time. It steadily becomes less decorative and more moralistic until the once-pristine portrait depicts a grinning satyr with blood dripping from its hands, a pure embodiment of sin and judgment. Thus it comes as no surprise that, like many an heirloom that clashes with the prevailing decorative scheme, the portrait is banished to a remote part of the house and cloaked with an object that more closely approximates Dorian's taste—a sumptuous purple tapestry that has previously served as a shroud. But for all Dorian's secrecy, there is no concealing the strange aesthetic inversion that the painting seems to have set in motion: in the picture of Dorian Gray, despite Wilde's preemptive claims in his preface, art comes to life, becoming moral, ethical, sordid, and unavoidably consequential. This aesthetic inversion is matched by its complement, since in the novel life also turns into a form of art, becoming decorative, atemporal, isolated, and aesthetically determined.

Wilde's concept of the aestheticization of everyday life drew heavily on the ideas of his friend, painter and designer James McNeill Whistler. Though a disciple of Ruskin's at Oxford, when Wilde came down it was Whistler he sought out in London. Whistler's biographers, Elizabeth and Joseph Pennell, note that: "For two or three years, Oscar Wilde was so much with Whistler that everybody who went to the studio found him there, just as everybody who went much into society saw the two men together."[16] Unlike Morris, Whistler saw no intrinsic value in patterns based on nature or in natural materials. Both Morris and Whistler appreciated simplicity and emphasized the importance of being surrounded by beauty in the home. But if Morris's conception of simplicity stemmed from a romanticized medievalism based on craft and country life, Whistler's aesthetic was cosmopolitan and favored abstraction, a broad use of color, and an emphasis on form, each of which became a hallmark of modernist art and design.[17] And if Morrissian simplicity came from the use of modest materials, Whistler preferred the simplicity of Japanese art and design, designs that filled Wilde's home, and later, Dorian Gray's.

Whistler's theories of design were given a full exposition in the White House, the home and studio built on Tite Street in Chelsea by architect and theatrical designer E. W. Godwin. The design of the façade was so ostentatiously simple that the Metropolitan Board of Works refused to license the construction until additional moldings were appended. Of the interior nothing remains, but the Pennells conclude that a section of a room Whistler entered in the Paris International Exhibition of 1878 was intended for the White House. This room was titled, after the fashion of his paintings, "Harmony in Yellow and Gold." According to the *American Architect and Building News*, it was suffused in different shades of its title colors to the point that it took on a haze: "Yellow on yellow, gold on gold, everywhere."[18] One visitor to the White House commented that "one felt in it as if standing inside an egg."[19] This synesthetic atmosphere enlarged the sphere of art from the wall to the room, drawing observers into an aestheticized realm where they became part of Whistler's totalizing artistic scheme.

If Whistler's atelier represented a place where private life has become an art form, then it seems apt that *The Picture of Dorian Gray* opens in an artist's home, reminding the reader that the story we are reading is an artistic contrivance and not an attempt to realistically portray the events of daily life. *The Picture of Dorian Gray* begins in Basil Hallward's garden, as seen through the eyes of Lord Henry Wotton, the mouthpiece of aesthetic philosophy who will influence Dorian so profoundly. Here is the scene:

> From the corner of the divan of Persian saddlebags on which he was lying, smoking, as was his custom, innumerable cigarettes, Lord Henry Wotton could just catch the gleam of the honey-sweet and honey-coloured blossoms of a laburnum, whose tremulous branches seemed hardly able to bear the burden of a beauty so flamelike as theirs; and now and then the fantastic shadows of birds in flight flitted across the long tussore-silk curtains that were stretched in front of the huge window, producing a kind of momentary Japanese effect, and making him think of those pallid, jade-

faced painters of Tokio who, through the medium of an art that is necessarily immobile, seek to convey the sense of swiftness and motion.

(7)

We enter the world of *Dorian Gray* through the viewpoint of Lord Henry,
who is seated inside, looking out the window and past the silk curtains to the
flowers and birds outside. The scene is richly synesthetic, and the mingling of
sense impressions is joined by a mingling of art forms. The large window with
curtains hanging to the floor is at once a picture frame and a stage set for the
action, and though Lord Henry is looking out on what might be called nature,
he sees artifice and art. What is real is hard to discern—he can just "catch the
gleam" of the flowers, and of the birds he sees only "fantastic shadows." It is the
note of art that dominates the passage—the "momentary Japanese effect."
From the very first, the preference for the aesthetic over the natural and for performance over spontaneous action is stressed, a shift that in this scene is made
possible by the framing effect of the window that simultaneously obscures the
outdoors and translates it into art. There is more than a little of Lord Henry's
will involved here; it might be said that Lord Henry is an artist of spectator-
ship—a flaneur—since it is his educated gaze that culls the form, pattern, and
beauty that equal art for him.

Basil, the artist, is the first in the novel to suggest that in an age where life is
becoming more aestheticized, art experiences an inverse transformation: "Men
treat art as if it were meant to be a form of autobiography" (15). Dorian's portrait is a biography that becomes an autobiography, since after Basil has finished it Dorian records the events of his life upon its surface. Basil's comment
shows that the portrait is not unique but part of a more general change in the
nature of art. Lord Henry, for example, has channeled his artistic expression
into his life. His explication of his personal philosophy is compared by Wilde
to an allegorical painting, in which

> Philosophy herself became young, and catching the mad music of Plea-
> sure, wearing, one might fancy, her winestained robe and wreath of ivy,
> danced like a Bacchante over the hills of life, and mocked the slow Silenus
> for being sober. Facts fled before her like frightened forest things. Her
> white feet trod the huge press at which wise Omar sits, till the seething
> grape-juice rose round her bare limbs in waves of purple bubbles, or
> crawled in red foam over the vat's black, dripping, sloping sides.
>
> (37–38)

We know only vaguely the substance of Lord Henry's conversation, for in its place we receive a vivid and imaginary Dionysian scene where pleasure overmasters sobriety and fact. One of the listeners suggests that Lord Henry might readily translate his talk into a more conventional art form: "You talk books away," he said; "why don't you write one?" (38). But Lord Henry chooses to pour all his art into his daily life: the book will not be written and the allegorical scene will not be painted; instead, his artistic production is channeled into his conversation and into Dorian, whose personality Lord Henry forms like a sculptor modeling clay. As he tells himself, "To a large extent the lad was his own creation. . . . now and then a complex personality took the place and assumed the office of art, was indeed, in its way, a real work of art, Life having its elaborate masterpieces, just as poetry has, or sculpture, or paintings" (49). Dorian has become an artwork while his portrait has taken on the properties of a living thing.

Many characters in the novel attempt to see the events of their own daily lives as expressions of art, most apparently in the Sibyl Vane affair. Sibyl is Dorian's first love, a young stage actress who performs Shakespearean drama nightly in a cheap theater. Sibyl's mother, also an actress, carries her stage techniques into her private life, making herself both subject and spectator of her art with "false theatrical gestures" (52) and self-conscious posturing to create effective tableaux. Sibyl, too, explains to Dorian that before meeting him she felt alive only while on stage but that now she knows him she can no longer feign emotion on stage. "You had brought me something higher, something of which all art is but a reflection. You had made me understand what love really is" (70). But in draining the life from her performance, Sibyl loses the quality that had gained her Dorian's affection, since Dorian's regard is all for art. Dorian has transmuted his romance into art, something that imparts profound and dramatic feelings of catharsis that lack lasting consequences. But the conventional affect and moral responsibility Dorian has evacuated from his life find their way into his portrait, passing through the frame that Basil has created for his work into the painting itself. It is only after Dorian's affair with Sibyl that the portrait begins perceptibly to alter. Dorian's reaction to her death, missing in life, plays out on the canvas; if for Dorian "Life itself was the first, the greatest, of the arts" (100), then it seems that in exchange art must become a repository for what the novel defines as art's antithesis, the unpremeditated, consequential, quotidian fabric of daily life.

This swap leaves art drained of beauty, enmeshed in a moral framework and constrained by the passage of time, a transformation exemplified by the portrait.

The portrait is "conscious of the events of life as they occurred" (83) and full of "some strange quickening of inner life" (122). After Dorian murders Basil in the room that houses the portrait, even the dead body seems a more aesthetically pleasing object than the portrait: the body is a "silent thing," a "grotesque misshapen shadow," an abstract object defined in formal terms. A shadow is two-dimensional, and so the body also seems to have lost the interiority and depth that the painting has gained. The painting is all too visceral and immediate; it is full of affect, with "loathsome red dew that gleamed, wet and glistening, on one of the hands, as though the canvas had sweated blood" (134). The portrait seems on the verge of liquefying and pouring out of its frame. Its bloody dew, symbolizing life and regeneration, harks back ironically to the spring garden where the novel opens and where the flowers pour forth pollen. The painted surface is not just a representation of Dorian's polluted soul but of his body as well, replete with sweat glands, organs, and the rest. The painting has acquired insides; it has gained depth, with "foulness and horror" that come "from within" (122). Basil's body, in other words, has become a painting, while the portrait, with its temporality and its interiority, has become a narrative. The portrait carries the burden of telling the story of Dorian's life, a burden Dorian refuses.

The transfiguration of life into art, and vice versa, finds its ultimate expression in the living tissue of Dorian's picture, but this inversion is propelled by the quiet workings of the picture's frame. The narrative of Dorian's life inheres in the portrait by virtue of its frame, for when the frame is breached it becomes the narrative of Dorian's body once again, a transfer that has the effect of bringing Dorian's life to an abrupt close. Frames, as I explain below, have traditionally served as bridges or barriers between art and life. But the new, modern style of framing—exemplified by the frames E. W. Godwin created for Wilde's own home—permits the idea that the frame is part of the surrounding environment and that, by extension, the picture is too. This is not to say that the frame is all that imbues Dorian's portrait with its protean nature but rather that the portrait's nature is consistent with and even suggested by the discourse on the decorative arts that runs through the novel. In the hands of Whistler and his contemporaries, the frame becomes a porous boundary, a shift taken even further in *Dorian Gray*. In the novel, the painting overflows its frame, coloring life according to the rules of art. Likewise, the substance and sequence of life pours into the painting, hybridizing both realms so that what develops is not a simple swap but a complex exchange. In order to understand the origin and significance of this process it is necessary to consider frames and framing more broadly as well as the role of frames in Wilde's time and in his home.

"My frames I have designed as carefully as my pictures"

Compared to the fascinating portrait that gives the novel its name, the frame may not seem very interesting, though the text does mention it a few times. Indeed, it is hard to keep your eyes on picture frames in general, because of the way they erase themselves, because they can sometimes seem so ordinary as to become invisible. Frames humble themselves before works of art, existing only to flatter and set off their more precious contents. The frame is generally considered of secondary importance to the painting, or it is executed with techniques so common that they seem beneath notice, such as gilding, carving, or fluting, and in a range of predictable and repetitive designs. The work of art demands attention for its originality, while the frame sometimes relies on unoriginality to shift the gaze past it. Yet the frame is an integral part of the experience of looking at art. It announces the painting as a painting; it completes the painting and even converts it into a work of art. As Ortega y Gasset observes, "A picture without a frame has the air about it of a naked, despoiled man. Its contents seem to spill out over the four sides of the canvas and dissolve into the atmosphere. By the same token, the frame constantly demands a picture with which to fill its interior, and does so to such an extent that, in the absence of one, the frame will tend to convert whatever happens to be visible within it into a picture."[20] As the frame helps to transform its contents into a work of art, it makes certain powerful and specific claims about the nature of art. The frame declares the work of art to be a thing of value; it announces that its contents need and are worthy of protection, and it distinguishes the world of the artwork from the world of the viewer.

In the latter part of the nineteenth century in England, a group of artists turned their attention to the frame and tried to reinvent its appearance and function, influenced in part by the changing status of decorative objects and in part by a desire to align the work of art with its surroundings. Whistler signed his frames as well as his paintings, an implicit argument for the coequal status of the frame with the work of art. In like fashion, the frame that surrounds Dorian Gray's image is characterized by Wilde as an elaborate frame designed by the artist. The new frames were generally designed by artists in concert with the individual painting, their plans executed by frame makers who were both craftsmen and merchants. Such a frame maker plays a small but important part in *Dorian Gray*. The frame, as is its way, is quietly central to the novel, effacing itself while simultaneously contributing to and influencing the meaning of the story.

The frame has always had a dual nature, one that derives from its function as a mediator. The frame forms a bridge between the building that surrounds it and the painting it surrounds. Like the wall on which it hangs, the frame partakes of architecture, as is suggested by the many frame motifs, such as columns and moldings, that make architectural reference. As a decorative object, it is part of the décor of the home in a way that the painting is not. While the painting's aesthetic is typically more self-contained, the frame participates in the overall design of the space that contains it. Meyer Schapiro observes: "The frame belongs then to the space of the observer rather than of the illusory, three-dimensional world disclosed within and behind."[21] The frame is with us, with the observer in the larger world of wall, room, house, world. The painting is elsewhere, a window into another domain. Yet though it partakes of the world around it, the frame also participates in the work of art. Schapiro continues: "[The frame] is a finding and focussing device placed between the observer and the image. But the frame may enter also into the shaping of that image." The frame is a kind of lens, amplifying without appearing to influence the viewing experience. But the frame is not transparent. Its design interacts with the work of art and affects the way that work is received by the observer. It can place a work of art within a particular class context, assert its relative value, comment on its aesthetic, or overwhelm it completely. The frame is indivisibly part of the work of art, a point that would seem incommensurate with its status as border. Jacques Derrida has articulated the internal contradictions that reside in the frame in *The Truth in Painting*: "The violence of the framing multiplies. It begins by enclosing the theory of the aesthetic in a theory of the beautiful, the latter in a theory of taste and the theory of taste in a theory of judgment. These are decisions which could be called external: the delimitation has enormous consequences, but a certain internal coherence can be saved at this cost."[22] The frame conceals its own work, and it also conceals the force that is necessary to establish its aesthetic hierarchy. But the frame does a lot of ideological work in contextualizing the work of art, enough, as Derrida wryly suggests, to tear itself apart.

The duality of the frame inheres throughout its history. But in late-nineteenth-century England, it takes on a particular importance, when, insofar as it is possible to look at the frame, frames were being looked at, taken apart, analyzed, and reinvented. Charles Eastlake, whose *Hints on Household Taste* was one of the bibles of home decoration in the 1870s and 1880s, lamented the new revolution in framing, and sought to return to the first principles of framing. In *Hints* he writes;

I have endeavoured to show that the only proper means of arriving at correct form in objects of decorative art is to bear in mind the practical purpose to which such objects will be applied. Now the use of a picture-frame is obvious. It has to give additional strength to the light "strainer" of wood over which paper or canvas is stretched. It may also have to hold glass securely over the picture. Lastly, it has on its outer face to form a border which, while ornamental in itself, shall tend, by dividing the picture from surrounding objects, to confine the eye of the spectator within its limits. These conditions seem simple enough, but how frequently are they violated in modern work![23]

In the context of a discussion of the decorative arts, Eastlake's emphasis on the frame's utilitarian role in supporting the painting's underlying structure reads like a willful refusal to consider aesthetic questions where they would normally be prominent. But his obstinacy was fueled by the unprecedented liberties that many prominent artists were taking with their frames. Eastlake's call for a return to the basics represents a reaction to a climate in which the frame was coming into its own as an artistic production, rather than a functional one. Tension was growing between aesthetics (the frame as part of the work of art) and utility (the frame as a functional object). This tension also structures *The Picture of Dorian Gray*, beginning with the series of epigrams with which Wilde opens the novel. The last epigram famously proclaims that "All art is quite useless," drawing a clear marker between everyday life, which is governed by utility and ethics, and art, which is governed by aesthetics. This is a division anchored by the work of the frame, but it is work that the frame was becoming increasingly unfit to perform. The frame came to epitomize the merger of the decorative arts with the fine arts. As designers began to merge the frame with both the wall and the painting, the boundary between these seemingly distinct realms grew more and more porous.

The reconceptualization of English picture frames began in the mid-nineteenth century with the pre-Raphaelite painters, who, dissatisfied with the conventional Victorian models, began designing their own frames. The primary goal of the new initiative was to bring the picture into a unity with its surroundings, a result pursued in several directions. Stock plaster patterns were set aside in favor of oak and other more "honest" materials commonly used in other parts of the home. The amount of gold leaf gilded onto the frame was reduced so that the grain of the wood showed through, an innovation that Eastlake (among others) praised and that quickly became a standard Arts and Crafts practice. Painters like Rossetti and Ford Madox Brown flattened out the frame, giving it low relief or no relief at all, smoothing the transition from wall to frame. Other artists looked to extend the lines and colors of the painting into the frame. Some frames made a thematic connection to their contents as well as a visual one through the use of symbolic emblems or quotations.[24] As the frame was increasingly customized to suit the painting, it became not a stock item but one as individualized as the artwork it surrounded; the frame became its own work of art.

Whistler's picture frames and exhibition design techniques were among the most radical at the time. Ira Horowitz argues that what set Whistler apart from the pre-Raphaelites was his pure commitment to the decorative. Unlike Holman Hunt and Rossetti, Whistler did not make frames with political or cultural content; his frames were intended to make an exclusively visual impact.[25] Whistler's frames bore out the aesthetes' commitment to art for art's sake, art for the sake of beauty without symbolic invocations of extraneous matters. His innovations in framing were of a piece with his philosophy of art and interior design, and both had a profound influence on Wilde, who was his frequent companion in the early 1880s. As early as 1873, Whistler was taking credit for one of the signal innovations in framing at the time, as shown in his letter to George A. Lucas:

> You will notice and perhaps meet with opposition that my frames I have designed as carefully as my pictures—and thus they form as important a part as any of the rest of the work—carrying on the particular harmony throughout. This is of course entirely original with me and has never been done. Though many have painted on their frames but never with real purpose and knowledge—in short never in this way or anything at all like it. This I have so thoroughly established there that no one would have to put any colour whatever (excepting the old black and white and that quite out of place probably) on their frames without feeling that they would at once be pointed out as forgers or imitators; and I wish this to be also clearly stated in Paris that I am the inventor of all this kind of decoration in colour in the frames; that I may not have a lot of clever little Frenchmen trespassing on my ground.[26]

As his defensive tone indicates, Whistler's claims may well have been overblown; for example, biographer Dudley Harbron gives E. W. Godwin credit for originating the same practice.[27] Still, beginning as early as the 1860s,

Whistler was designing individual frames for his portraits that departed sharply from the large, heavily carved and ornate frames that had previously been the norm. Whistler's frames used simple, architectural techniques like reeding and striation and were decorated, if at all, with medallions or restrained Chinese or Japanese motifs. His frames were painted in a single color that harmonized with the painting and then gilded, with the gilding rubbed and thinned to allow the color underneath to emerge. On some frames he placed repeated geometric patterns such as checkerboards, parallel lines, herringbone, or basket weave to complement the overall effect.[28] The frame most associated with Whistler was the simplest of all. The Pennells note: "In after years, he not only ceased almost entirely to use these painted frames, but he designed a simple gold frame, with parallel reeded lines on the outer edge, for the paintings, now universally known as 'the Whistler frame.' "[29]

Whistler, whose innovations in frame coloration and in the integration of frame and picture were of a piece with the design reform movement, saw his frames as important artistic precedents that would shape present and future avant-garde practice. Whistler's preference for formalism over socialism was evident merely from the titles of his paintings, which, despite their figural content, were generally given abstract or musical titles such as "Arrangement" or "Nocturne." Whistler's frames were an expression of an overall design philosophy that, in broad outline, he shared with many of his fellow artists and designers. That philosophy included integrating art into the ordinary objects of the domestic interior and a concomitant fusing of painting with frame. For example, after the first few days of work on his 1891-92 painting *Arrangement in Black and Gold: Robert, Comte de Montesquiou-Fezensac*, Whistler placed the portrait inside the frame and worked on it in that state, presumably in order to focus on the relationship between painting and frame (fig. 2). Edgar Munhall suggests that only the frame accounts for the reference to "gold" in the painting's title, since there is no use of gold in the portrait itself.[30] If that is so, then the title gestures to the integral relationship between painting and frame, which together compose the work of art.

Whistler's experiments in pure color and form were rarely confined within the frame of a painting but instead sprawled out into entire rooms. Like Godwin, Whistler favored interior designs that took account of a built space in its entirety. As Deanna Marohn Bendix notes: "instead of stressing rural charm or homely domesticity like the Morris company, Whistler and Godwin were interested in creating a chic theatrical aura of suggestive mood and exotic drama in their interiors."[31] A room was a total work of art, and everything in it needed to harmonize. The Anglo-Japanese environments of Whistler and Godwin favored strong silhouettes over dense and colorful patterning. Whistler was a collector himself and valued craftsmanship, but he used a monochromatic palette and favored objects with relatively simple lines, enabling an overall consistency. Such rooms presented statements in formal composition that were somewhat at odds with conventional Victorian interiors, where objects were chosen individually and then heaped together, resulting in an eclectic environment. Victorian art galleries tiled artworks up and down and across walls, producing a visually cluttered environment in which bulky frames, hung end to end, formed the only separation between the images. Indeed, this style of display predominated from the Renaissance onward. In Samuel Morse's *Gallery of the Louvre* (fig. 3), the walls of the dimly lit gallery are barely visible between the paintings.

Whistler dismantled this tradition of display and designed exhibitions that contemporary galleries continue to replicate. He hung his works well apart, provided strong lighting, and integrated every aspect of the gallery interior into the show. Since Whistler's personal decorative ambitions often exceeded his financial grasp (the White House was broken up and sold by bailiffs), his solo public exhibitions gave him the fullest opportunity to create ambitious interiors.[32] He mounted a number of such shows throughout his career, all of which attracted public and press notoriety even when the work went unsold. Among Whistler's most influential exhibitions was his 1883 "Arrangement in White and Yellow," held at the Fine Art Society in London and designed to display fifty-one etchings he completed in Venice. The exhibition subsequently traveled to a range of American cities, including New York, Boston, and Chicago. The Freer Gallery of Art re-created the exhibition in 2003 and, though aspects of their installation are necessarily based on conjecture, co-curators David Park Curry and Kenneth John Myers constructed an approximation of the show Whistler mounted (fig. 4).

The contrast with the Louvre Gallery is decided, for Whistler's show instantly feels modern. With plenty of white space and strong natural light, the room presents a total environment for the viewing of the artworks. Whistler was proud of the level of detail he brought to this exhibition design, as he enthused to his friend Waldo Story:

> I can't tell you how perfect—though you would instinctively know that there isn't a detail forgotten—sparkling and dainty—dainty to a degree my dear Waldino—and all so sharp—White walls—of different whites—

Figure 2. James McNeill Whistler, *Arrangement in Black and Gold: Robert, Comte de Montesquiou-Fezensac,* 1891–92. © The Frick Collection, New York.

Figure 3. Samuel F. B. Morse, *Gallery of the Louvre*, 1831–33. Courtesy of the Daniel J. Terra Collection, Terra Foundation for the Arts, Chicago.

Figure 4. Gallery view, "Mr. Whistler's Gallery," Freer Gallery, 2003–4. Freer Gallery of Art, Smithsonian Institution, Washington, D.C.

with yellow *painted* mouldings—not *gilded!*—yellow velvet curtains—pale yellow matting—yellow sofas and little chairs—lovely little table yellow—own design—with yellow pot and *Tiger* lilly! Forty odd *superb* etchings round the white walls in their exquisite white frames—with the little butterflies—large white butterfly on yellow curtain—and yellow butterfly on white wall—and finally servant in yellow livery (!).[33]

Whistler controlled every aspect of the space of the exhibition, from the furniture to the wall surfaces to the attendants' apparel. The environment was so enveloping that the artworks became not the focal point but one of a range of harmonized elements. Thus the show staged the collapse of the boundary between what lay inside the frame and what outside of it. Visitors passed through an entrance draped in yellow silk and velvet into a gallery where the walls were covered with white felt and festooned with a large gauzy yellow ceiling drape. The fuzzy walls gave the interior a soft focus and together with the filtered yellow light created by the drape, combined to produce a sense of texture. The show also played with the viewer's sense of scale. To look at the small and delicate artworks, it was necessary to stand quite close to them. Since many of the etchings had either long vistas or shadowed doors as focal points, as viewers moved toward the etchings, they found themselves pulled into them. And as viewers stepped away from the individual works they moved out into another Whistlerian creation, the frame of the exhibition. As Myers points out, the title that Whistler gave the exhibition announced it as an artwork in its own right, one that was completed by the viewer. Myers observes:

Even as the act of naming drew attention to the installation as being a nonrepresentational art object, it also suggested Whistler's distinctively modern recognition that no painting or art object is ever fully and finally complete in itself. The completeness, the beauty, of an art object lies less in the object itself than in the eye of the sympathetic beholder or, more precisely, in the momentary subjective, congruence of beholder and object.[34]

At the same time that the gallery was elevated into a work of art, it was domesticated, personalized. Furnished with a yellow sofa and a set of caned chairs, the gallery became a zone of comfort and individual taste. At the opening Whistler, playing host, moved through the crowded room, adorning a few chosen guests with yellow satin and velvet butterflies, the butterfly being his trademark and signature. Playing to all of the viewer's senses, the show was a sensuous experiment in performance more than it was a conventional exhibition, an expression of personal vision as much as a commercial show. It received extensive publicity and reviews ranging from laudatory to mocking to downright suspicious, as some critics seemed to feel that the saturated yellow environment Whistler created in the gallery interior could pose risks to the viewer's physical, psychological, or moral health. Wilde attended the show and wrote enthusiastically of it to Waldo Story: "I saw a great deal of Jimmy in London *en passant*. He has just finished a second series of Venice Etchings—such water-painting as the gods never beheld. His exhibition opens in a fortnight in a yellow and white room (decorated by the master of colour) and with a catalogue which is amazing."[35]

The frames that Whistler designed for the exhibition played an important, if understated, role in the total experience. The etchings were custom framed by Whistler in frames with narrow white borders striped with a pair of light brown lines. One contemporary critic wrote that "the etchings with their broad white margins and glazed frames are seen dimly, as if a mist had risen up between them and the spectator."[36] The entire exhibition space served as the frame for the etchings, a frame so dominating that the artwork seemed to recede into a dizzying yellow haze. Where the artwork began and ended was difficult to judge. Wilde recaptured Whistler's sensuous yellows in poems like his own "Symphony in Yellow," which opens: "An omnibus across the bridge / Crawls like a yellow butterfly."[37] It might be said of many of the works done by Whistler and his contemporaries that the work of art had overflowed the frame, impressing its tones, composition, and subject matter onto the surround. But in Whistler's exhibition, the yellow surroundings spilled over into the artworks—if not blotting them out, then certainly obscuring them. The integration of the space overruled the primacy of the artwork; as Henry Heydenryk asserts, "displaying the painting to its best advantage was no longer all-important."[38]

Certainly today it is not unusual to find a gallery or museum space in which the entire environment has been assimilated to the artistic project. But it is important to stress that the roots of this expansion began at the edge of the frame. The picture frame was a key element in the erosion of the space between the aesthetic terrain of the picture and the sphere of everyday life. In some cases the site of the frame was expanded to include the wall or the room, while in others, like Whistler's "White and Yellow" show, the mediating role of the frame seemed to be eliminated entirely. Wilde too advocated the use of frames that occupied a midpoint between picture and architecture in his "House Beautiful" lecture.

I hate to see the ruining of so many fine pictures in the framing, by reason of the frame being all out of keeping with the picture. I don't like to see the great, glaring, pretentious gold frames for fine pictures; use gold frames only where the picture can plainly bear it, and in all other cases picture frames should be tinted a middle tone between the picture and the wall.[39]

Wilde's idea of using the frame to mediate between picture and wall was one he took in a more radical direction in the decoration of his own home. Unlike Whistler, Wilde never had the financial security to build from the ground up. But when he married in 1884 and prepared to set up housekeeping, he followed Whistler's example to the extent he could afford. Wilde selected a modest house on the same street as Whistler's, Chelsea's Tite Street, and hired Godwin as his decorator. The selection of Godwin made sense for other reasons as well.[40] Godwin was esteemed by Max Beerbohm as "first among the aesthetes." His previous commissions had included the Tite Street house a few doors down that Wilde had shared with Frank Miles, another house that provoked the Metropolitan Board of Works to mandate additional decorations for the façade. In addition to Whistler, Godwin was another of Wilde's models for thinking about the unity of the arts, for his work ranged among architecture, furniture and textile design, stage and costume design, criticism, and more. Lionel Lambourne writes that Godwin's "importance in the evolution of . . . the lectures of Oscar Wilde and the Aesthetic sensibilities of J. M. Whistler cannot be overestimated."[41]

Godwin's work had featured prominently in the first edition of William Watt's influential commercial catalog, *Art Furniture* (1877), published in London. Godwin contributed the preface to the catalog, in which he noted:

To furnish a home, four things should be considered, economy, utility, fitness or suitability, and beauty. We have no set rules for furnishing a home, for every man's house should not only be to him a castle for security, but a field for the display of individual taste and through it of individual character.[42]

Godwin's resolve to "have no set rules" for home decoration was daring. Lengthy household manuals such as Eastlake's *Hints on Household Taste* set out explicit rules regarding the right way to organize and decorate a home. Respectability, status, social hierarchy, etiquette, and comfort: these were the values enshrined in the Victorian domestic interior, and taste and self-expression were subordinate. But for Godwin, as for Whistler, the house was an extension of personal style, a forum for displays of personality and individuality. From Godwin Wilde learned how the home could be made into a place of beauty, and more, how it could embody, through its aesthetic commitments, the personality of its owner. For Wilde, who calculated every aspect of his appearance and self-presentation to produce a desired effect, a house decorated by Godwin seemed an ideal frame for his personality.

A successful public lecturer and a recently married man, Wilde's new domestic establishment allowed him to put into practice his advanced notions on the subject of house decoration. MacCarthy notes: "It was in the 1880s that the choice of special objects with which to live surrounded, one's furniture and furnishings, one's wallpapers and carpets, glass, pottery and silver, became established, in sophisticated circles, as a considerable skill, if not an art."[43] Wilde went to plenty of expense and trouble over his house—including a lawsuit with his contractor—but he and Godwin produced something original, replete with Whistlerian notes and Japanese elements. Richard Ellman writes of Wilde's desire to move beyond the innovations of his contemporaries: "Gone were the Morris wallpapers and other vestiges of Pre-Raphaelite décor. In came the new era of white high-gloss enamel, varied by golds, blues, greens."[44]

The house on Tite Street is no longer extant, and its contents were sold off to pay creditors in Wilde's lifetime, but some plans and descriptions of the interior remain. The surviving designs are perhaps the single most important non-authorial artifacts for understanding Wilde's relationship to framing and interior design. Of most interest to this account is the plan for the drawing room, a double room separated by folding doors on the second floor of the four-story house. Among the few surviving drawings that Godwin did for 16 Tite Street are two sketches for the picture frames in the front half of the room, and those drawings are of a strikingly original nature even considering the time and Wilde's avant-garde advisers. Godwin's notes describe the overall color scheme for the room as follows: "Woodwork ivory white. Walls distempered flesh pink from skirting to cornice. The cornice to be gilded dull flat lemon colour gold and also the ceiling margin to Japanese leather which latter will be provided by Mr. Wilde and is to be properly fixed by Contractor. The wall bank to be moulded wood as per sketch pt ivory white."[45] The color scheme was readily explained, but the wall design was strange enough to require notes to the contractor. Godwin's sketches, though rough, show plans for two walls, one to hold Whistler etchings, and the other Burne-Jones drawings (figs. 5 and 6).[46] For both wall banks Godwin designed moldings that reach out from the wall to enclose the artworks. If a picture is normally set back into a frame, Wilde's pictures were to be set back into the wall itself. The wall was built out around the pictures in concentric framing squares with wide margins between frames. Seen from the side, the effect is even clearer. The existing picture frame was augmented to produce a double frame that blended picture and frame together. The pictures were submerged in the wall, smoothly joined with the architecture of the room. Rather than ornamenting the wall, the pictures seemed to become the wall, part of the sustaining structure of the building. The boundary between picture and frame, between frame and wall, was greatly diminished.

This design integrated the fine arts with the decorative and architectural. The frame both disappeared into the wall and assumed a new primacy, consuming the picture's depth. And as the paintings were dissolved into the room, the room dissolved into a painting, a feature that W. B. Yeats observed when he visited the Wildes at home: "I remember vaguely a white drawing room with Whistler etchings 'let into' white panel. . . . It was perhaps perfect in its unity and I remember thinking that the perfect harmony of his life, with his beautiful wife and his two young children, suggested some deliberate composition."[47] Wilde's family life was a performance he offered to himself and to the world, and this was only one of the ways in which his house embodied and reinforced the image of himself Wilde had composed. The integration of the frame with both the architecture and the artwork it encircled had the effect, as Yeats observed, of aestheticizing Wilde's family life. Godwin, a noted stage designer (his notes for a production of *Hamlet* are scribbled on the reverse side of his frame designs for Wilde's house), had created a stage set for his clients: beautiful, artificial, and illustrative of the consequences of breaking through the frame. It was a step Wilde took account of in the note he sent to Godwin when the house was finally completed. He praised his designer "for the beautiful designs of the furniture. Each chair is a sonnet in ivory, and the table is a masterpiece in pearl."[48] Wilde's compliment made connections among different art forms, integrating literature, design, and the fine arts. Just so, the "House Beautiful" Godwin designed was a living painting, where the distance between art and life decreased until it seemed to disappear into an aesthetic moment. With the help of the designer, Wilde had gone to live inside a work of art.

When, a few years later, Wilde wrote his "essay on decorative art," *The Picture of Dorian Gray*, he returned to the question of the interrelationship among the arts, to the evacuation of ethics from art, and again, to the problem of the frame as a bridge between worlds. Drawing on Godwin and Whistler's examples, Wilde created a residence for his main character much in the style of his

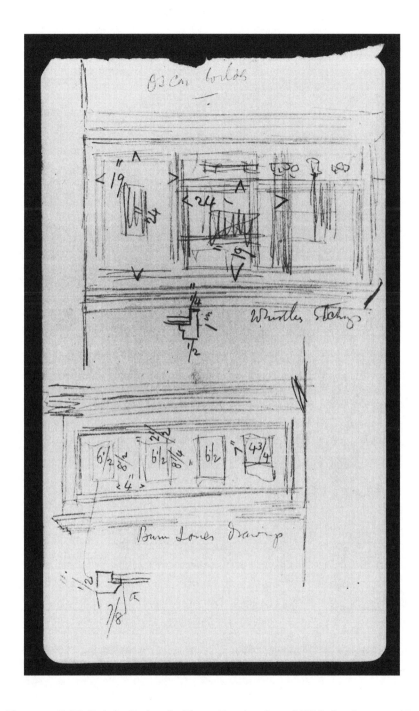

Figure 5. E. W. Godwin, Designs for Picture Framing, Oscar Wilde's drawing room, Tite Street, Chelsea, 1884. The Hyde Collection, Four Oaks Farm.

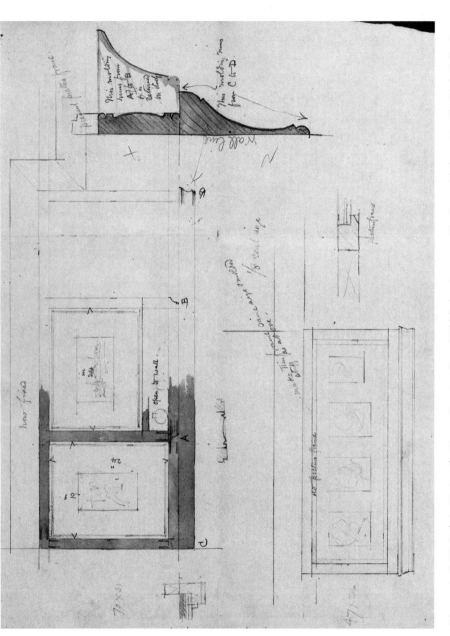

Figure 6. E. W. Godwin, Designs for Picture Framing, Oscar Wilde's drawing room, Tite Street, Chelsea, 1884. The Hyde Collection, Four Oaks Farm.

own. Like Wilde, Dorian has a home that is a product of his creative vision, filled with things that are both decorative objects and works of art. Like Wilde, too, Dorian's home is a kind of stage set for those aspects of his personality and those items in his collection that he is prepared to offer for public enjoyment. Dorian is the kind of collector described by Walter Benjamin, one who "makes the transfiguration of things his business."[49] He collects for a transfigurative purpose: to drain objects of any ethical content and place them into a purely aesthetic setting. For this mission the frame is central because of its traditional role in separating the ethical realm of life from the aesthetic realm of art. At Wilde's home the frames have retreated into the wall, a decorative choice that, as Yeats noted, contributed to the derealization of family life. Similarly, at Dorian's the picture frame has ceased to perform its role of dividing life from art, or the wall from the canvas, and the result is the work of artifice that Dorian Gray becomes.

For Wilde, the frame was more than a container for the work of art—it was the means by which the painting could be brought into a relationship with the surrounding wall, and with the built environment generally. The frame exemplified Wilde's contention that "all the arts are fine arts and all the arts decorative arts."[50] In Wilde's house, despite all the showy furnishings, it is the integration of the frame with the wall that most suggests the aestheticization of the family, its "deliberate composition." The amorality that was consequent on the transfiguration of life into art suggested intriguing literary possibilities for Wilde, preparing the way for Dorian Gray to merge with his portrait just as the painting had merged with its frame. As these apparently distinct entities come together, Dorian's picture becomes less of an image to be looked upon than a text to be read. Let us now finally turn to the representation of picture and frame in *Dorian Gray* and track the increasing identification among private self and public self, decoration and art, and picture and frame.

"You shall be varnished, and framed, and sent home"

The picture of Dorian Gray is fitted with what its subject describes as "the most wonderful frame, specially designed by [Basil Hallward]" (48), the painter, to suit the portrait. This custom frame might be compared to the metaphorical frames that surround Dorian himself. From the outset Dorian is more framed than his picture, defined by Basil and his friend and mentor Lord Henry Wotton's competing visions of him as a living artwork. Basil admits to Lord Henry that Dorian is "all my art to me now" (14), while Lord Henry sees Dorian as "a real work of art" (49). Basil also conflates Dorian with his portrait from the moment the painting is completed, telling Dorian that "as soon as you are dry, you shall be varnished, and framed, and sent home" (27). This framing is echoed by a second one, instigated by Lord Henry and his gift to Dorian of a hand mirror. When Dorian first discovers his portrait has altered, he turns to this gift for reassurance: "He winced and, taking up from the table an oval glass framed in ivory Cupids, one of Lord Henry's many presents to him, glanced hurriedly into its polished depths" (73). At this moment, the portrait effectively splits into two competing aesthetic visions: Basil's, in which Dorian figures as a motive for art and the painting responds to Dorian's private behavior; and Lord Henry's, in which Dorian *is* art, and the mirror reflects Dorian's public identity. Wilde argues in the novel's preface that "all art is at once surface and symbol" (3), and the mirror, in spite of its "polished depths" records the surface, while the portrait registers the symbol. If art has often been called a mirror for life, here art and a mirror offer competing reflections. The mirror is itself more of a work of art than we might normally expect of such an object because of the sculpted Cupids that compose its frame.

The myth of Narcissus provides another link between Dorian's two portraits, since both the portraits nod to this story in similar ways. Dorian is plainly a type of Narcissus, beloved by many but able to feel love only for himself. Like his self-involved ancestor who stared at his own reflection in a pond, Dorian sits adoringly before his portrait and tries to gain its affections: "Once, in boyish mockery of Narcissus, he had kissed, or feigned to kiss, those painted lips that now smiled so cruelly at him. Morning after morning he had sat before the portrait wondering at its beauty, almost enamoured of it, as it seemed to him at times" (83). Similarly, the Cupids surrounding the mirror affirm the love of the gazer for his reflection. When the portrait begins to deform, the mirror becomes as much—if not more—of a work of art as the portrait, since the portrait shows the alterations wrought by age and experience, and the mirror reflection remains true to the vision that Basil recorded in paint. In the Narcissus story, Narcissus and his reflection decay together as Narcissus's devotion to his reflection leads him to neglect his physical well-being. In Dorian's case, his two portraits testify to the growing separation between the outer Dorian, whose mirror image remains young, beautiful, and pure, and the inner Dorian who is revealed by his painted portrait to be hideous and corrupt. The increasing divide between the two portraits is indicative of the increasing distance in the novel between art and life, as the mimetic power of art increases in inverse proportion to the reflective power of the mirror.

This division is mapped onto an equally counterintuitive division in the novel between public and private life: Basil's portrait represents Dorian's private self, soon to be permanently hidden away in the recesses of his home, while Lord Henry's portrait becomes Dorian's public self, reflecting to society what is beautiful—which is what it wants to see. But while Dorian's portraiture is divided, Dorian himself remains whole. The Dorian who commits unspeakable sins is perfectly continuous with the Dorian whose sense of style is widely imitated and who travels in high social circles. Dorian does not separate his worlds. He brings society gentlemen like Adrian Singleton with him to opium dens, and he asks his friend Alan Campbell to help him conceal evidence of a murder. His "private" life of sin and shame is not separate from his "public" life as a gentleman and an aesthete.

As a novel, *Dorian Gray* is widely associated with secrecy. Many critics have tried to guess at the substance of Dorian's secrets. Eve Sedgwick argues for a secret within a secret, same-sex desire camouflaged by drug addiction.[51] Alan Sinfield sees the text as directing the Victorian reader to imagine masturbation as Dorian's dreadful vice.[52] Elaine Showalter suggests that Dorian's unrevealed shame is venereal disease, while Jeff Nunokawa claims: "there is still a secret left to be told" about the novel—that it's boring.[53] Most critics don't make the mistake of assigning any single specific referent to Dorian's secret, but they do search for buried treasure when what is hiding is in plain sight. For what really is Dorian's secret but the painting? All his fear of exposure is localized in Basil's portrait, which he protects with locks and metal bars. Dorian's secret is not moral but aesthetic, and similarly his sense of a (divided) self is grounded not in moral terms (conscience vs. will, good vs. evil) but in aesthetic ones (surface vs. symbol, realism vs. allegory).

The model of the split self is a resonant one in Victorian culture. As Showalter observes, "we think of the late nineteenth century as the age of split personalities who solve their social and sexual problems by neatly separating mind and body, good and evil, upstairs and downstairs."[54] One of the clearest literary examples of this splitting can be found in the story of another well-to-do nineteenth-century man who is frequently compared to Dorian Gray: Robert Louis Stevenson's *Strange Case of Dr. Jekyll and Mr. Hyde* (1886).[55] Dorian's split is on the level of representation, while, by dint of drinking a potion, Dr. Jekyll physically changes into his double, who, unlike the tall, good-looking, and generous Jekyll, is short, ugly, and vicious. If Dorian's doubles are distinguished from each other on aesthetic grounds—one handsome, one hideous— Dr. Jekyll and Mr. Hyde are primarily separated by their ethics. Hyde gives way to every impulse, while Jekyll holds himself in a state of constant restraint. Further, Dorian's self remains integrated, while the two parts of Jekyll's personality can never coexist: when Hyde surfaces, Jekyll submerges. Jekyll's split is along public/private lines, since Hyde's indulgent private life is what makes Jekyll's restraint possible.[56]

But this is not Dorian's story. Although he might deny it, Dorian actually maintains a modern continuity between his private and public lives, choosing his partners in secret perversity from among his society friends. Yet while his friends are ostracized for their behavior, Dorian's name remains, for the most part, clear. Dorian holds his head up because he believes in the inviolability of his private life, a life he symbolically sequesters in the portrait. It is art that is marshaled to support this rapprochement between the public and private. More specifically, the frame of the portrait serves to help distinguish the realm of art from that of life; note that Dorian's portrait does not begin to change until it has been framed. But the frame is an unreliable border guard, one that threatens to allow for the reconciliation of art and life and indeed does so in the scene that provides the novel with its violent climax.[57] The split self arises to cope with irreconcilable aspects within an individual. To displace the splitting into art is to understand art as divided between mimetic realism and subjective impressionism, a division critical to the birth of the modernist novel. The modernist novel rejects naturalism in favor of experimental techniques that give rise to a new literary interiority; it reflexively foregrounds its own techniques of representation, interweaves ethics with aesthetics, and emphasizes the quotidian. Dorian's portrait—if not Wilde's novel—has all these qualities. In addition, like the modernist novels suppressed by the courts on the grounds of obscenity, Dorian's picture seems to corrupt its viewers. More even than *The Picture of Dorian Gray*, the picture of Dorian Gray is itself a protomodernist literary work, and Dorian is a reader of that work.

If the picture isn't very picturelike, however, the frame is irreducibly an artifact of visual art. Wilde's most extensive meditation on the role of the frame in his novel occurs shortly after Dorian discovers that the portrait has begun to alter and determines to hide it away. Wilde devotes an unusual amount of exposition to the portrait's relocation, especially considering that the scene is a set piece that contributes nothing to the plot. To move the portrait he invites a frame maker and his men to come to his house—"Mr. Hubbard himself, the celebrated frame-maker of South Audley Street" (93–94). For all that his role in the story appears incidental—the character appears only in this one scene—he seems to have lingered in his creator's imagination. When Wilde published

Dorian Gray as a novel, he changed the manuscript substantially from the version that had first appeared in *Lippincott's*. After the book was complete, Wilde's editor received a telegram from Paris: "Terrible blunder in book, coming back specially. Stop all proofs. Wilde." On arrival Wilde disclosed that the blunder lay in the name given to the frame maker in the *Lippincott's* text, Ashton. Wilde told his editor: "Ashton is a gentleman's name. . . . And I've given it—God forgive me—to a tradesman! It must be changed to Hubbard. Hubbard positively smells of the tradesman!"[58]

For all its tradesman status, the professional reputation of the frame maker was on the upswing in Wilde's time. Some frame makers enjoyed artistic prominence consistent with the new esteem accorded to design generally and frame design in particular. As *Dorian Gray* demonstrates, frame makers typically not only created and fitted frames but also arranged for transport of their work and sometimes hung the finished pictures.[59] The picture's progress to the top of the house is a labored one because the elaborate frame on Dorian's portrait adds bulk and weight. So heavy is the picture that Dorian allows the framer and his assistant to take the wide front staircase upstairs, and even helps carry the painting: " 'Something of a load to carry, sir,' " Mr. Hubbard apologizes, and Dorian acknowledges, " 'I am afraid it is rather heavy' " (94). Evidently it is the weight of conscience that bears the portrait down. This brief journey might serve as an allegory for the novel as a whole: Dorian, burdened by his conscience, shifts the weight onto an artwork that bears it for him. He cannot accomplish this shift without help, which is provided by the frame, keeping the realm of art safely away from that of life, and by a frame maker whose job it is to mediate between the two realms. Dorian also insists on dragging other individuals down with him, making them bear the weight that should be his alone. But the frame maker, for all the necessary support he provides, poses a threat to Dorian. He asks to look at the work of art, which has been carried upstairs covered by its shroud: "Dorian started. 'It would not interest you, Mr. Hubbard,' he said, keeping his eye on the man. He felt ready to leap upon him and fling him to the ground if he dared to lift the gorgeous hanging that concealed the secret of his life" (96). The murderous passion Dorian suddenly feels toward the frame maker, surpassed only by his hatred of the portrait's artist (whom he will eventually murder) has something in it of the rage of the parricide. Dorian hates the men whose art makes his life possible.

If Dorian harbors conflicted feelings toward Mr. Hubbard, the frame maker's feelings toward Dorian are less complex—he simply loves him. In addition to his physical support, Mr. Hubbard, together with his assistant, bring a touch of eros to the humdrum task of moving the portrait upstairs. Mr. Hubbard, Wilde tells us, "never left his shop" (94). The only customer for whom he will alter his habits is Dorian, because "it was a pleasure even to see him." Though Mr. Hubbard has a shop in Mayfair and is no doubt anxious to cultivate an image of himself as an artist rather than a manual laborer, for Dorian he throws over his afternoon and does whatever he is asked to do. Mr. Hubbard's assistant is even more taken with their client, glancing "back at Dorian with a look of shy wonder in his rough, uncomely face. He had never seen any one so marvellous" (96). As framers, Mr. Hubbard and his assistant appreciate Dorian as a work of art, something to be looked upon with admiration whenever possible. Nevertheless, the work they perform for him is arduous and by the time they reach the top of the stairs, the frame maker is "gasping for breath." His exertions are like those of the frame around the portrait, which is hard-pressed to perform its task of keeping Dorian's degraded appearance within its bounds.

Though the picture frame seals off the picture, it also provides an increasingly viable route for its reintegration into the larger world. In the novel's last scene, the portrait's frame is breached, and the painting leaps out of the frame. This moment is presaged in the novel by the destruction of the portrait's double, the framed mirror given to Dorian by Lord Henry. Following a painful interview with Lord Henry, Dorian's gaze falls upon the hand mirror:

> The curiously-carved mirror that Lord Henry had given to him, so many years ago now, was standing on the table, and the white-limbed Cupids laughed round as of old. He took it up, as he had done on that night of horror when be had first noted the change in the fatal picture, and with wild, tear-dimmed eyes looked into its polished shield. Once, some one who had terribly loved him had written to him a mad letter, ending with these idolatrous words: "The world is changed because you are made of ivory and gold. The curves of your lips rewrite history." The phrases came back to his memory, and he repeated them over and over to himself. Then he loathed his own beauty, and flinging the mirror on the floor, crushed it into silver splinters beneath his heel.
>
> (167)

Dorian has shattered Lord Henry's portrait, the portrait that told Dorian who he was and that made him into a living work of art. With its carved cupids, this frame accords with conventional Victorian taste in both its imposing size and its generous ornament. But the Victorian frame lacks the power of the frame around Dorian's picture, which Dorian will find he cannot destroy. Unlike the mirror, Dorian treats the portrait as though it were alive—which he believes it is—setting out to "kill" it with the same knife he used to stab Basil.[60] When Dorian's knife touches the picture, the painting overflows its frame and life returns to the aestheticized space that Dorian has inhabited since the portrait was painted. Evacuated of life by Dorian's attack, the painting reverts to an ageless work of art and regains the appearance it had on the day it was completed. Dorian falls dead to the floor, bearing the disfigurements of age and sin that moments ago covered the portrait.

In Dorian's final struggle with his portraits, he can defeat one but not the other. In breaking the hand mirror, Dorian rejects his polished surface: his beauty, his public persona, and his status as living artwork. The function of the Victorian frame is to wreathe its subject in ornament and status and isolate it from the world beyond the frame. That is Lord Henry's Dorian—beautiful, adored, incapable of doing wrong, but in many ways a fragile relic. Having smashed the mirror, Dorian believes he has set aside the portion of himself that worships youth and beauty and can begin a new life. Yet the portrait is more difficult to leave behind, though it too is a kind of mirror, "the mirror of my soul," as Dorian calls it more than once. The portrait is the enabler of Dorian's private life; it is the log of his activities, of the impact of time's passage on his personality. It is also his aide-mémoire, recording past actions through the dual symbolic registers of art and physiognomy, blood on his hands to represent a murder, a leer to represent an act of hypocrisy. While the mirror's frame is designed to mount an impermeable (Victorian) barrier between art and life, the portrait's (modern) frame allows for Dorian's deeds to leave their traces on the canvas. But the frame is a poor choice of ally for Dorian, since he enlists its aid in keeping his public and private selves distinct at precisely the moment when the frame is in the process of becoming less of a barrier and more of a bridge. Dorian attempts to negotiate between his public and private lives, to keep them in a precarious balance that is sustained by the frame. While Dorian's attack on the mirror leaves his appearance intact, his attack on the portrait is enough to unbalance and invert the delicate relationship between art and life maintained by the frame. Dorian's dead body is still a double for his portrait, with identities reversed.

As the frame sinks into the painting, the secret, unacceptable self merges with the presentable, socialized self. The precondition for this internalization is created by the changing nature of the frame, which is introjected by its own alter ego, the work of art. The private self is a fragile construct in the world of

Dorian Gray, as in Wilde's own home; in whatever aesthetic context it appears, the private self seems always on the verge of being revealed as identical with its apparently distant source. And when it does, the realms of ethics and aesthetics are poised to collide. When Dorian attacks the portrait with the same knife he has used before to murder, he treats the portrait as a living being, not as an artwork. He expects that he can kill off the private self, the "monstrous soul-life" who lives in the frame, as readily as he killed its creator. He depends on the artist-designed frame to contain the "soul-life" in the picture, but the frame fails to do so because what Dorian asks of the frame is exactly what the frame no longer is designed to do. So perhaps we cannot fault the frame for abandoning its responsibilities as a border guard. Though Dorian is not fully prepared for the changing times, his story presages the collisions of art and life, public and private, fine art and decoration, and ethics and aesthetics that are central to the relationship between modernist literature and design.

The narrative frame of *Dorian Gray* is perhaps of as much interest as the picture frame. As I began by observing, the narrative describes an act of framing, moving from the unframed portrait on the artist's easel to the framed portrait on its owner's wall. As Mary Ann Caws has noted about literary frames, "the distance from the earlier tendency toward the isolation of a picture or a scene as framed to stand out from the rest, or to stand still in the center of the narrative flux, to the later thrust toward the notion of the frame itself as the principal object of interest, represents the distance from premodernism to modernism at its height."[61] Modern literature foregrounds its narrative frame and structure over its content or theme, and the same emphasis holds true in the development of picture frames. In Wilde's novel the two teleologies of framing coincide: the novel's narrative frame tells of how a picture frame determines the story's shape, and the novel's picture frame(s) represent the main character's narrative journey from art to life. The narrative frame points to the picture frame, and the picture frame points to the narrative. Both types of frame are as modest as frames prefer to be, always pointing elsewhere—to a picture, to a moral, to any alibi that will distract from their critical power to mark the limits of art.

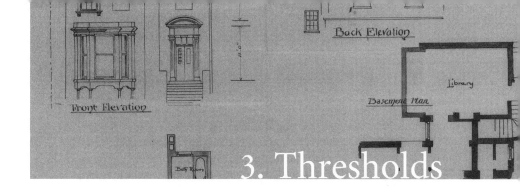

Why not sense that, incarnated in the door, there is a little threshold god?
—Gaston Bachelard, *The Poetics of Space*

Few spaces are more formative than a childhood home. It is a crucible of identity, a place that teaches both overtly and implicitly who we are, what things mean, and how life is to be lived. Many of us may recall the places where we grew up with a complicated mixture of emotions, but biographer and critic Lytton Strachey had a particularly intense response. In an autobiographical essay named for his childhood home at 69 Lancaster Gate, and written many years after his family had moved, he confesses that the house is the subject of his only recurrent dream. In the dream, he and his family find themselves mysteriously re-occupying the house. Realizing this:

> A feeling of intimate satisfaction comes over me. I am positively delighted. And this is strange because, in my working life, I have never for a moment, so far as I am aware, regretted our departure from that house, and if, in actuality, we were to return to it, I can imagine nothing which would disgust me more. So, when I wake up, and find myself after all at Gordon Square or Tidmarsh, I have the odd sensation of a tremendous relief at finding that my happiness of one second before was a delusion.[1]

Strachey responds viscerally to the house with a combination of attraction and repulsion that is as strong as it is mysterious. "Those curious contraptions of stones or bricks, with all their peculiar adjuncts, trimmings, and furniture, their specific immutable shapes, their intense and inspissated atmosphere, in which our lives are entangled as completely as our souls in our bodies—what powers do they not wield over us, what subtle and pervasive effects upon the whole substance of our existence may not be theirs?" (16). The power of houses arises from their architecture and furnishings, from the things that fill them. Strachey's alliterative, polysyllabic words bristle with corners, crevices, and doodads.

The objects that fill Lancaster Gate may be Victorian, but Strachey considers his response to them modern, and more than that, a sign of a generational divide: "Our fathers . . . were more interested in the mental and moral implication of their surroundings than in the actual nature of them. . . . the notion that the proportions of a bedroom, for instance, might be significant would have appeared absurd to them" (16). By contrast, "We find satisfaction in curves and colours, and windows fascinate us, we are agitated by staircases, inspired by doors, disgusted by cornices, depressed by chairs, made wanton by ceilings, entranced by passages, and exacerbated by a rug" (16). Why does Strachey feel so stirred by domestic trappings? What hidden meanings are preserved in the innocent surfaces of domestic life, and why do they preoccupy the adult as much as the child?

The circumstances in which Strachey first uttered his claims have a bearing on these questions. "Lancaster Gate" was written for and read aloud to the Memoir Club sometime in 1922. Beginning in 1920, the club members would meet two or three times a year, dine out, and then by prearrangement, one or two of the company would read a memoir. The other regular members were Clive and Vanessa Bell, E. M. Forster, Roger Fry, Duncan Grant, Maynard Keynes, Desmond and Molly MacCarthy, Adrian Stephen, Saxon Sydney-Turner, and Leonard and Virginia Woolf. These formed a good portion of the loose coterie known as the Bloomsbury Group, many of whom had known each other from young adulthood or before. His inclusive "we" embraced his listeners not only on the basis of familiarity but on the basis of a shared interest in home design. Several of them had worked on projects in the decorative arts at the Omega Workshops. In the past year, as well, the Woolfs had purchased Monks House in Sussex, and were remodeling and modernizing the house. Bell and Grant were at work on their own Sussex home, Charleston Farmhouse, which was becoming incrementally covered by their designs. Fry was living in Durbins, a modern house of his own design. Strachey himself had recently set up housekeeping at Tidmarsh Mill for himself and Dora Carrington, who decorated the house. Thus Strachey's comments had a potent resonance for his audience, who shared his interest in the influence houses could exert on their inhabitants.

Strachey's architectural approach to life-writing was shared by Virginia Woolf, whose own memoir seems to have inspired his. A year or so earlier, Woolf had read the Club an essay named after her childhood home, "22 Hyde Park Gate." She also discussed this house at length in two other pieces; the first, "Old Bloomsbury," was a continuation of "22 Hyde Park Gate" and was read to the Memoir Club a year later. The second, longer essay was "A Sketch of the Past," written at the end of her life.[2] For both writers, the rejection of Victorian domestic life runs alongside their paradoxical impulse to memorialize and reanimate their childhood homes, neither of which is still owned by their families at the time of writing. Strachey and Woolf were lifelong friends, correspondents, and important readers of each others' work. Although describing experiences that occurred long before they knew each other, their memoirs share a common tone, subject matter, and technique. Struggling to define themselves against the legacy of their parents' generation, both writers find themselves drawn back into a world they find cannot be easily left behind.

These "household memoirs," as I will term them, provide an important clue toward understanding Bloomsbury's challenge to its heritage, its assault on the conventions of private life. They are not merely period pieces that recall the bygone customs of Victorian childhoods.[3] Rather, these works have an anthemic importance for their writers, who offer them as a kind of explanation for their identity and creative direction. The households they depict provide a shaping influence and an adverse model that both writers, in different ways, react against throughout their careers. Michael Holroyd, Strachey's biographer, writes that "Lancaster Gate" provides "the clue to Strachey's attitude toward the Victorians; here is the clue to so much in his life."[4] For Woolf her old home explains her present, since, as she writes, "though Hyde Park Gate seems now so distant from Bloomsbury, its shadow falls across it" ("Bloomsbury," 182). This shadow can be traced through many of Woolf's works, which, like Strachey's, revive the Victorian world in a spirit that combines fascination with critique.

Bringing their old households back to life in these memoirs, Woolf and Strachey describe homes where the division of rooms reflected a carefully conceived vision of social order, based in large part on a class-bound definition of clean and proper family life. Middle- and upper-class Victorian households were organized into rooms named and allocated for particular individuals or activities, but a way of life built around separation and specialization encounters difficulty when faced with transitional or in-between states that resist categorization. Such states are architecturally embodied in the threshold, the space that forms a bridge between two discrete rooms. In what follows I focus on the threshold and examine how this space figures as an unsettling intermediary in the otherwise black-and-white world of separated spheres. Mary Ann Caws writes of the threshold that "Liminal perception chooses its framework, hallowing an otherwise mundane space and setting it apart, as in a game whose rules oppose what happens therein to the normal customs of day-to-day work."[5] For Woolf and Strachey, in different ways, the threshold comes to both embody and counter a set of ideas about cleanliness, propriety, and transition.[6]

Thresholds are as important to household memoirs as they are to houses. Household memoirs interweave architectural details and domestic routines to render the story of a life inseparable from its material environs. They take account of what Woolf calls "invisible presences" in "A Sketch of the Past," social forces that impinge on the subject and that have "never been analysed in any of those Lives which I so much enjoy reading, or very superficially." Woolf lays out the project of accounting for these social forces in the act of coining the term "life-writing": "Consider what immense forces society brings to play upon each of us, how that society changes from decade to decade; and also from class to class; well, if we cannot analyse these invisible presences, we know very little of the subject of the memoir; and again how futile life-writing becomes" ("Sketch," 80).

Attacking the autonomous subject of life-writing, Woolf proposes an alternative approach that replaces the subject in the social milieu. "Life-writing" is a broad term and includes genres such as biography, autobiography, diary, and memoir. I use it here in order to bring Strachey and Woolf's personal writings together with their biographical work. Woolf defines modern life-writing in opposition to the Lives of Great Men tradition associated with writers like her father, Leslie Stephen, and his *Dictionary of National Biography*. As self-defined modern life-writers, Woolf and Strachey reject what they see as the Victorian preference for the public, the exterior, and the world of action and turn toward private life in several forms: the domestic sphere of the home, the inner life of thoughts and emotions, and the intimate details of embodiment. Resistance to Victorian domestic practices and resistance to Victorian life-writing intertwine in these memoirs. Writing against the Victorian convention of an autonomous subject who was defined by his activities in the public sphere, these writers tell stories of the quotidian, focused on daily domestic life. Woolf and Strachey are themselves threshold creatures in their memoirs, looking back to their Victorian childhoods in order to imagine different, modern futures. But the threshold, as I will show, both creates difference and collapses it, and a moment of oppositional self-invention can also become one of mimetic identification.

The Gentleman's House

The Victorian home was ordered above all by its room divisions. These divisions found their fullest expression in the elite environs of the Victorian country houses, with their innumerable rooms, but were represented on a reduced scale in the urban row houses like those where the Stephen and Strachey families lived. As Stefan Muthesius explains, "The overriding principle in the planning of a nineteenth-century house whether country mansion or cottage was the same: the differentiation of functions, the allocation of a separate room for each and every purpose."[7] Rooms were designated by gender, by class, and by function; these designations helped to model relationships between the house's major constituencies, the family and servants. The house plan assigned varying levels of convenience, space, privacy, and importance to different members of the household according to their age and station. In their function as room dividers, walls served as physical realizations of social divisions. The architecturally mediated social system of the country house has long been an object of fascination: television shows like *Upstairs, Downstairs* (1971–75) and films like *The Remains of the Day* (1993) and *Gosford Park* (2001) have exhaustively reproduced the nuances of this way of life. Most recently, in the reality television show *The Edwardian Country House* (2002), nineteen volunteers re-created the country house lifestyle.

Class was the most marked consideration guiding the plan of the house. Robert Kerr, one of the most popular and influential writers on domestic architecture in the mid-nineteenth century, laid particular stress on separating the house along class lines; in his much-reprinted work *The Gentleman's House* (1871) he writes: "It is a first principle with the better classes of English people that the Family Rooms shall be essentially private, and as much as possible the Family Thoroughfares. It becomes the foremost of all maxims, therefore, however small the establishment, that the Servants' Department shall be separated from the Main House, so that what passes on either side of the boundary shall be both invisible and inaudible to the other."[8] Kerr's words imply a certain equality between family and servants, with each group seeking the same insulation from the other. But although the family and servant wings of the house might be similar in overall size, the resemblance ended there: the servant wing was far more densely populated and divided up into many little rooms dedicated to particular tasks ("Boots," "Knives," "Coals," etc.), while the rooms of the family wing were larger and given over to leisurely pursuits ("Music-room," "Smoking-room," "Sitting-room," etc.).

Gender was another key value informing the logic of room divisions. Gendered division was expressed through the broad "zoning" of male and female regions of the home, the designation of individual rooms, and the contents of the rooms. Masculine rooms (such as the study, the billiard room, or the gentleman's room) were associated with isolation and privacy, while feminine rooms (such as the drawing-room or breakfast room) were considered more social and open. The popular notion of the "Angel in the House" imagined the home as sacred feminized domain. As Mrs. Eustace Miles, author of a popular 1911 domestic manual, wrote, "Home is above everything else the house (of rooms, or even a single room) in which the individuality of the woman as wife, or mother, or sister, finds expression."[9] Yet more rooms were given over to the gentleman of the house than to its mistress—as many as seven, according to Kerr. A sustaining tension lay in the contradiction between the overall sense of the home as feminine and the large amount of space specifically coded as masculine in many homes. Mark Girouard speculates that this proliferation was occasioned by Victorian chivalry: "Male preserves were the natural result of this 'remember-there-are-ladies-present-sir' attitude."[10] The extensive constraints on what middle and upper-class women might see and hear also provided a disinterested basis for masculine secrecy and isolation at a time when these qualities were increasingly bound up with a claim to power.

The plan of the Victorian home articulated class and gender through each other. Male and female servants, for example, might be allotted separate staircases so as not come into unnecessary contact with each other in the performance of their duties. Similarly, unmarried male guests might be provided with a "Bachelor's Stair," both to facilitate covert entrances and exits and to sequester unmarried female guests from contact with their male counterparts. In Bear Wood, an extremely large house designed by Kerr that was finished in 1874, "women" are apportioned a work room, while "ladies" withdraw to a boudoir dedicated to leisure. Such distinctions helped to manage the diverse household community, creating a domestic space that stratified the many different social groups that lived in such close proximity.[11] The Victorian home has sometimes been described as a repressive space, but it seems more accurate to identify it as compartmentalized, a characteristic that in many ways only drew attention to the importance of the contact zones between men and women, family and servants.

Thresholds of rooms, or junctures between different areas of the house were a particularly sensitive concern, since these architectural transitions also distinguished different household constituencies. Separations between rooms participated in the creation of gendered or class-based distinctions as well as attempting to distinguish between the proper and improper, public and private, clean and dirty. Robin Evans's work on architectural transition spaces identifies Kerr as an important figure in the history of the threshold: "with Kerr, architecture in its entirety was mobilised against the possibility of commotion and distraction,"[12] mobilized, in other words, in the service of privacy. Kerr seems noticeably preoccupied with the issue of what he calls "intercommunication" between rooms. His frequent criticism of such intercommunication is that it can weaken the individual character of a given room. For example, discussing the relationship of the drawing room (a feminine and social space) to the library (a masculine and solitary room), he writes: "Intercommunication is frequently made with the Drawing-room, and sometimes intimately, and this carries with it no doubt a certain sort of convenience, because the two rooms can be thrown together occasionally for the evening; but it is a question whether, in a good house, and looking at such a question broadly, it is not on the whole a serious loss to both rooms as regards their more proper purposes."[13] Thresholds can threaten domestic order because they are sites of intersection and difference. Individual rooms, to extend the metaphor of intercommunication, ought not to speak to each other; they should model circumspection for their occupants. A "good" house, a proper house, is one in which rooms maintain social and spatial discretion.

Thresholds can also unsettle another principle of domesticity that Kerr holds dear: privacy. Privacy, for Kerr, "the basis of our primary classification," helps to secure the oppositions of the gentleman's house. He defines it as seclusion, or freedom from interruption. Threshold spaces are potential sites of interruption, junctures that can diminish the individual's access to privacy or secrecy.[14] Kerr is less severe regarding intercommunication among rooms of a similar nature, such as the library and the study. But even in these cases he withholds full approval, noticing, for instance, that two feminine rooms such as the boudoir and drawing room are compromised by the presence of a connecting door: "if the Boudoir be properly used, so ready an access from the Drawing-room may be very inconvenient as regards the privacy of the lady."[15] Kerr lingers suspiciously on the question of intercommunication because, although doors or passageways are necessary to the plan of the house, such threshold spaces impair the stability and perfection of the plan.

In her well-known work *Purity and Danger*, Mary Douglas cites sociologist Van Gennep, who compares society to "a house with rooms and corridors in which passage from one to another is dangerous."[16] Douglas's subject is not house planning, but something she argues is organized according to a similar logic, dirt. Like the house that contains it, dirt is defined and organized in specific ways. Anxiety about dirt was a strong current in Victorian domestic life. Countering the image of the middle-class home as a sacred, feminized retreat from the pressures of public life was a prevailing sense that the home could be a breeding ground for dirt and disease, invariably accompanied by moral decay. As Annmarie Adams explains, "The house was *not* a safe, protective shelter, removed from a dangerous and unpredictable Victorian city. Between 1870 and 1900, middle-class houses were considered much more poisonous and dangerous than public spaces or working-class neighborhoods, the subject of earlier reforms."[17] Like the threshold, dirt is neither one thing nor another but defined only through reference to its surroundings; dirt is associated with threshold states. For Douglas, "Danger lies in transitional states, simply because transition is neither one state nor the next, it is undefinable."[18] Openings in the body are often considered dirty and governed by boundary-policing rituals, because they mark the places where the body is subject to transitions, such as assimilating food or discharging waste. Dirt, in other words, partakes of the threshold, as is plain in Woolf's and Strachey's household memoirs, where dirt, secrecy, and thresholds create a grid of social order and disorder that locates the subject of life-writing.

Douglas focuses in particular on how dirt is identified and managed in relationship to the body, but one might also turn the issue around and ask: What does dirt do? What does it do to things, to persons? How does dirt separate from the body, and how does it return to the body? The dirt that will interest me in this chapter is of a particular order: household dirt, a ready presence in everyday life in the late-nineteenth-century middle-class British home. As Dominique Laporte argues, dirt "must certainly have played a role in the emergence of the family and familial intimacy."[19] Before the advent of central heating, rooms were heated individually by wood or coal, producing quantities of soot and ash; ventilation was relatively poor since keeping heat in was more important than circulating fresh air. The walls of many Victorian parlors were painted dark blue or black, a decorative choice that accommodated the inevitable presence of heating residues. Further, before the ready availability of flush toilets and running water, bodily dirt was a more visible presence in the household. Household dirt has a distinct and intimate relationship to home dwellers; it is both proprietary and individualized. In the household, the body must own up to its dirt through processes that have ontological implications for the domestic subject.

In the negotiation between hygiene and dirt, organization and disorder, the household servants played a critical role. As Anne McClintock writes, "servants stood on the dangerous threshold of normal work . . . and came to be figured increasingly in the iconography of 'pollution,' 'disorder,' 'plagues,' 'moral contagion' and 'racial degeneration.' "[20] Kerr specifies that domestic servants should remain as much as possible in parts of the house where the family rarely ventured. The role of the domestic servant contained numerous paradoxes: at once of the household and outside of it; both dirty and charged with ensuring cleanliness; simultaneously visible in labor and invisible in order to protect the family's privacy. Woolf's home at Hyde Park Gate employed seven housemaids, all of whom had their bedrooms on the top floor of this tall house. Their sitting room, however, was in the basement, so that the housemaids were pushed to the margins of the house in both directions. Woolf remembers this basement as "a dark unsanitary place for seven maids to live in" ("Bloomsbury," 116).[21] Her accounts of the housemaids are few and far between, but one anecdote stands out for its detail and force. She recalls how once one of the housemaids unexpectedly spoke up about the grim basement conditions:

> "It's like hell," one of them burst out to my mother as we sat at lessons in the dining room. My mother at once assumed the frozen dignity of the Victorian matron; and said (perhaps): "Leave the room"; and she (unfortunate girl) vanished behind the red plush curtain which, hooped round a semi-circular wire, and anchored by a great gold knob, hid the door that led from the dining room to the pantry.
>
> ("Sketch," 116–17)

The threshold between the family and servant portions of the house is concealed to the point that to an outsider's eye the servant quarters seem not to exist. Such draping covers the workings of the household class structure, masking the threshold that awkwardly links the worlds of family and servants. When the servant accuses her employer, she violates this code of invisibility, invoking the tremendous discrepancy between life on one side of the curtain and the other. Woolf's sympathies may be with the girl, whom she calls "unfortunate," but the story ends there. Having vanished behind the curtain, that girl never finds her way back into the memoir, which recounts life on only one side of the curtain.

Strachey too associates the household servants with dirt and concealed horrors. He describes the butler of the house, Bastiani, as "a fat, black-haired, Italianate creature, who eventually took to drink, could hardly puff up the stairs from the basement, and, as he handed the vegetables, exuded an odor of sweat and whisky into one's face" (26). Sweat and heavy breathing are signs of excessive labor, but on the servant's body Strachey reads them as decrepitude. Puffing and perspiring, with stinking breath, Bastiani's body is insufficiently able to contain itself; in Strachey's reading, the servants, rather than controlling and eliminating dirt from the home, are carriers of it. The threshold matter of servants—a token of their humanity—was particularly unwelcome to the masters of the house. In Kazuo Ishiguro's *The Remains of the Day* (1989), set before the Second World War, when the under-butler waits at table with a large bead of sweat dangling from the tip of his nose he is relieved of his table-waiting duties.

Going back and forth between the basement (which, as in the Stephen household, is restricted to the servants) and the family zone of the dining room where he waits at table, Bastiani brings the world of the servants, where intimacy with dirt is expected, into the supposedly hygienic family sphere. When Strachey and his siblings peer into the butler's sideboard, Strachey recalls finding "tangled masses of soda water-bottle wires, broken corkscrews, napkins, and the mysterious remains of disembowelled brushes" (26) abandoned by Bastiani. Strachey has stumbled upon something like a crime scene. The offense is one of excessive presence, since the servants should be as invisible as possible. The leaving behind of filthy traces violates this rule, as does the display of emotion; the outburst of the Stephens' housemaid is matched by Bastiani, who "disappeared—after a scene of melodramatic horror" (26). In both memoirs, servants are threshold figures, moving between zones of cleanliness and filth, visibility and invisibility, with a power and responsibility to purge the house of dirt.

In these memoirs, dirt becomes a symbol for household matters considered unspeakable, unseeable, and unwriteable in Woolf's and Strachey's childhood homes. Physical filth stands at one end of a spectrum of meanings for dirt that includes bodily secretions, socially inappropriate emotions, and sexual transgressions. The body, a powerful vehicle for intimate symbolism with its own set of threshold regulations, becomes a particular site of attention in the gentleman's house, and a wellspring of dirt and secrecy. As Woolf and Strachey show, the body is subjected to a pervasive discipline through the routines of household life, organized not around the elimination of the improper, the private, or the dirty but rather around the identification and regulation of these qualities. The dirt they describe is not homogeneous or abstract; it has qualities of its own and it asserts itself at key moments. At stake in these memoirs, in a sense, are competing claims to cleanliness across the generations. Is it preferable, as the older generation would have it, to define dirt as "matter out of place" and strive for cleanliness through proper management of the threshold? Or is dirt simply another name for secrecy, and total exposure the only way to make a clean breast of it? Or—is there an argument to be made for dirty living?

"Life within walls"

The house at 22 Hyde Park Gate was built in the early nineteenth century, one of a series of architecturally undistinguished row houses designed as single-family homes for upper middle-class families. Leslie Stephen was born on the same street, at number 14; in 1878 he moved to 13 Hyde Park Gate South (later renumbered 22). At this address he married his second wife, Julia, who had been a Hyde Park Gate neighbor during his first marriage. Julia moved in with her three children from her previous marriage, while Leslie brought a daughter to the marriage. Leslie and Julia were to have four children of their own, and so the family quickly outgrew the house, which consisted, when Virginia was born in 1882, of only two stories, plus a basement and an attic. In 1886, Leslie and Julia sought to accommodate their expanding family by undertaking a substantial renovation, converting the attic into habitable space and adding a new top floor, as well as the house's first bathroom.[22] The builder on the project made no effort to harmonize the new floors with the existing facade, and the line demarcating the addition is plain even now, more than one hundred years later. The Survey of London comments, "The insensitive manner in which Sir Leslie Stephen added two extra brick-faced storeys to his otherwise stucco-fronted house at No. 22 provides an obvious case . . . of architecture . . . mutilated by inappropriate additions."[23] The plan for the addition (fig. 7) is the only surviving blueprint for the original house at 22 Hyde Park Gate, though the rest of the house can be imaginatively reconstructed if we rely on Woolf's description of it in her memoirs.[24]

Illustrating Kerr's contention that the plan of the house organizes its occupants, Woolf's vision of the house's plan was based on an architectural analogy to the body. She may well have drawn this idea from Geoffrey Scott, whose popular work *The Architecture of Humanism* was in her library. Scott wrote that "The tendency to project the image of our functions into concrete forms is the basis, for architecture, of creative design," and favored architecture that "transcribe[d] in stone the body's favourable states."[25] Woolf too saw the body reflected in the plan of her home, writing for instance that her father's study, located atop the house, was "the brain of the house" ("Sketch," 119). The remote location afforded maximal privacy for writing. Leslie Stephen wrote

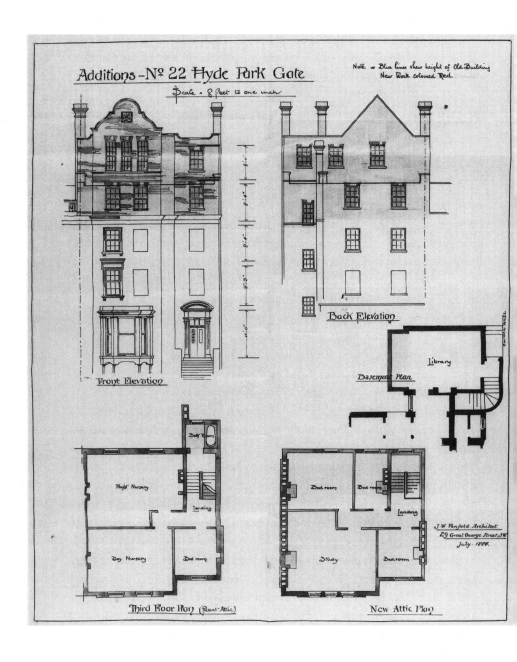

Figure 7. Additions to 22 Hyde Park Gate, 1886. The Royal Borough of Kensington and Chelsea Libraries and Arts Service.

from his rocking chair, at the room's center. It's not surprising to find the most private space in the home given over to its bookish master, but in Woolf's eyes the master's privilege was no guarantee of his virility. Ensconced in his chair, he is almost immobile; Woolf tells us, "He had written all his books lying sunk in that deep rocking chair; which swung up and down; for it was so deep that his feet were off the ground. Across it lay his writing board" ("Sketch," 119). Where some might see the distinguished writer in his study, Woolf paints her father as infantile. She also gestures to the "stack of rusty alpenstocks" heaped in a corner as further evidence of their owner's decline.

The father may be the house's brain, but the mother is its body. The tea table is "the centre, the heart" of the house, presided over by Julia Stephen. In addition to a heart(h), the house also has sexual organs, identified with the parental bedroom and its bed: "in that bed four children were begotten; there they were born; there first mother died; then father died, with a picture of mother hanging in front of him" ("Sketch," 118). The father belongs in the bedroom too, but in Woolf's view his activities are all circumscribed by the mother, who both begets and bears the children and who lingers after her own death to oversee her husband's. Julia Stephen is the central figure at 22 Hyde Park Gate in her daughter's eyes not because she has supreme authority in the house but because she embodies it, and family life, in the tradition of the Victorian domestic angel. Hers is the body governed by its complement, the paternal brain.

In Woolf's account, the house/body is organized according to the logic of oppositional divisions anticipated by Kerr: "It was a black and white world compared with ours; obvious things to be destroyed—headed humbug, obvious things to be preserved—headed domestic virtues" ("Sketch," 115). The credo of the gentleman was spelled out on a strip of cardboard hung over the fireplace and printed with a motto: " 'What is it to be a gentleman? It is to be tender to women, chivalrous to servants' " ("Sketch," 117), and so forth. Twenty-two Hyde Park Gate was a gentleman's house, with a firm distinction between public and private spheres. The most public part of the house was its ground floor, which contained the dining room, pantry, and kitchen, from which a staircase twisted off into the hall. Off the hall were the front and back drawing rooms, divided by a pair of folding doors, and on the first floor was the master bedroom. Above these rooms were two floors for the children's bedrooms, and above these, the study and servant's bedrooms. The best furnishings and decorative schemes were all reserved for the lower, public floors, where guests were admitted. Downstairs was decorated in rich red velvet upholstery, heavy oak carved furniture, woodwork painted black with thin gold lines running through it, and a prized portrait by Watts of Leslie Stephen hung facing the door. These rooms also contained the desks of Julia Stephen and her eldest daughter, Stella.

Each succeeding story after the basement had a progressively lower ceiling. From eleven feet on the parlor floor to eight feet on the nursery floor, walking up the stairs at 22 Hyde Park Gate meant moving into increasingly confined spaces. The sense of crowding was augmented by the clutter of objects: "Old letters filled dozens of black tin boxes. One opened them and got a terrific whiff of the past. There were chests of heavy family plate. There were hoards of china and glass" ("Bloomsbury," 182). It was a house "crowded with scenes of family life, grotesque, comic and tragic" ("Bloomsbury," 183). In a series of extended similes in "A Sketch of the Past" Woolf compares the operation of the household to a zoo (116), a shell (143), and an ant colony under glass (147), all claustrophobic enclosures that resolve into a final picture of threatening confinement in which domestic routine is likened to the action of a hydraulic press.[26] "Victorian society began to exert its pressure at about half past four. . . . The pressure of society made itself apparent as soon as the bell rang. . . . About seven thirty the pressure of the machine became emphatic" (148–50). From organic to mechanical, from protective to crushing, the progression of images shows individuals mass-produced by the social machine.

The pressure of convention was closely tied to Woolf's experience of Hyde Park Gate as a dirty place, where the struggle for cleanliness was constantly waged and lost. In houses without running water, bathing could be an uncomfortable process, often limited to those parts of the body on visible display. Bodies were seen as incorrigibly dirty, a state that cleansing could only mitigate. Every evening before dinner, Woolf recalls, she and her sister Vanessa washed: "However cold or foggy, we slipped off our day clothes and stood shivering in front of washing basins. Each basin had its can of hot water. Neck and arms had to be scrubbed, for we had to enter the drawing room at eight with bare arms, low neck, in evening dress" ("Sketch," 150). This washing was for the benefit of the family, who wished to see clean and feminine bodies at dinner unmarked by the work of the day. Women's cleanliness had a special importance, shoring up the image of the home as hygienic and beneficial. Adams writes: "Like the service pipe, house drain, and ventilating pipe that defined women's sphere, her body acted as both the protection against disease and the source of infection."[27] This position is represented in Woolf's and her sister's partial wash, bodying forth cleanliness and leisure and concealing both the signs of labor and the evidence of the unwashed body under the wrappings of femininity.

Woolf's descriptions of dirt conflate it with rumor, excessive emotional display, and social impropriety. Hyde Park Gate, Woolf remarked, "seemed tangled and matted with emotion" ("Bloomsbury," 183). Emotion was dirty, cloying, clogging; it impeded and polluted whatever it touched. Her characterization of her father's emotional displays mingles dirt with sex: "He had an illicit need for sympathy, released by the woman, stimulated; and her [Vanessa's] refusal . . . exacerbated him; checked the flow that had become necessary of self pity, and stirred in him instincts of which he was unconscious. Yet also ashamed" ("Sketch," 146). Emotion belongs to a fluid economy, regulated by patterns of repression and release triggered by unconscious drives. Feminine sympathy— once given by his wife, now inappropriately looked for from his daughter— stimulates an emission of self-pity that Woolf finds disgusting and incestuous. His displays are figured as a kind of perverse ejaculation; to turn them on Vanessa is a (socially acceptable) misuse of his daughter.

For Woolf, dirt was like a secret vein that ran through family life, and the superficial scrubbing of necks and arms did little to disguise its presence. The bathroom was the central space for negotiations with the body's dirt. At 22 Hyde Park Gate there were three water closets and a single bath, all located on stairwell half-landings, for the occupants to share. In London in the 1880s the bathroom was a recent innovation, introduced into the house by Woolf's parents at the time of the renovation. With the appearance of the bathroom in the nineteenth century came a reconceptualization of the significance of the body and its functions in the home. The existence of separate water closets and bathrooms (instead of portable chamber pots, washstands, and baths) sequesters bodily ablutions from the rest of domestic life, marking them as private and intimate activities.[28] The name "water closet" both refers to body wastes and to the liquid that carries these wastes out of the household. It is appropriate that the Victorians, famously if ambiguously committed to body modesty, popularized the relegation of bodily ablutions to a separate room in the house. This act of segregation links the secret with the dirty and identifies the body as a reservoir of both qualities. In the bathroom, the body owns up to its dirt and undergoes hygienic rites. From its origins, this room stood in the paradoxical position of promoting hygiene and purity while creating a welcoming space for the body's dirt.

In a telling simile, Woolf contrasts the regulation of social life in the drawing room with the regulation of the body: "But it is of the folding doors that I wish to speak. How could family life have been carried on without them? As soon dispense with water-closets or bathrooms as with folding doors" ("22

Hyde Park Gate," 164). Woolf's comparison of the bathroom to the folding doors of the drawing room draws specifically on associations with both secrecy and dirt. The drawing room, writes Mike Hepworth, "was the acme of [respectability]: a purified social arena subject to constant surveillance dictated by the proliferating rules of etiquette."[29] The idea of the drawing room as an unsanitary place is jarring, and here, in both drawing rooms and bathrooms, dirt creates the need for privacy. The folding doors kept the dirt of inappropriate emotion private; their purpose, Woolf explains, was to screen off from general sight the more unseemly tales of women's lives:

> A servant dismissed, a lover rejected, pass books opened, or poor Mrs. Tyndall who had lately poisoned her husband by mistake come for consolation. On one side of the door Cousin Adeline, Duchess of Bedford, perhaps would be on her knees—the Duke had died tragically at Woburn; Mrs. Dolmetsch would be telling how she had found her husband in bed with the parlour-maid or Lisa Stillman would be sobbing that Walter Headlam had chalked her nose with a billiard cue.
>
> ("22 Hyde Park Gate," 164)

Household dirt takes many forms, as Woolf drolly observes. One of the incidents she mentions, the nose chalked with a billiard cue, draws on a classic material definition of dirt, that of out-of-place matter. Lisa Stillman's sobs show that she feels herself to have been "stained." Like the bathroom, the space beyond the folding doors concealed what was considered inappropriate for public view and provided a space for the outlet of dirt. On one side of the doors, all was "dark and agitated," while the other side would be "cheerful enough"; the divider effectively banished the improper. Or did it? It is hard to imagine the folding doors as an impermeable barrier against sound. Again, like the walls of the bathroom, the folding doors are a threshold that responds to the requirement that dirt be visually screened off.

Women appear to have been the ones who sought the refuge of the folding doors, and the topic of conversation was frequently women's troubles in their relationships with men. In this sense, the nether half of the drawing room served as an impromptu boudoir, a room for the lady of the house that was typically designed, as J. J. Stevenson noted in *House Architecture* (1880), for "the very commendable purpose of allowing ill-humour to be got rid of in private."[30] The word *boudoir* comes from the French *bouder*, meaning to pout or sulk. The boudoir was a women's room, and the restriction on public emotion was primarily limited to women. By contrast, Woolf recalls her father's theatrical displays of emotion: "My father strode up and down the drawing room, groaning, swearing . . . without caring if the victim . . . overheard" ("Sketch," 112). The boudoir, like the bathroom, was a place for private relief, but women's dirt—both emotional and physical—demanded extra protection against revelation.

Woolf writes that "family life" could not have been "carried on" without the folding doors, yet this arrangement was not a sanctioned organization of the middle-class domestic interior. Kerr describes an arrangement exactly like the Stephens' and condemns this form of "intercommunication": "When Boudoir and Drawing-room are connected by folding-doors, so as to be capable of being thrown into one, this must be considered as an arrangement at variance with the requirements of the Boudoir, and only adopted as a means of enlarging the Drawing-room at its neighbour's expense."[31] The Stephens' compromise, as Kerr warns, preserves a larger drawing room at the expense of a private space for Julia Stephen that would correspond to her husband's study. Despite this deviation, Woolf's impression that the folding doors were critical to family life derives from Kerr's most basic tenet about Victorian domesticity: that every activity housed by the home be allotted a separate domain. What Woolf emphasizes and Kerr disregards is the premise that such domestic arrangements meant that social improprieties (such as sobbing on your knees in the drawing room) were rendered tacitly permissible by spatial segregations. In this sense, the house neatly parallels its occupants, for both segregate "dirt" in lieu of banishing it. The threshold space of the folding doors was less a solid barrier than a symbol of the requirement for separation, marking a domestic commitment to make dirt undetectable in the absence of sufficient space to make it vanish. Like any threshold, the doors were a pressure valve, a restraining measure that could give way, allowing the contents of one room to stream into the next. Household dirt creates the threshold, with the segregation of dirt offered in lieu (or by way) of purification.

The plan of the house provides guidelines for what can be spoken of and where, guidelines that vary according to who is speaking. When it comes to sensitive disclosures such as secrets, confessions, or histrionics, the rules become explicit. Servants are enjoined from speaking personally at all in the family quarters of the house; when the Stephens' maid does so she is dismissed from the room (and when the Stracheys' butler does so he must leave the house). For the women of the family and female visitors, a special room is allotted for this purpose, providing little real privacy but preserving the tranquility of the rest of the house. Woolf is critical of the literary output produced by this domestic system, which in her home put her father's needs literally above all else: "The Victorian manner is perhaps—I am not sure—a disadvantage in writing. When I read my old *Literary Supplement* articles, I lay the blame for their suavity, their politeness, their sidelong approach, to my tea-table training. I see myself, not reviewing a book, but handing plates of buns to shy young men and asking them: do they take cream and sugar?" ("Sketch," 150).

In the drawing room, as in Woolf's early writing, there is much that could be said but is not. The room demands discretion to the point of concealment, which may make for a placid home but can produce insipidity. "Clean" conversation gives the home a luster of sanitation and propriety, but Woolf suggests in her memoirs that good writing is dirty. This is a surprising claim, coming from the writer who famously criticized *Ulysses* as reminiscent of a "queasy undergraduate scratching his pimples." Like many people, Woolf didn't care for the dirt of others, but she liked her own.

"The framework of our being"

Bridget Cherry and Nikolaus Pevsner describe the street Lancaster Gate as spanned by "tall well-to-do houses" that were built around 1856–57 in the mid-Victorian style.[32] From 1884 to 1908, the Strachey family owned and occupied number 69. The house was indeed tall, rising six stories above ground with a basement below. It was built by an uncelebrated architect, and Strachey remembers it as having been "designed extraordinarily badly" (19). It was narrow and deep, with no courtyard, and the only source of natural light was the row of windows in the front. Yet excellence of design is not necessarily what gives a childhood home its power, and the house certainly made a considerable impact on Strachey. "To reconstruct, however dimly, that grim machine, would be to realize with some distinctness the essential substance of my biography" (27), he claims, and this is the project of his household memoir. Strachey's home, like Woolf's, is a social machine for stamping out uniform products. His essay moves between loathing and longing, for while he portrays his childhood home as fetid, dim, and choked by custom, his tone conveys nostalgia and fondness for the years he spent there.

The essay "Lancaster Gate" is a heady, hysterical read. Though he lived there for twenty-five years, Strachey never felt at home, and his essay rings with intimations of the uncanny. Here is his opening description of the house:

Its physical size was no doubt the most obviously remarkable thing about it; but it was not mere size, it was size gone wrong, size pathological; it was a house afflicted with elephantiasis that one found one had entered, when, having mounted the steps under the porch, having passed through the front door and down the narrow dark passage with its ochre walls and its tessellated floor of magenta and indigo tiles, one looked upwards and saw the staircase twisting steeply up its elongated well—spiraling away into a thin infinitude, until, far above, one's surprised vision came upon a dome of pink and white glass, which yet one judged, with an unerring instinct, was not the top—no, not nearly, nearly the top.

(18)

In contrast to Strachey's typically measured prose style, this passage rings with vertigo and phobia, a sense of space twisted, bulging, and out of control. Like Woolf, Strachey models his home on the human body, but his is sick and deformed. This house presents symptoms of swelling and bruising. If Woolf's home squeezed her out of existence, Strachey was so estranged from his that it seemed to him profoundly unhomely. Anthony Vidler's comments on modernist architects resonate with Strachey's perceptions; he writes that for the "modernist avant-gardes, the uncanny readily offered itself as an instrument of 'defamiliarization' or *ostranenie*: as if a world estranged and distanced from its own nature could only be recalled to itself by shock."[33] Strachey's is a productive estrangement of the kind described by Vidler, since it allowed him to turn a critical eye upon what was most familiar to him. To Holroyd, Lancaster Gate remained Strachey's "personal symbol of Victorianism," an object of fascination at the back of his later dissections of the Victorians in biographies such as *Eminent Victorians* and *Queen Victoria*. By making familiar things strange, Strachey denaturalizes the Victorian world and renders it an artifact of the past rather than a living representation of personal history. The source of this estrangement is, in Vidler's terms, the shock of modernity, the jolt of discord that launches Strachey forward from his Victorian past into a modern future.

Like Woolf's, Strachey's household memoir is preoccupied with secrecy and filth. Like hers, his memoir presents a portrait of a large house tended by many servants and teeming with children—thirteen altogether, including three who died in infancy. Lancaster Gate stretched higher and enclosed itself tighter than Hyde Park Gate, with seven stories and few windows. The earliest plans I have uncovered for the house date from 1929, twenty years after the Stracheys moved out. Judging from the discrepancies between these plans and Strachey's account, some changes to the interior occurred in the interim, including the addition of more bathrooms and the division of the drawing room into three separate rooms. As is the case with Woolf's memoirs, it is possible to piece together the original plan of 69 Lancaster Gate on the basis of Strachey's memoir, with additional details supplied by the 1929 plans. These plans show a house roughly twenty-five feet wide and eighty feet deep, beginning in the basement with the servants' quarters and kitchen, and moving upward to a ground-floor dining room and first-floor drawing room. The stories further up were carved into bedrooms, and the entire household shared a single lavatory on the half-landing above the drawing room.

Privacy was a hard-fought privilege in this house because, in spite of its size, it had few rooms not primarily dedicated to sleeping. As at Hyde Park Gate, only General (Sir) Richard Strachey had his own sitting room; the daughters of the house shared a sitting room, called the "young ladies' room." Strachey is dubious about this arrangement: "privacy there, I suppose occasionally there must have been, but privacy arranged, studied, and highly precarious" (20). "Strangest of all," from Strachey's point of view (though identical to the Stephens's arrangement), was that Lady Strachey had no room of her own and attended to her voluminous correspondence and household accounts from a desk in a corner of the dining room. Lancaster Gate allocated its limited non-bedroom space to a room where the entire family could gather. This space, the centerpiece of the house, "the seat of its soul," in Strachey's words, was the drawing room.

Unlike the Stephens' drawing room with its folding doors, the Stracheys' drawing room made no concession to privacy; the room, with its vast open space, seemed to deny the very need for it. The room occupied the majority of the first floor of the house, and faced front, with three windows along the road hung with voluminous pale green curtains. If the scale of the 1929 plans is accurate, the drawing room was approximately 25 by 40 feet, or about 1,000 square feet. It contained a piano for family concerts and large quantities of upholstered furniture, but its most striking decoration was a large mantelpiece (one of two in the room) designed by Halsey Ricardo; Strachey describes it as a "bulk of painted wood with its pilasters and cornices, its jars and niches, its marble and its multi-coloured tiles" (21). Strachey remembers the mantelpiece as a Victorian hodgepodge of ornament, but this seems doubtful on the basis of Ricardo's career. He was a progressive figure in English design, an architect who worked with the better-known W. R. Lethaby. But as Strachey admits, his view of the room is biased: "the decorations were undoubtedly, for the time, slightly advanced. But it is almost impossible for me to come to an impartial judgement on it" (21). For him, the room's significance lay in its status as a preserved specimen of Victorian society.

Even without the empirical evidence of the plans and information about the

designers, Strachey's description of the drawing room appears dense with dis-
tortions.

> When one entered the vast chamber, when, peering through its foggy dis-
> tances, ill-lit by gas-jets, or casting one's eyes wildly towards the infinitely
> distant ceiling overhead, one struggled to traverse its dreadful length, to
> reach a tiny chair or a far-distant fireplace, conscious as one did so that
> some kind of queer life was clustered thick about one, that heaven knows
> how many eyes watched from just adumbrated sofas, that brains
> crouched behind the piano, that there were other presences, remote,
> aloof, self-occupied, and mysteriously dominating the scene—then, in
> truth, one had come—whether one realized it or no—into an extraordi-
> nary holy of holies. The gigantic door, with its flowing portière of pale
> green silk, swung and shut behind one. One stepped forwards . . . one sat
> and spoke and listened: one was reading the riddle of the Victorian Age.
> (20)

The twisting and elongated syntax of these phrases mimics the space they
represent and brings the reader into a looking-glass world where size and shape
fluctuate. Strachey is overwhelmed by simultaneous feelings of agoraphobia—
as the room seems to stretch out endlessly before and above him, causing him
to throw his gaze "wildly" about—and claustrophobia, in his overpowering
sense of intruding eyes that crowd him into place. The space exerts its own
potent power, pressuring Strachey to conform. This spatial anxiety is also
related to the uncanny effect, as he writes, "up to my last hour in it, I always felt
that the drawing-room was strange" (21).

Strachey's self-consciousness is overwhelming. His portentous estrangement, in his view, marks him as modern, but surely it also marks him as Victorian. For as Strachey moves through the drawing room, what is he if not one of
the "presences, remote, aloof, self-occupied"? He is every inch a product of the
drawing room, a heritage confirmed by the continued appearance of the room
in his dreams, where it symbolizes his conflicted longing to return to this space.

Though the law of the drawing room favors self-involvement, it also governs
social behavior, including the display of affection between relatives. In an anecdote that must have drawn a laugh from his audience, Strachey relates a memory he finds, like so many others, "strange":

> Is it conceivable that Dorothy [Strachey], evening after evening, in that
> room, kissed me a hundred times, in a rapture of laughter and affection,

counting her kisses, when I was six? that, in that same room, perhaps twenty years later, sitting on a sofa alone with [his nephew] Andrew, I suddenly kissed him, much to his surprise and indignation—"My dear man! Really! One doesn't do those things!"

(22)

The rules of kissing seem clear to everyone but Strachey, who follows the inclination of his feelings only to be rebuked. The drawing room, for all its propriety and aura of disembodiment, accommodates only heterosexual family romances. His willed naïveté perhaps stems from a desire not to have to take the rules of the drawing room as natural law.

As in Woolf's memoir, Strachey's desire to expose the scandals and secrets of the seemingly proper house is symbolized by a preoccupation with household dirt and the futile effort to eliminate it. Household dirt for Strachey is evidence of the decay of the Victorian household. He and his siblings, representing a new generation, welcome this decline and search for traces of the dirt lurking in the seemingly presentable home: "*we* knew by heart all the camouflaged abysses, taking a sardonic delight in the ruthlessness of the introspective realism with which we plumbed and numbered 'filth-packet' after 'filth-packet'—for such was our too descriptive phrase" (25). Strachey's "filth-packets" conflate dust bunnies with more illicit materials: the Strachey children could be either looking under the bed or in their parents' bedroom drawer. "Filth-packet" also conveys deliberation, a composition of household detritus, assembled perhaps by Bastiani. As at the Stephens', where only visible parts of the body need be clean, housekeeping at the Strachey residence focused on surface appearances.[34] If the code of the Victorian household is one of superficial propriety, Strachey substitutes a new ethic of "introspective realism," which might also be called confession, or hanging out the dirty laundry, a literary style as well as a mode of housekeeping.

At Lancaster Gate, as at Hyde Park Gate, the presence of the lavatory is a reminder of the constant proximity of dirt, of what should not be seen. The lavatory intrudes on drawing-room life with a reminder of the intractable dirtiness of the body. The single lavatory in the Strachey household was placed "in an impossible position midway between the drawing-room and the lowest bedroom floors—a kind of crow's nest" (19). At Lancaster Gate, the lavatory is relegated to a threshold location, between one floor and the next, but it belongs to neither. The threshold proves more permeable than the occupants would like it to be; in spite of the effort to keep the lavatory away, it invades the drawing room. In a parallel that again seems to reference Woolf's memoir, Strachey invokes the unexpected relationship between lavatory and drawing room. On a typical evening, he relates, the family might gather in this room after dinner to be entertained by a guest's piano playing. Describing a representative evening spent listening to music with his family, Strachey writes, "all at once yet *another* sound—utterly different—burst upon their ears—the sound, this time, of rushing water. There was a momentary shock; and then we all silently realized that someone, in the half-way landing upstairs, was using the w.c." (23). The flush produces a double shock: in a house recently endowed with indoor plumbing the sound was still new. It also marks the aural intrusion of household dirt into the drawing room. The eruption of the body's dirt in a space dedicated to disembodied creatures— "remote, aloof . . . presences"— violates the integrity of the threshold. The sound of rushing water also announces that dirt is being evacuated from the home and its inhabitants, a proper function of domestic order that is nevertheless an embarrassment. Like the servants themselves, the elimination of dirt should be invisible, inaudible. The flush brings together mind and body, clean and dirty, value and waste, and reminds its hearers that they were never separate.

Woolf and Strachey are both drawn to the moment when the integrity of the threshold collapses—when the lavatory flushes in the drawing room, or the drawing room splits in two—because in that moment the structuring contradictions of the household are exposed. The plan of the house deploys walls as barriers that stratify the home, defining and organizing social groups and domestic activities into a hierarchical relationship. But there is a difference between the blank spaces of the floor plan and the lived experience of the household. When the thresholds that join these rooms (and by extension their occupants) are compromised, convention is apparently breached. These breaches are an unavoidable part of daily life, so that it is not the breach itself that matters so much as the individual's response to it: the embarrassed silence, the order to leave the room, the conscious disregard of the voices on the other side of the folding doors. This response reinscribes the subject's subservience to a social system that remains an imperfect version of itself. The domesticated Victorian body is not a clean body, but rather a body that willingly conceals its dirt. The proper Victorian household is not a household with nothing to hide, but one where secrets are well kept.

"Lancaster Gate" and "22 Hyde Park Gate" end with similar acts of exposure that undermine the logic and ideals of Victorian domesticity. The Stephen and Strachey households value the close-knit and well-regulated family and so these memoirists land on the deepest and dirtiest secret of intimate family life: incest. An almost universal human taboo, incest had a particular place in the imaginative life of the Victorians as a fatal flaw in the enshrined image of the family. As James B. Twitchell writes, "The 'family cult of friendship' was a central part of the early-nineteenth-century *Weltanschauung* for the middle class as well as for the aristocracy. The family was such a solid social and financial unit that it was quite normal for a girl to think of refusing to marry a man she loved because her brother might not like it."[35] Leslie Stephen strongly resisted the marriage of his eldest daughter, Stella, on similar grounds. Incest is a psychological horror, but it is also a relationship that invokes the instability of the threshold, since it unites people who are closely related but forbidden to fully mingle with each other. The avoidance of incest depends on maintaining appropriate boundaries in family relationships. In Edgar Allen Poe's short story "The Fall of the House of Usher," the thresholds of family relationship and the thresholds of domestic architecture intertwine when an incestuous relationship between a brother and sister causes their ancestral home literally to split apart and collapse, mirroring the decline of the family itself.

Woolf's memoir makes no secret of the incestuous assaults of her stepbrother George Duckworth, which she casts in terms of an attack on the threshold of both family and home.[36] After an evening of making the social rounds of fashionable parties in decorous drawing rooms, Woolf is retiring for the evening when she is interrupted:

> Sleep had almost come to me. The room was dark. The house silent. Then, creaking stealthily, the door opened; treading gingerly, someone entered. "Who?" I cried. "Don't be frightened," George whispered. "And don't turn on the light, oh beloved. Beloved—" and he flung himself on my bed, and took me in his arms.
>
> Yes, the old ladies of Kensington and Belgravia never knew that George Duckworth was not only father and mother, brother and sister to those poor Stephen girls; he was their lover also.
>
> ("22 Hyde Park Gate," 177)

The violation, terrible as it is, is exacerbated by George's personation of every family member—this act of incest carries the signature of the whole family. Other portions of the memoir make the case that George's liberties were not an isolated aberration from social norms, but one encouraged to an extent by other aspects of family life. George appeals to his sister specifically on the grounds of sisters' moral responsibility to their brothers: "I could only conjure up in my virgin consciousness, dimly irradiated by having read the 'Symposium' with Miss Case, horrible visions of the vices to which young men were driven whose sisters did not make them happy at home" (172–73). George tries to appeal to filial love, a moral obligation of family members, in support of his desires, because he sees incest as an extension of that sanctioned affection rather than a monstrous, isolated violation.

For Woolf, George's ability to disguise his misconduct in familial terms is partially enabled by the principles of Victorian domestic life. His advance is an extreme and distorted version of the same code of behavior that places the young women of the house at the beck and call of their male relatives everyday. The cliché romantic rhetoric Woolf uses to describe the encounter ("took me in his arms"; "those poor Stephen girls") ventriloquizes George's point of view while her irony exposes his perverse self-justification. Her description of the incest functions as a larger social critique in a way that critic Henry Miles characterizes as typical. Miles writes: "There is little doubt that the fictional treatment of incest in the nineteenth century served as a form of protest literature, whether conscious or not, opposing the cosy artificial world of the Victorian family."[37] Woolf appropriates this literary convention to conclude her essay and shock her readers. The revelation of incest is the final exposure of the hypocrisy of the household, a kept secret that demolishes the family rather than consolidating it.

Strachey's conclusion also uncovers an incestuous bedtime scene, but one quite different from Woolf's. Strachey's concluding anecdote is another light-hearted sequel to his drawing-room encounters with his sister and nephew. As a young man of about twenty-four, he returns home late one evening to find the second bed in his bedroom occupied by his cousin Duncan Grant, who has evidently stayed on at Lancaster Gate past a convenient hour for departure. Strachey concludes:

> As I was getting into bed I saw that all the clothes had rolled off Duncan—that he was lying, almost naked, in vague pyjamas—his body—the slim body of a youth of nineteen—exposed to the view. I was very happy; and smiling to myself, I wondered why it was that I did not want—not want in the very least—what the opportunity so perfectly offered, and I got into bed, and slept soundly, and dreamt no prophetic dreams.
>
> (28)

The double refusal opens the possibility that Strachey might welcome a tryst with his cousin, but then repudiates it. Strachey no doubt presumes a little on the knowledge of his audience, who would have known of Strachey's long-standing crush on Grant and their affair. Concluding on a scene of chastity, Strachey offers one clue to his ongoing estrangement from Lancaster Gate: the implicit heterosexual logic of the household, which appears to deem homosexuality more unacceptable than heterosexual incest (note that George asks Virginia to save him from homosexuality) and seems to place a damper on the writer's normally energetic libido even when privacy and a desirable partner are available. Hampered by the house that he described as an "incubus . . . upon my spirit" (27), Strachey gently alludes to an illegal desire most noticeable for its absence, foreclosed before it has hardly been imagined. His allusion to "prophetic dreams" also circles back to the dream that opened the essay, in which his dream is a false prophecy of a return to Lancaster Gate.

For Strachey and Woolf as family members, to reveal family secrets is to break with family tradition. But as writers, to reveal family secrets is also to break with the tradition of nineteenth-century life-writing. Woolf's and Strachey's memoirs respond in form as well as in content to their forebears; they claim to redefine the genre of life-writing to accommodate the kinds of stories they want to tell. Rebellion against Victorian domesticity and Victorian life-writing occur in tandem. Woolf's and Strachey's household memoirs formally repudiate the lives chronicled by Victorian life-writers to tell a more private, fractious, and sometimes anguished story. This act of repudiation is claimed as the basis for modernism, but it also reinscribes the centrality of Victorian mores. Woolf puts it well: "While we looked into the future, we were completely under the power of the past" ("Sketch" 147). The inescapable irony of these household memoirs is that their chief achievement lies in their vivid re-creation of a way of life they were created to discredit.

"This room explains a great deal"

The plan of the house, with its carefully secured divisions between private and public spaces, offers an extension of the doctrine of separate spheres. The nineteenth century in England saw a growing divide between the spheres of home (understood as feminized, spiritual, and private) and work (understood as masculinized, profane, and public). As Mary Poovey observes, the impetus for this separation was largely economic: "The segregation of the domestic ideal created the illusion of an alternative to competition; this alternative, moreover, was the prize that inspired hard work, for a prosperous family was the goal represented as desirable and available to every man."[38] The opposition between public and private also secured the social and architectural organization of the domestic interior, creating another set of separate spheres within the home itself. The plan of the house demarcated its public sections, where the family assembled and entertained, in opposition to the private spaces where they slept and dressed. The opposition between public and private also informs the logic of that substantial portion of Victorian life-writing which represents its subjects as independent and largely impervious to outside influences.[39] In Regenia Gagnier's account, the Victorian subject of life-writing maintains a "belief in personal creativity, autonomy, and freedom for the future"—he has a power of self-definition and a strength of personality that separate him from the surrounding environment.[40] Life-writing was primarily a vehicle for recounting the public achievements of its subjects, with far less attention given to personal details or family life. Biography in the late nineteenth century, writes Paul Murray Kendall, became increasingly monumental, but also increasingly empty: "What was known to be important in a life had become enormously enlarged; but what was permissible to acknowledge had shrunk to the innocuous."[41] The life-writing of Charles Darwin, Thomas Carlyle, and Matthew Arnold focused on intellectual growth and style, with the life of the mind represented in isolation from the material world, and the life of the body nearly absent.[42]

One could hardly find a more relevant example of these principles than in the work of Leslie Stephen. Stephen's lifelong project, the *Dictionary of National Biography*, recaps the careers of the great men of England with a focus on public deeds. Stephen's autobiography, *The Mausoleum Book* (1895), on the other hand, is a far more private variety of life-writing.[43] Written after Julia Stephen's death as a token of remembrance for her children, *The Mausoleum Book* was conceived as an intimate document to be circulated within the family, though Stephen told his children they might publish it after his death. In spite of the private nature of this work, in it Stephen refrains from intimate disclosures and even takes a certain pleasure in concealment. He opens the work with a disclaimer that seems strange for an autobiographer, especially one writing to a limited and confidential audience: "I do, indeed, remember certain facts about myself. I could give a history of some struggles through which I had to pass—successfully or otherwise: but I have a certain sense of satisfaction in reflecting that I shall take that knowledge with me to the grave."[44]

Rather than skipping over what he does not wish to reveal, Stephen underlines the omissions in his narrative as if to display nothing more conspicuously than his powers of discretion. About the death of his first wife, Minny Thackeray, he writes: "I remember only too clearly the details . . . but I will not set them down." Or, in recalling Minny's words about her daughter Laura, "I can remember, though they are too sacred to repeat, little words of Laura's mother." And regarding Julia's death: "I cannot venture to speak of the last terrible time."[45] Stephen's discretion has a certain nobility to it, a willingness to muster his own emotional reserves to protect the well-being of his children and to keep family business in the family. At the same time, the absent moments of particular intimacy, crisis, or conflict that might have been staged as the climaxes of *The Mausoleum Book* become conspicuous by dint of Stephen's refusal to record them. Like the *Dictionary of National Biography*, *The Mausoleum Book* is informed by a strong sense of what ought and ought not to be said and done, of what is public and what private, and of respect for and enjoyment of custom and formula. Stephen's work provides an important benchmark for tracing codes of exposure and concealment as they pass from one generation to the next.

Strachey and Woolf argued that the summary of career accomplishments and acts of self-determination did not themselves capture the spirit of an individual life. To get at that spirit, life-writing needed to delve into matter. Strachey writes: "to our fathers the visible conformations of things were unimportant; they were more interested in the mental and moral implication of their surroundings than in the actual nature of them. . . . Our view is different" (16). Things have an existence independent of their metaphysical properties and for Strachey it is the irreducibly material aspect of things, not their hidden transcendent nature that counts. As Woolf too seeks to demonstrate, the individual's development cannot be separated from apparently inconsequential details of the materiality of domestic life. In their household memoirs, these writers reject not only a way of life but also a way of writing about life, the former for its emphasis on the division between public and private, the latter for passing over the kind of quotidian events that, Woolf argues, make up "a great part of every day" ("Sketch," 70). Of course, it might be argued with equal justice that it is the monumental and not the everyday that defines the subject of life-writing—that individuals are revealed by the extraordinary decisions and events of their lives, not by the way they get dressed in the morning. Yet for Woolf, who never refrained from propagandizing on behalf of the moderns, Victorian life-writers (in spite of the lengthiness of their works) were simply lazy:

> It is obvious that it is easier to [transmit personality] by considering that the true life of your subject shows itself in action which is evident rather than in that inner life of thought and emotion which meanders darkly

and obscurely through the hidden channels of the soul. Hence, in the old days, the biographer chose the easier path.[46]

Writing household memoirs was only one way these writers rebelled against nineteenth-century life-writing as they understood it. Both Woolf and Strachey sought to integrate public and private lives in much of their life-writing, drawing on two distinct definitions of privacy. The first was what might be called the "extraordinary private," the kinds of secrets and scandals about which Leslie Stephen pointedly kept his counsel. For example, in her 1940 biography of Roger Fry, composed concurrently with her longest memoir, "A Sketch of the Past," Woolf dedicated a chapter to Fry's disastrous marriage and his wife's mental illness.[47] The second kind of privacy was the "ordinary private," the habits of everyday life. *Roger Fry* also offers an extended description of Fry's home. The value and import of ordinary life was foundational in Woolf's work as any reader of her novels immediately perceives. *Mrs. Dalloway* (1925), though not a work of life-writing, takes the form of a single day in the life of its characters; *To the Lighthouse* (1927) depicts two days, separated by a brief passage into which years are compressed. Strachey too was interested in the story that a single ordinary day could tell. His essay "Monday June 26th 1916" recounts in detail the events of that single day in his life, a project he deems of supreme aesthetic value: "to realize absolutely the events of a single and not extraordinary day—surely that might be no less marvelous than a novel or even a poem, and still more illuminating, perhaps!"[48] Particular kinds of insights accrue in the "day in the life" approach—personal exchanges, rhythms of mental life, motivations, and desires—above all the continuities of daily experience in which the spheres of public and private weave together.

Perhaps this willingness to see deep import in the incidental was a product of a Freudian age. In psychoanalysis, the individual stood most revealed in the trivialities of daily life such as dreams, jokes, or slips of the tongue. Woolf and Strachey preferred finding significance in the incidental to a more traditional notion of signal events. Freud's influence can certainly be felt in another aspect of modernist life-writing: the principled commitment to reveal what a Victorian life-writer might have kept secret. As with the turn to the quotidian, this confessional tendency was not limited to life-writing: the modern novel famously shocked its readers (and was frequently censored by legal authorities) for its frankness about topics that ranged from scatology to sexuality to sexology. Unlike Stephen, who kept secrets from his readers on principle, for Woolf and Strachey, secrets—like dirt—had to be revealed in order to enact the individual's refusal to be defined by the social standards that demanded secrecy.

Both Woolf and Strachey were explicit about the grounds for their decision to reveal what had previously been excluded from life-writing. In her essay "The Art of Biography," Woolf traces the development of the genre in the nineteenth century, positing the great man's widow as the source of all tactful elisions: "Suppose, for example, that the man of genius was immoral, ill-tempered, and threw the boots at the maid's head. The widow would say, 'Still I loved him—he was the father of my children. . . . Cover up; omit.' The biographer obeyed."[49] It is in the domestic sphere that secrets emerge, and the Angel in the House who hides them; Woolf either doesn't worry about or doesn't conceive of possible scandals in public life. She continues: "Then, towards the end of the nineteenth century, there was a change. Again for reasons not easy to discover, widows became broader-minded, the public keener-sighted. The biographer certainly won a measure of freedom." This development in biography, Woolf writes, reaches a turning point with the works of Lytton Strachey, whose work shows the future for biography in which "The biographer is bound by the facts—that is so; but, if it is so, he has the right to all the facts that are available."[50] Strachey defined the task of the biographer as one of exposure; his preface to *Eminent Victorians* concludes: "Je n'impose rien; je ne propose rien: j'expose."[51] His stated aim in the book was to "lay bare the facts." It is a select group of facts that he presents as he puts the lives of four prominent Victorians into the space of a few hundred pages, and by design the facts he chooses are often those previous biographers had chosen to omit. In the beginning of his essay on Florence Nightingale, for example, he writes that "everyone knows the popular conception of Florence Nightingale . . . But the truth was different."[52] Strachey wants to reveal the truth about his subjects, but he also wants to point out the omissions in previous accounts of their lives.

I follow Woolf and Strachey in their claim that their life-writing had different emphases and pursued different methods than that of Leslie Stephen and his ilk; I also follow their claim, which I explore further in the last chapter, that the households they established differed from those in which they were raised. What I want to question is the status of dirt in the creation of modernism, the idea that the new life-writing had a different relationship to dirt than its predecessors. There is probably no Bloomsbury anecdote better known than the story of what Woolf considered the group's defining moment. The presence of dirt was announced one evening in the drawing room at Gordon Square, where

Woolf and her sister Vanessa made a home after the death of their father and the dispersal of the Hyde Park Gate household.

> Suddenly the door opened and the long and sinister figure of Mr Lytton Strachey stood on the threshold. He pointed a finger at a stain on Vanessa's dress.
>
> "Semen?" he said.
>
> "Can one really say it?" I thought and we burst out laughing. With that one word all barriers of reticence and reserve went down. A flood of the sacred fluid seemed to overwhelm us. Sex permeated our conversation. The word bugger was never far from our lips.
>
> ("Bloomsbury," 195)

Here is an exemplary threshold moment. Strachey, standing on the threshold, delivers a remark that breaks down the barrier that has erased the body from the drawing room. The stain on Vanessa's dress, once exposed, is taken as evidence that dirt has invaded the formal confines of this space; Strachey's comment appears to uncover not just another filth-packet but a sexual secret as well. Both are suddenly made subjects for social discourse, and for life-writing too, since Woolf records the conversation in her memoir. For her, the moment is epochal: the restrictions on drawing-room conduct collapse and semen (figuratively) floods the room.

But let us scrutinize the questions this anecdote asks more closely. There are two, the first from Strachey and the second from Woolf. Strachey's question, "Semen?" surely points to the speaker's desire more than to his power of observation. A semen stain has no visibly unique character. Strachey has not uncovered evidence of a sexual encounter, just a stain on Vanessa's dress that he uses as a pretext for saying "semen" in the drawing room. The scandalous secret here is likely a product of the speaker's imagination. It is not sex that is being introduced to the drawing room but sex talk. So Woolf's question actually seems more pivotal—"Can one really say it?"—this being the question that Woolf and Strachey go on to ask throughout their work. Woolf's question carries all the delight of the child who has at last broken away from parental supervision and can explore her new liberty, the liberty to talk like a bad girl, if not to act like one.

How different is this scene from the moment when the rushing waters of the water closet invade the Strachey drawing room? The two questions recoup the focus on dirt, the body, scandal, in short, on all the threshold matters that organized life at Lancaster Gate and Hyde Park Gate. If Woolf never heard the word "semen" at 22 Hyde Park Gate, she did hear its equivalents: the maid's "It's like hell!," her stepbrother's "Beloved!," and Lisa Stillman's staining encounter with Walter Headlam's billiard cue. If Woolf wants to stake a claim for her generation's difference on the verbal introduction of semen into the drawing-room, she is on shaky ground. Her claim is founded on a questionable proposition that in the Victorian drawing room the walls are impermeable and the thresholds fully regulated. As Strachey and Woolf themselves describe, at Gordon Square, as at Hyde Park Gate, dirt has a way of entering the drawing room; in fact, dirt has always been inseparable from the drawing room; dirt makes the drawing room what it is. The stain on Vanessa's dress, pointed out by the delighted Woolf and Strachey, has always been there, and these writers have as much fun saying so in their new homes as they did in their old ones. Strachey, in other words, is still turning up filth-packets. As a founding moment of modernism, the stain seems to point up some of what it seeks to deny: Woolf's and Strachey's continuity with the Victorian tradition and their reliance on the distinction between public and private life, between propriety and scandal, to give their work meaning. In some sense, then, these writers are caught up in the logic of the threshold where they love to linger.

It should come as no surprise that Strachey and Woolf have difficulty leaving the past behind, that their most stirring repudiations of their heritage coincide with their most complete reanimations of it. Modernism's rhetoric of parthenogenesis is, after all, sometimes just a rhetoric. The past finds a way to leave its trace in Bloomsbury's most impassioned denials of it. In Strachey's threshold encounter with Vanessa, that trace takes the form of dirt. This seems appropriate, since dirt is sometimes nothing more than something old that has outstayed its welcome, like the crust of yesterday's dinner on today's frying pan. Dirt is residue, one of the ways the past manages to hang on. There are in fact two stains in the story Woolf relates, of which the anonymous stain on Vanessa's dress is only the first. The second is the "Can one really say it?" the stain of the past on the present, the question Woolf continues to ask of the older generation even when they are no longer there to answer.

4. Studies

If he be at his book, disturb him not.
—Ben Jonson, *Every Man in His Humour*

The study is a good place to go when you want to be left alone. In *Sido* (1929), Colette recalls how her father passed the days of his retirement alone in his study writing his memoirs and binding the volumes himself. While her father was alive, neither Colette nor any other member of the family was ever tempted to open one of the books, because of their unprepossessing titles: *My Campaigns, The Lessons of '70, Marshal Mahon Seen by a Fellow-Soldier,* and so forth. After her father died, however, the library was converted into a bedroom, and Colette's elder brother made a discovery: "The dozen volumes bound in boards revealed to us their secret, a secret disdained by us, accessible though it was."[1] Except for a dedication, the books contained all blank pages. Their seemingly literary father, closeted in his study, never wrote a word. This discovery epitomizes the father's impotence, which is also suggested by his missing leg and his failed political career. But the blank books are most shameful of all. How could they have remained secret for so long? And what other secrets might the study conceal? Colette's seemingly idiosyncratic anecdote exemplifies a broader relationship between the study, authorship, and secrecy.

It is startling to discover that the accoutrements of authorship are enough to make an author of Colette's father. Authorship has always had a plainly material basis, with trappings that can be readily enumerated: books, pens, paper. It has also been closely associated with the spaces of writing throughout its history from St. Jerome onward. "The writer in his study" continues to be a staple of authorial iconography. Many things about the scene of authorship Colette describes resonate with the history of the study. First, the perfect privacy that allowed Colette's father to keep his secret safely has long been a feature of this room. The masculine aura evinced by the military titles lining the walls is equally well represented in the historical record. What is uniquely modern about Colette's anecdote is the will to power expressed by a woman writer who wishes to claim the study for her own. For it is hard to read this anecdote without noting that the daughter has become the writer that the father only pretended to be, his writer's block succeeded by her prolific output. Colette has filled her father's empty pages, is filling them now in the act of testifying to her father's comparable inadequacy. This act of usurpation, defined by and through the history of the study, is a founding moment for the modern woman writer.

Referred to sometimes as studies and sometimes as libraries or by other names, all the rooms I will discuss in this chapter are spaces dedicated exclusively to reading and writing, rooms closely identified with the male writer or scholar's profession and personality. Even as the identity of this space as the seat of authorship and authority in the home was being consolidated in the nineteenth century, the exclusivity of the male claim to this space came under attack. As we have seen, the doctrine of separate spheres that underwrote the organization of the home faced challenges from within and without, but the study or its equivalent has always been somewhat at odds with the framework of separate spheres that locates paid labor in the public domain. Walter Benjamin has pointed out that the private sphere is largely an invention of the nineteenth century when, for the first time, "living space becomes . . . antithetical to the place of work."[2] But this distinction does not extend to the writer who frequently works at home in the study.[3] Thus the study offers a space for sanctioned professional work within the domestic sphere, a space that—were it not for its thoroughly masculine character—might seem tantalizingly proximate to the budding woman writer. Critics have written extensively about the construction of female authorship in the early twentieth century, formulating authorship—not surprisingly—in largely literary terms.[4] But here I want to take a different approach, recognizing that the source of the modern writer's authority is as much bound up with material conditions as it is with influence, affiliation, or style. The possession of a study can affirm and protect its owner's literary efforts to such an extent that, as in the case of Colette's father, little or no evidence of actual writerly production is required to justify ownership of the space. The question I want to explore is a simple one: given that in the late nineteenth century the spaces of reading and writing are associated with a privilege and power that is exclusively masculine, what happens when ambitious women set out to claim these spaces for themselves?

Answering this question requires briefly tracing the history of such spaces with particular attention to the intertwined histories of gender and privacy. Following this discussion, I will turn to a group of texts that stage women's desire to usurp the privileges of the study to support their own acts of writing: Arthur Conan Doyle's short story "A Scandal in Bohemia" (1891), Radclyffe Hall's novel *The Well of Loneliness* (1928), and Virginia Woolf's essay *A Room of One's Own* (1928), the last being the most famous articulation of the study's power. These texts stage the historical collision between the masculine confines of the study and the ambition of the woman writer, a collision that has an impact on gender identity, authorship, and private life. So strong is the connection between masculinity and the study that women with studies are invariably defined (and see themselves) as manly. Crossing genders to cross the study's threshold affects both the way these women construct their authorship and the way they understand the authorial work they do in the domestic sphere. Their crossings also shed light on how privacy is constructed in the home: what it means, who is entitled to it, and what it covers. The secret Colette's father kept in his study is not an exception to the history of this space but rather its enabling condition. When Colette writes of "a secret disdained by us, accessible though it was," she is pointing at the emptiest of spaces, the space of the blank page. The paternal secret is in this sense an empty secret, its content a distant second in importance to the significance of the father's ability to have secrets, an ability conferred by the study and associated exclusively with masculinity.

The study is typically a space for one person alone. It is the perfected space of privacy, a privacy that enables a heightened degree of autonomy within the symbiotic structure of the household. As I described in the previous chapter, modernist writers critiqued the way in which the ideology of separate spheres set the master of the house at the top of domestic hierarchy and argued for a more egalitarian division of household space. But that critique apparently grinds to a halt at the study door. The generative power of this space and the autonomy it bestows prove so tempting that the writers I discuss want only to co-opt it for their own use, to take the study on its own terms. The history of the study in the late nineteenth and early twentieth centuries bespeaks not a transformation of the meaning and function of this space but a mere transfer of ownership. Thus, as we will see, when women enter the study, so strong is the shaping power of this space that they find they can only do so *as men*, that is to say, by reconstituting the triangulated dynamic of secrecy, masculinity, and scholasticism that animated the Victorian study.

"A place of reading and writing for one person alone"

The first European interior spaces devoted to reading and writing were probably located in monasteries. In the private home, the earliest such spaces were small compartments directly off the bedroom called studies or closets. Though men were far more likely to have such spaces than women, there were exceptions: Christine de Pizan's *Book of the City of Ladies* (1402) opens with a woodcut of the author working in her private study (or as Christine calls it, her "cele"), and Roxbury's *Life of St. Catherine* (1430) mentions "hir secreet study where no creature vsed to com bot hir self allone."[5] Whether the room in question belonged to a man or a woman, this space does seem to have connoted privacy and secrecy from its inception. The *OED* signals the association in its entry for "study," which it defines in part as a term "often applied to the 'private room or office of the master of a house, however it may be used.' " It offers the following example: "1574. 'I gave a deed to be ingrossed with speed, and yt must be done very secretly in a Close studdie.' "[6] The single-owner nature of the study naturally lent itself to secrecy, a feature that could cause other household members to grow curious, as is evident from a scene in the popular Spanish courtesy book *Libro Aureo de Marco Aurelio* (1527) by Antonio Da Guevara:

> The emperour had the study or closet of his howse in the mooste secrete place of his palays, wherin he neyther suffred his wyfe, seruant, nor frend to entre. On a day it chanced, that Faustyn thempresse desyred importunatly to se that study, sayenge these words: my lorde, let me se your secrete chaumbre. Beholde I am greatte with chylde, and shall dye, yf I see it not.[7]

The privacy of the study or closet was central to its identity as a space; specifically, the room seems to have long been a place for keeping secrets, especially those related to sexual transgression. In this anecdote, it transpires that Faustyn believes her husband to be concealing a lover in the study and wants entry in order to learn the truth. In distinction from the women I discuss below, Faustyn does not want a study of her own; she just wants to know her husband's secret.

The book closet offered unparalleled opportunities for keeping secrets in the early modern household, so much so that some scholars have placed this space at the origin of the notion of domestic privacy.[8] As Lena Cowen Orlin writes, "Closeting himself inside, the householder discovered a space that was unique to him, that accepted his exclusive imprint upon it, that rejected the incursions of others, that welcomed him into the comforting embrace of his proofs of possession, that celebrated an identity independent of relational responsibility, and that put ready to hand the impedimenta of authorship."[9] Authorship, privacy, masculinity: these terms mingled together in the architectural genesis of the study. The room grew into a power center in the home, a space that helped structure the forbearance that was understood to be due the master of the house. The masculinity forged in conjunction with the space of reading and writing was of a particular type: autonomous, knowledge-based, and resistant to both physical and psychological penetration.

Though women occasionally had a study or its equivalent, for the most part such spaces of solitary retreat and labor were seen as incompatible with women's role at the center of family life. It would not be considered seemly for a woman to wish to hide herself away in a study when she might be interacting with family members, servants, and visitors. Further, the overtones of power connected with private spaces of reading and writing were masculine in flavor; as Jacqueline Pearson notes, "the private library figures male power, especially patriarchal authority over the sex-lives of women and younger men."[10] If women wished to read and write they could do so in the library, which by the eighteenth century had grown into a social space to be distinguished from the more private environs of the study.[11] The eighteenth century library allowed the space of reading and writing to be divided into two different kinds of spaces that reflected two different ways of relating to books, one social and one private. Larger houses might have both a study that contained books and was the private sanctuary of the master of the house and also a library that held books but was used for entertaining.[12] Mark Girouard writes that by the end of the eighteenth century, "libraries were . . . essential adjuncts to the entertainment of a house party," worlds away from the somber monk's cell that was the study's ancestor.[13]

Roger Chartier has observed that in the eighteenth century the typical figure of the reader shifts from a solitary and hermitlike man to a secular and gregarious woman.[14] As this transition suggests, reading for women was represented as a more social activity than it was for men. Public-oriented libraries in the home offered women an appropriate space for their reading while leaving the study for men to commune with books in private. This solution endured into the nineteenth century, as women were encouraged to treat reading as a social activity. Reading aloud was particularly praised because, as Kate Flint notes, "this practice would necessarily check the dangerous delights of *solitary* reading."[15] Despite its proscribed nature, the gendered disparity between reading practices could produce dissonance. Peter Thornton describes the change in the home library in a manner which symptomizes the anxiety that accompanied the transition: "Increasingly, as the eighteenth century came to a close, the library was invaded by the women of the family who gradually turned it into a family drawing-room, introducing all kinds of additional comforts. . . . It was as if the English womenfolk, by taking over this gentleman's sanctum during the day, were taking their revenge for being sent off to the drawing-room after dinner."[16] Thornton's account represents both the possessiveness that girded the study and the way gender divisions in the home could produce turf disputes. In the nineteenth century, the study seemed more than ever desirable and more than ever inaccessible to bookish women. Its place in the hierarchy of rooms was unique and increasingly entrenched.

As intimated in chapter 3, the well-to-do nineteenth-century British home was a highly gender-differentiated space. Floor plans for English country houses collected in home-design books showed the house divided into male and female zones, with designations like "Young Ladies' Entrance," "Bachelors' Stairs," "Gentleman's Room," "Gentleman's Dressing Room," carefully demarcating who might tread where.[17] The gendered divisions in the home operated on every level, from the broad "zoning" of male and female regions of the home, to the gendered designation of individual rooms, to the contents of the rooms.[18] Although the house itself was considered a feminized space, the masculine regions of the home were generally larger than the feminine regions. Girouard writes: "One curious feature of Victorian houses is the increasingly large and sacrosanct male domain, an expansion in size and time of the after-dinner aspect of the Georgian dining room."[19] Robert Kerr names seven possible rooms dedicated to the needs of gentlemen: library, study, billiard room, smoking room, gentleman's room or business room, gentleman's odd room, and saloon (the last more characteristic of seventeenth- or eighteenth-century homes). By contrast, Kerr names only two rooms specifically ascribed to the lady of the house: the drawing room and the boudoir. According to Kerr, the drawing room was the main social space of the house, but the boudoir could also be social in nature; it was "a Sitting-room" to be accessed from "the principal Corridor of the house."[20]

Within this hierarchy of rooms the study often served as a center for the governance of the household. Often physically situated in the house on the border between the family and servant quarters, the study simultaneously afforded the gentleman privacy and gave him access to the household community. In the plan Kerr provides for the ground floor of Toddington (fig. 8) the maximally separated quarters for the family and the servants are joined by an adjacent private library, study, and record room. These rooms are all placed within easy reach of both a garden entrance and the back stairs, allowing the occupant to come and go privately. The private library that is part of this suite is distinguished from the main library, located between and connected with both the drawing room and the dining room. This "public" library, the likely domain of the woman reader, does not afford anything like the privacy of the study and private library; in fact, the study is the only room in the family wing that is not accessible from a public corridor. Even in a smaller mid-Victorian home like Midelney Place (fig. 9), a similar structure is replicated on a reduced scale: servants' quarters are linked to the family quarters by the study. The library is accessible from the drawing room and the hall, but the study has only one entrance and a separate lobby from which its owner can come and go in secret or admit guests for whom admission via the house's main entrance is not appropriate or desirable. As at Toddington, at Midelney Place accommodations are created for readers other than the master of the house, accommodations that have the not-incidental effect of eliminating possible reasons to disturb the gentleman in the study.

Well shielded but also centrally sited, the study could be a fearful place for anyone but its owner. In George Eliot's *Daniel Deronda* (1876), Gwendolen Harleth pauses nervously at the study's threshold: "An enormous log-fire with the scent of Russia from the books made the great room as odorous as a private chapel in which the censers have been swinging. It seemed too daring to go in."[21] The study has an air of masculine ritual, secrecy, and sensuality, all of which tend to exclude women. And if the Victorian library was a more social space than the study, it too was sometimes only grudgingly opened to women, as represented in Sarah Grand's New Woman novel *The Heavenly Twins* (1893). When the heroine insists on writing her letters in the library, her husband inwardly fumes: "Why did she choose . . . his own private *sanctum* . . . when there were half a dozen other rooms at least where she might have been quite as comfortable?"[22] Though the library was theoretically open to women, its bookish, quiet nature made it functionally masculine in some households, especially those without separate studies. Kerr articulates this aspect of the

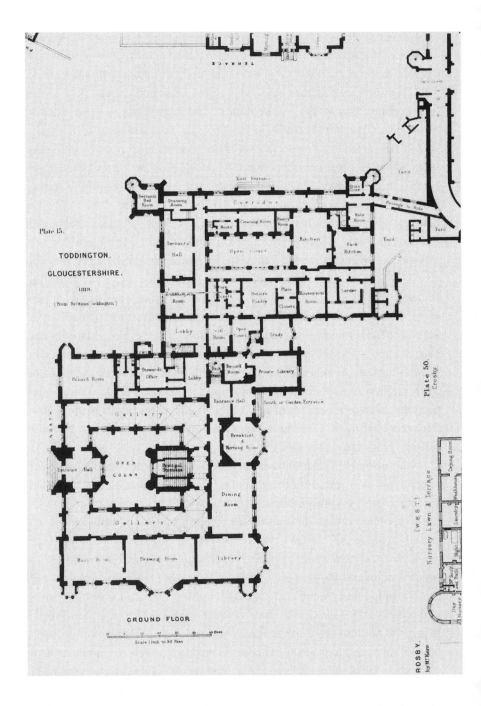

Plate 15.

TODDINGTON.

GLOUCESTERSHIRE.

1819.

(from Britton's Toddington.)

GROUND FLOOR

Scale 1 Inch to 30 Feet

Figure 8. Toddington, from Robert Kerr, *The Gentleman's House,* 3rd ed. (London: John Murray, 1871). By permission of the British Library.

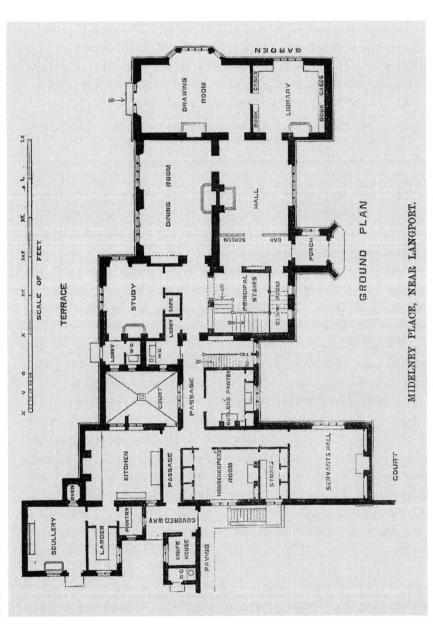

Figure 9. Midelney Place (ground plan). *The Builder,* November 1868.

library's nature when he calls this space "a sort of Morning-room for gentle-men rather than anything else. Their correspondence is done here, their read-ing, and, in some measure, their lounging;—and the Billiard-room, for instance, is not infrequently attached to it. At the same time the ladies are not exactly excluded."[23] And not exactly welcomed. Even in the library, women might be admitted only grudgingly. In the Victorian study, by contrast, women were even more rarely admitted in person, though visual or written represen-tations of women could be found there. In George Gissing's *New Grub Street* (1891), for example, the study was a place where John Yule sat and "contem-plated the portraits of those female [friends of his] who would not have been altogether at ease in Mrs. Yule's drawing room."[24] In the study, the subject of women was contemplated and debated, but women themselves were excluded, almost by definition. In his 1964 history of such spaces, Raymond Irwin writes that women "rarely furnish [studies] in the true tradition; when the study becomes feminine, it quite rightly changes its character."[25] A study that belongs to a woman is somehow not a study at all.

The study's private nature also confirmed its masculinity, since the house construed women as essentially social creatures who belonged in drawing rooms. For Kerr, "a study, in whatever circumstances, may be defined to be a place of reading and writing for one person alone."[26] If this formulation does not explicitly prescribe the gender of that "person," the iconography of late-nineteenth- and early-twentieth-century spaces of reading and writing fre-quently suggested their masculine nature. In Gloag and Mansfield's 1923 illus-tration of the study (fig. 10), prescriptively titled "The House We Ought to Live in," the room has only one chair;[27] anyone besides the "one person" would have to sit on the floor. A safe is visible in the corner, designed to conceal yet advertising its secretive function to the reader's eye. In Lewis Day's 1881 illus-tration "Scheme for Arrangement and Decoration of a Room" (fig. 11), the reading occupant keeps his face turned away from the spectator, a posture that hardly diminishes his authority over the scene. The motto running around the paneled walls—partially visible, like the man—is taken from Francis Bacon and urges the cultivation of a scholarly masculinity: "Reading maketh a full man, conference a ready man, and writing an exact man." Though most men with studies were not, of course, writers, the study was the place where they culti-vated—or at least cultivated the appearance of—the scholarly accomplish-ments considered fitting for a gentleman.

Even as the bookish, exclusive nature of such rooms was being touted in the late nineteenth century, popular contemporary writers on interior design were

The Study

Figure 10. "The Study," from Leslie Gloag and John Mansfield, *The House We Ought to Live In* (London: Duckworth, 1923). Illustrations by A. B. Read. By permission of Gerald Duckworth and Co. Ltd. and the British Library.

Figure 11. "Scheme for Arrangement and Decoration of a Room," from Lewis F. Day, *Every-day Art* (London: B. T. Batsford, 1882). By permission of the British Library.

Figure 12. "A Study Mantel Piece," from Robert Edis, *Decoration and Furniture of Town Houses* (London: C. Kegan Paul, 1881). By permission of the British Library.

lamenting their decline. Robert Edis's well-known *Decoration and Furniture of Town Houses* (1881) illustrates the mantel of his own library (fig. 12), with masculine accoutrements like guns, fishing rods, swords, and smoking gear prominently displayed. He speaks approvingly of the "man who really uses his library as a work-room . . . for real literary work and study" but seems concerned that fewer and fewer men are living up to their studies. Edis advises that the room

> should be surrounded with bookcases, the lower portion made to take large books . . . the shelf which this lower projection forms will do admirably for the arrangement of . . . personal things, with which a man crowds the room he really lives in; of course I am speaking to those who make a den or working room of their library, and not to those who fit a back room up with various tiers of shelving, on which are arranged a library of books which are seldom looked at.[28]

In this account, the man of the house ought to want to spend time alone reading and writing, ought to seek frequent refuge in this private retreat—but perhaps does not. R. A. Briggs in his 1911 *The Essentials of a Country House* was similarly disconsolate about the seeming decline of the study. He writes: "A large room, to house the books we read, has rather grown out of fashion. The Study, except for the clergy and for writers who really work in their Study and study, has—sad as it is to relate—descended into being a 'den,' where indeed a few books may be kept."[29] When the gentleman gives up his hold on the study, the fortress of masculinity has been breached—and from within. Reassuringly, the photograph of a study provided by Briggs (fig. 13) as an example is well stocked with books. The study, according to Edis and Briggs, seems to have gone into decline and is in need of defense. But perhaps the study should be seen as *never not* in decline—that is, as the symbolic stronghold of masculinity, the study creates manliness and the need for its protection all the more vigorously by presenting it as embattled. By portraying the study as in danger of falling prey to feminine encroachment through absorption into the drawing room, Edis and Briggs make the preservation of the study a point of honor and dedication to the tradition of all-male spaces.

If the masculine predilection for reading and writing, advertised by house planners like Edis and Briggs, offered one justification for the study's existence, another lay in the need for privacy in homes populated by a diverse community of family members, servants, and guests. The study was the place where private family documents would most likely be kept: photographs, wills, family trees, records of parentage, and even love letters. Generally speaking, documents

Figure 13. Library, Manor House, Wormley, from R. A. Briggs, *The Essentials of a Country House* (London: B. T. Batsford, 1911). By permission of the British Library.

relating to the history of the family and its continuity, or threats to the same, were the private papers kept in the study. Documents of a socially questionable nature—like John Yule's pictures of his "female friends"—could be well masked by the seemingly chaste apparatus of scholarship and record keeping.[30] Mary Haweis's description of the study's contents in her popular 1881 household manual emphasizes the mysteries this room guards for its owner: "books and ancient belongings, photographs of inscrutable people who were his early friends, gifts from unknown quarters which he still fancies he values."[31] For Victorian gentlemen, the ability to keep their secrets safe in a private room was part of a privilege associated with masculinity. The study was the architectural realization of this privilege.

The texts to which I now turn offer a twist on the formula of secretive, writerly men because they feature women. These texts are disparate: a popular detective story, a scandalous novel, and a literary essay. Yet their very disparity points to the centrality of what they share: in all these texts, a woman's claim to a private space for reading and writing is underwritten by the possession of an important secret. All offer similar constellations of female masculinity, authorship, and secrecy organized around the possession of such a private space. Secrets are at the center of all these texts, secrets bound up with transgressions of gender and sexuality. Keeping these secrets locked in a study would seem to minimize the threat of exposure, a fantasy of eluding social determination that is tied to a broader set of fantasies associated with Victorian masculinity: control over one's space and the abilities to act unobserved and to resist penetration by others. Taken together, these fantasies reveal the lineaments of a masculinity that is, with relative ease, assumed by women, suggesting that the secret the study conceals is more far-reaching than any individual family secret and that the construction of early-twentieth-century female authorship relies on a masculine ability to hide one's secrets from the world's penetrating gaze in the study's interior.

"Women are naturally secretive"

In "A Scandal in Bohemia," the first Sherlock Holmes story published in *The Strand*, Holmes is hired by the King of Bohemia to cover up a sexual indiscretion in his past that now threatens his imminent royal marriage. Upon hearing of his engagement, one of the king's past mistresses, a retired diva named Irene Adler, has threatened to expose him by publishing letters he wrote to her and a photograph of the two of them together. "The well-known adventuress Irene

Adler,"[32] as the King describes her, is a force to be reckoned with; indeed, Watson opens the story by telling us that "To Sherlock Holmes she is always *the woman*" (5). What is the source of Adler's power? As a single woman living alone, she would seem something less than a match for the team of a reigning monarch and Europe's greatest detective. Holmes's interest in her is notable, as he never allows himself a sexual relationship lest it compromise his mental powers: "Grit in a sensitive instrument, or a crack in one of his own high-power lenses, would not be more disturbing than a strong emotion in a nature such as his" (5), Watson tells us. The penetration of emotion into the machine-like mind of Holmes would cause a breakdown, or worse: in thrall to Adler, the King admits, "I was mad—insane" (13). Yet Adler's sexual powers alone don't explain her ability to defeat Holmes.[33] Adler possesses another asset that makes her a formidable opponent: a space of her own to write, read, and conceal important papers.

Such a space is tantamount to the usurpation of a masculine prerogative, and it gives her the power to act as a man and, when necessary, pass for one. The King warns Holmes early on that Adler "has the face of the most beautiful of women, and the mind of the most resolute of men" (14). The "man's mind" is materialized in the space of Adler's architectural power base: a private room in her house where she keeps both love letters and important papers related to issues of familial succession (since the King's letters and photograph must remain hidden in order for his dynasty to continue). Adler's masculinity is a logical inference for the King: if she has a place to keep a secret, she must be a man. And he's not wrong. Adler claims several masculine liberties in the story, each made possible by her capacity to inhabit space as only a man ought to be able to. Conversely, throughout "A Scandal in Bohemia" Holmes repeatedly tries to defeat Adler by treating her like a woman. In the end, Adler's masculinity allows her to usurp authorial privileges, wresting control of the narrative away from the text's sanctioned author figure.

Confident in his abilities, Holmes believes that men (like himself) are better able to keep secrets than are women, a fact he plans to exploit to find Adler's cache. Though he tells Watson that "Women are naturally secretive, and they like to do their own secreting" (22), he clearly believes himself to be a better secret keeper than Adler. Holmes thinks women like to *have* secrets but aren't equipped to *keep* them. Holmes's pun on secrets/secretions suggests women's leaky bodies aren't made for discretion. Masculine secrecy, by contrast, rests on impenetrability, affirming the heterosexual man's role as one who penetrates and the woman's role as the one who is penetrated. This bodily logic takes architectural form when penetration is prevented by walling off a space and keeping others outside. Correspondingly, a special piece of the study was often split off and made into a strong room, tailor-made for secreting. This space was called a "Strong-closet" by Kerr, who described it as "a fire-proof closet for deeds and documents of importance."[34] The fear of fire Kerr mentions is not incidental; important papers would be most vulnerable to flames, something Holmes exploits in this story by faking a blaze in order to fool Adler into revealing her secret hiding place.

Like many detective stories, "A Scandal in Bohemia" is about privacy and who has the right to it. Holmes protects his own privacy by adopting multiple disguises; his claim to masculinity depends on preserving a privacy that is equated with invisibility and impenetrability, even as he seeks to deny Adler these qualities. Dressed as a stable groom, he goes to spy on Adler's house, where one room immediately strikes him as vulnerable. He tells Watson about a "Large sitting-room on the right side, well furnished, with long windows almost to the floor, and those preposterous English window fasteners which a child could open" (16). Holmes does not call this room a "study" or a "library," though we do learn that it is furnished with a "comfortable sofa," many shelves and drawers, paneled walls, a bellpull for summoning servants, and a secret hiding place. Adler doesn't have a study, but she seems to need one. A sitting room was a place where secrets would be leaked, not kept. What she has is a sitting room that acts like a study, just as its owner is a woman who acts like a man.

This room is the focus of Holmes's attack on Adler's environs. It is the physical site of her privacy, the place where until now she has kept her secret safe. Holmes assumes yet another disguise for his second attempt. Though he failed to conquer as a groom, he adopts another role available only to men: a clergyman. This role is one specifically associated by contemporary writers with studies. In Kerr, for example, the study is deemed best suited to "a studious man, for instance a Parsonage."[35] For Briggs, the study is especially "for the clergy and for writers."[36] Holmes masquerades as the ideal masculine study owner, and his costume is consistent with his apparent gender. Likewise, he expects Adler to behave true to hers. He instructs Watson to throw a smoke bomb through the window, reasoning that under threat of fire Adler will rush to save her treasure. He tells Watson: "When a woman thinks her house is on fire, her instinct is at once to rush the thing which she values most. . . . A married woman grabs at her baby—an unmarried one reaches for her jewel box" (25).[37] The plan works—Adler goes for her hidden treasure—but turns and rushes from the room when she realizes there is no danger. In the smoky confusion, Holmes reconnoiters with Watson on the street corner, and the two stroll home, but as they reach Holmes's door, a voice calls out, "Good-night, Mister Sherlock Holmes" (26). Looking around, Holmes sees that the greeting has come from "a slim youth in an ulster who had hurried by," but he can't place the face. Nor does it occur to him to wonder at the fact that he is hailed while still in his theoretically impenetrable clergyman's disguise.

The greeting comes from Adler, who has followed them home disguised as a man and eavesdropped on the conversation, having guessed the clergyman's true identity. Holmes never suspected he might be followed by a woman since, after all, genteel women in 1890s London did not walk the streets alone in the evening. What Holmes overlooks (again) is Adler's ability to *not* be a woman. As Adler later explains, cross dressing is a common strategy for her. "Male costume is nothing new to me. I often take advantage of the freedom which it gives" (28). She refers to her man's outfit as her "walking clothes."[38] As a result of her surveillance, when Holmes appears at Adler's house the next morning to collect the plunder he finds Adler has decamped from her house, having seemingly left England for good. Most critics read Adler's marriage and subsequent flight as signifying the recuperation of Holmes's authority and the containment of the insurgent feminine power Adler represents. However, there is another possibility that seems more consistent with the rest of the story: that the "elderly woman" with "a sardonic eye" who represents herself as Adler's housekeeper and tells Holmes of her mistress's flight is Adler herself, disguised again in order to throw Holmes off her trail.

When Holmes reaches into the secret panel where he believes the King's letters and photograph are concealed, he finds they have been replaced by a photograph of Adler and a letter from her to Holmes.[39] The letter Adler writes to Holmes has a curious status in the text. In it, she explains the chain of reasoning by which she penetrated Holmes's disguises and the actions she took to thwart him. Detective stories often end with such an account but it is generally provided by the detective. Even when a criminal confesses at the tale's end, the detective unpacks additional obscure details afterward, performing his role as the restorer of social order. But Adler takes the detective's role on herself, supplanting Holmes's chain of reasoning with her own. By writing this letter she reverses roles with Holmes (as she has already done by shadowing him) as well as with Watson. In the Holmes stories Watson is a kind of stand-in for the author, chronicling Holmes's adventures for the public. But here, in a fashion unusual for the series, Adler assumes the chronicler's function with her written account of events addressed to the detective. Adler has already reversed roles with the King: by hiding her representations of the King in her room, Adler makes the King the feminine subject of secrets, instead of the masculine keeper of them. In sum, Adler takes on three roles distinctly associated with masculine power and authority—that of detective, author, and king. Her assumption of each of these roles is predicated on her ability to keep her secret safe in her home. There she writes her letter, hides her secret, and pieces together Holmes's plot.

The study as such is never named in "A Scandal in Bohemia," yet I have included it in my discussion because it presents an early constellation of the issues associated with the study some years later: women's authorship, female masculinity, and secrecy. "Scandal" both worries and delights over the ease with which prerogatives purportedly tied to masculinity—privacy, mobility, authorship, and logic—can be assumed by a woman. The story disrupts the logic of heterosexual masculinity by playing with the stakes of penetration: Holmes fears being penetrated and prefers to penetrate others, but Adler (in spite of being "*the* woman") both penetrates Holmes's disguise and has her home penetrated, all the while preserving her secret intact. Moving between masculine and feminine roles, Adler defeats Holmes by upsetting his definitions for gendered behavior, definitions that Holmes treats as natural law. In fact her prerogatives emanate primarily from the autonomy conferred by her possession of private space in the home. This possession is so profoundly associated with masculinity that Adler's assumption of masculine roles is an inevitable consequence. So closely does one follow on the heels of the other that it is difficult to say whether masculinity or private space is the antecedent factor.

In Radclyffe Hall's novel *The Well of Loneliness*, private space again becomes pivotal to the secretion of information that runs counter to what these texts identify as masculinity's master narrative. Like "Scandal," *The Well* emphasizes the importance of having a private place to house secrets about sex. But whereas shifting gender roles create the subtext for "A Scandal in Bohemia," in *The Well*, gender instability forms the crux of the story. My reading of "Scandal" cuts against the grain of the text, since Adler neither has a study nor considers herself a writer. But in *The Well*, as in *A Room of One's Own*, authorship, the study, and masculinity come directly to the fore. Hall is the first English writer to put before the reading public a fully developed portrait of a masculine woman, and this character lays claim to masculinity by acquiring a study and launching a successful career as an author.

"Her father's study"

Published in 1928, *The Well*'s first printing sold out quickly. But the novel was banned after a well-publicized obscenity trial for its explicit discussion of what Havelock Ellis had recently described in 1897 as "sexual inversion." *The Well* tells the story of Stephen Gordon, who, from childhood on, feels trapped and out of place in her woman's body.[40] Stephen is described repeatedly as an "invert," a blanket term that broadly referred to cases of one sex taking on the appearance or behavior of the other. Esther Newton writes that "the true invert was a being between categories, neither man nor woman."[41] Sexology's case studies named the invert and made this figure representable in literature, albeit curtailed by censorship. But if Hall's protagonist was on the cutting edge, her setting was retrograde: Morton, a Victorian country house.[42] Morton is an extraordinarily nostalgic space, harking back to homes that were built to preserve strict gender divisions.[43]

> Not very far from Upton-on-Severn—between it, in fact, and the Malvern Hills—stands the country seat of the Gordons of Bramley; well-timbered, well-cottaged, well-fenced and well-watered, having, in this latter respect, a stream that forks in exactly the right position to feed two large lakes in the grounds.
>
> The house itself is of Georgian red brick, with charming circular windows near the roof. It has dignity and pride without ostentation, self-assurance without arrogance, repose without inertia; and a gentle aloofness that, to those who know its spirit, but adds to its value as a home. It is indeed like certain lovely women who, now old, belong to a bygone generation.[44]

Many Victorian country houses were expansions of Georgian homes, with the old house retained at the core of the expanded dwelling. As a house that has survived its proper era, Morton is imagined through a haze of nostalgia and bygone days. *The Well* is uncomfortably placed in time, for it combines a Victorian backdrop, antiquated from the novel's first paragraph, with a heroine whose textbook case of sexual inversion marks her as a paradigmatic child of the modern era. Unfortunately for Stephen, in the anthropomorphic house where she is born, individuals are supposed to reflect the character of their homes. As the forked stream and two lakes mentioned in the novel's first sentence imply, gender is formally presented as a choice between two opposite positions, and Stephen uncomfortably straddles the fork. Against such a back-drop, Stephen's masculinity is accentuated but also completely submerged, and her inversion becomes her family's deepest and most shameful secret. Appropriately, this secret finds its home in the study, where it takes the form of foundational sexological texts by Krafft-Ebing and Ellis, stored there and inscribed by her father with Stephen's name.

Gender, like class, is constructed as a binary choice via the architecture of the domestic interior. In the traditional plan of the country house, the servants' wing forms almost a separate house, divided along gendered lines. For Kerr, the basic division in the private house is between the servants' quarters and family quarters. "The family constitute one community: the servants another."[45] While Stephen does not fully articulate the class division at Morton, she feels it keenly. As a child seeing her parents' pleasure in each other, she yearns to have a share of this happiness herself, but her first love is Collins, the housemaid.

> All [Stephen] would know was that seeing her parents together in this mood would fill her with longings for something that she wanted yet could not define—a something that would make her as happy as they were. And this something would always be mixed up with Morton, with grave, stately rooms like her father's study, with wide views from windows that let in much sunshine, and the scents of a spacious garden. Her mind would go groping about for a reason, and would find no reason—unless it were Collins—but Collins would refuse to fit into these pictures; even love must admit that she did not belong there any more than the brushes and buckets and slop-cloths belonged in that dignified study.
>
> (36)

The "brushes and buckets and slop-cloths" do belong in the study, as does the housemaid, but only as invisible presences with no proprietary claim to the space they maintain. Stephen intuitively grasps the connection between *being* and *dwelling* in Morton's rooms.[46] Stephen is no class rebel: she participates happily in aristocratic rituals like riding to the hunt, and she loves the things her money can buy. But she fits uneasily into Morton's rooms.

This misalignment peaks when Stephen reaches young adulthood, when she must leave the relatively gender-neutral schoolroom behind and join her mother in the feminine drawing room. Instead, she feels herself increasingly drawn to her father's study. Stephen doesn't often go into Lady Anna's drawing-room. Sitting there, hands folded, Lady Anna is the perfect lady: "In the vast drawing-room so beautifully proportioned, so restfully furnished in old polished walnut, so redolent of beeswax and orris root and violets—all alone in its vastness would Anna be sitting, with her white hands folded and idle" (80). Anna sits alone in this scented shrine to the idea of femininity because her husband and daughter are always in the study together, living the life of the mind— which cannot be separated from the life of the male body. The two sit together for hours in the study, discussing "the feel and the smell and the essence of books" (79). As sensually scented as the drawing room, the library, with its books, attracts Sir Philip erotically as well as scholastically: "Surrounded by his books, caressing their bindings, Sir Philip would look care-free again and light-hearted" (86). Husband and wife each find his or her own solitary pleasure: while Anna sits with hands folded in her lap, Philip uses his hands to touch his books so that he can relax. Philip's learning forms a counterpoint to his wife's ignorance; she is described as a woman of little learning and less interest in books. Anna's lack of education even explains "why Sir Philip had loved her, that was why he found her so infinitely restful" (80). Stephen, on the other hand, receives a full education, both from her governesses and from her father.

If Irene Adler's study is a never-named species of the room, Sir Philip Gordon's study is an outright classic of the genre, with a gravitas derived in part from its aristocratic pedigree. Large, grave, dignified, quiet, Sir Philip's study has a desk with a locked drawer, and many bookcases, at least one of which can also be locked. It contains writing materials, and a distinguished library—"one of the finest libraries in England" (26)—as well as an old armchair, in which its owner is always to be found. This is a real working study, not just a room for custom or show. Like the idealized studies described by Edis and Briggs, it contains both books and guns. Sir Philip's study also contains a secret that is essential to Stephen. "Alone in that grave-looking, quiet study, he would unlock a drawer in his ample desk, and would get out a slim volume recently acquired, and would read and reread it in the silence. The author was a German, Karl Heinrich Ulrichs" (26). Ulrichs was the first to describe the phenomenon of sexual inversion, and as Philip reads he makes tiny marginal notes that refer to his daughter. Thus Stephen's marginal gender identity finds a textual mirror in actual marginalia. Sir Philip is a careful and close reader, but it is his daughter who will fulfill the study's most important purpose. As he finds Stephen's gender identity in his books, he finds her future career reading one of his daughter's so-called queer compositions: " 'So that's it, you want to be a writer. Well, why not? You've got plenty of talent, Stephen; I should be a proud man if you were a writer' " (79). Stephen's career as an author is launched in her father's study. By becoming a writer, Stephen commits herself professionally to the masculine sphere of the study and withdraws from the drawing-room life her female body reserves for her. *The Well* is famous for its representation of female sexual inversion, but the text also offers a developed portrait of female authorship.

Philip protects the secret of Stephen's inversion all his life. After her father's death, her mother receives a threatening letter from the husband of Stephen's lover and exiles her daughter from Morton. Leaving Anna in the drawing room, Stephen retreats to her father's study:

> As though drawn there by some strong natal instinct, Stephen went straight to her father's study; and she sat in the old arm-chair that had survived him; then she buried her face in her hands. . . . She must go— she was going away from Morton. . . . Getting up, she wandered about the room, touching its kind and familiar objects; stroking the desk, examining a pen, grown rusty from long disuse as it lay there; then she opened a little drawer in the desk and took out the key of her father's locked book- case. Her mother had told her to take what she pleased—she would take one or two of her father's books. She had never examined this special book-case, and she could not have told why she suddenly did so. As she slipped the key into the lock and turned it, the action seemed curiously automatic. . . . Then she noticed that on a shelf near the bottom was a row of books standing behind the others; the next moment she had one of these in her hand, and was looking at the name of the author: Krafft Ebing—she had never heard of that author before."
>
> (203–4)

Inscribed in the pages of *Psychopathia Sexualis*, Stephen finds her own name and quickly realizes the implications. The "natal instinct" and the "automatic . . . action" that are described as driving Stephen toward the study's secret underscore the biological reflex that inspires the discovery. Hall seeks to underline the inborn nature of Stephen's difference, but her gesture opens a crucial space for the cultural aspect of that difference. Stephen, in Hall's logic, was born an invert, but she must still become a "man." She was born with some of the attributes of masculinity—intellect, athleticism, and broad shoulders—but she wants more. When the young Stephen queries, " 'Do you think that I *could* be a man, supposing I thought very hard—or prayed, Father?' " (26; italics in original), she looks for a cultural remedy to a bodily insufficiency, attempting to compensate for what she perceives as a natural lack with a cultural supplement. The two activities she identifies as crucial to the project of becoming man—thinking and praying—recall the study's ideal owners, the writer and the clergyman.

Stephen's steadfast drive to become masculine is articulated through her desire to emulate her father. Stroking his desk, handling his pen, Stephen reawakens a sensual connection to the necessary objects of a writer and a gentleman. Indeed, she realizes her identity through a readerly identification with her father; thanks to her father's marginalia Stephen is the subject of *Psychopathia Sexualis,* but she is also a close reader of that work. In choosing that text as the founding volume of her own library, Stephen chooses private masculine reading practices over social feminine ones. Newton writes that Stephen is denied "patriarchal legitimacy" because she is not a boy; whatever else she inherits from her father, "she cannot be his true heir."[47] But insofar as masculinity is revealed in *The Well* to be as much a set of acquired practices as an accident of embodiment, Stephen is her father's heir. What draws her to her father's secret bookshelf is the call of the paternal legacy, the law of primogeniture—what Stephen herself calls her "intolerable birthright." Mature masculinity in *The Well* is understood as the ability to have and keep secrets—and thus her transition to manhood takes place through inheritance of these books.[48]

With the need to keep a secret comes the need for a study. The discovery of the secret volumes concludes book 2 of the novel; book 3 opens with Stephen in London, "in her large, long, rather low-ceilinged study whose casement windows looked over the river" (209). By moving the narrative directly from Sir Philip's old study to Stephen's new one, Hall draws a distinct line from the father's study to the daughter's. The child has taken up the father's mantle; she has cast herself and her masculinity in her father's mold. She shops for jewelry for her lover in the same store where Philip bought Anna's engagement ring; she copies his love of books and horses; she shares her father's code of honor; and like him, she is a secret keeper. Though the books she takes from her father's study act as talismans for her, they mean something different to Stephen than they did to her father. For Philip, the books—together with the jottings he added—are a real secret, a discovery about his daughter's nature that he refuses to reveal to his wife or daughter. But Stephen has no need to conceal these books. For her the books symbolize her father's secretive, bookish masculinity and thus they form the building blocks of her own study. Oddly, even without a secret of her own, Stephen clings to her father's secretive form of masculinity. This aspect of her demeanor is a marked contrast to the other inverts she encounters after leaving Morton, such as Jonathan Brockett and Valerie Seymour, who are relatively open about their same-sex desires. But Stephen prefers to remain a mystery. So strongly does she identify sexual secrecy with the possession of a study that her mind to her is a locked room. When Brockett pushes his question about her sexuality, she thinks, "it was almost as though [Brockett] had peeped through a secret keyhole into her mind" (234). Central to Stephen's masculinity is a resistance to penetration, even when hers is plainly an open secret.[49]

Having hidden away her secret books in her new study, Stephen justifies her right to this space by writing a novel. *The Furrow* is a critical success, but the work emerges from an authorial self-destruction cast by Hall as perverse motherhood: "Like infants [her characters] had sucked at her breasts of inspiration, and drawn from them blood, waxing wonderfully strong" (214). This grisly image demonstrates Stephen's inability to anchor her authorship in any version of the feminine; femininity is far more unnatural to her than masculinity. Returning to writing after *The Furrow,* she finds even this source for inspiration diminished, experiencing simultaneously exhausted maternality and male impotence: "her brain felt like over-stretched elastic, it would not spring back, it was limp, unresponsive" (216). Like Adler with her man's mind, Stephen's brain represents the physical seat of her masculinity, hence her attempt to "think" herself male ("Do you think that I *could* be a man, supposing I thought very hard?"). After the first novel, her inspiration declines and she produces a book reviewers find insufficiently virile. Stephen, too, feels that her work suffers from "a lack of grip" (218). Feminine authorship is construed as self-sacrificing to the point of self-destruction; in the parental mode, apparently only masculine authors can create without deforming themselves.

By the time she comes to write her third novel, inspiration has failed her altogether. And one night she realizes what is missing:

> She turned, looking wearily round the study, and it came upon her with a slight sense of shock that she was seeing this room for the very first time, and that everything in it was abnormally ugly. . . . How had she endured this room for so long? Had she really written a fine book in it? Had she sat in it evening after evening and come back to it morning after morning? Then she must have been blind indeed—what a place for any author to work in!
>
> (233)

This shock is one of defamiliarization, of an intimate, everyday place made suddenly strange by an aesthetic awakening. Traditionally, the study is the author's fortress as well as his cradle, his spur to work and his zone of rest and retreat. Stephen's study cannot fulfill these functions because she has not imprinted her masculinity on it as prescribed by designers like Edis and Kerr. Unlike her father's study, which not only kept Sir Philip's secret safe but also provided a perfect outlet for its owner's bookish habits, Stephen's study, in spite of her having written two books in it, fails to provide a sustaining space for authorship. The resonant spaces of Morton that seemed so natural and timeless to Stephen as a child prove difficult to reproduce in a house without Morton's history. Space is not so readily manipulated as Stephen might wish. Becoming a man is hard and deliberate work.

And so, like many a writer, she goes into a self-imposed exile in Paris, a city known at that time for its relative tolerance of gender outlaws. She buys and renovates an old house on the rue Jacob, preferring, as is her way, to build on tradition rather than strike out anew. The first room planned is the study: "A fine room with a window that opened on the garden," which she decorates as "an Empire study with grey walls and curtains of Empire green, for she loved the great roomy writing tables that had come into being with the first Napoleon" (249–50). Here is a room perfectly suited to her: Stephen's prefer-ence for the Empire style over more up-to-date Parisian styles such as Art Deco signals her nostalgia for the nineteenth century, but more than that, it indicates another basis for her masculine identification. As a child, Stephen's favorite game was "playing Nelson," acting out the great battles of the naval commander. Once she is settled in France, her attention turns to a French ruler. In both roles, her performance is in a decidedly militaristic mode, and in both cases her models are men *manqué*: Nelson because of the eye and arm he lost in battle, Napoleon, because of his short stature. In Stephen's repeated casting of the invert as "maimed," we can trace her alliance with these men: hypermasculine yet physically diminished. Moreover, both Nelson and Napoleon rose from obscurity to become national heroes; as "self-made men," their example could provide encouragement to Stephen in her own self-fashioning.

Stephen's decision to furnish her study in the Empire style also ties her to the social foundations of that style, created by Napoleon's designers Percier and Fontaine between 1804 and 1814. For Siegfried Giedion, the Empire style illus-trates Napoleon's conviction that "every specific station in life had a corre-sponding environment."[50] This belief conforms well both to Morton's archi-tectural hierarchy and to Stephen's desire to make herself masculine by acquiring the furnishings of the role. With the study as her power base, Stephen can function in Paris society. She keeps her hair cropped short and wears men's clothes exclusively, she finds a moderately satisfying social sphere in the company of other inverts, and her writing becomes confident and successful. She also finds a romantic partner to share her home, from whom, just like her father at Morton, she retreats into the study.

> Stephen often called [Mary] into the study, comforted by the girl's loving presence. "Come and sit with me, sweetheart, I like you in here." But quite soon she would seem to forget all about her. "What . . . what?" she would mutter, frowning a little. "Don't speak to me for a minute, Mary. Go and have your luncheon, there's a good child."
>
> (340)

Stephen finds herself copying her father's behavior, staying up late in the study and then sneaking upstairs to bed. Where Philip "would steal up to bed, being painfully careful to tread very softly, fearful of waking his wife" (27), Stephen "would steal like a thief past Mary's bedroom" (343). The comparison confirms the inherited qualities of Stephen's relationship to both her partner and her privacy—both are strictly modeled on her father's practice. Both are secured by the possession of a study that posits masculinity as secretive and writerly.

Despite Stephen's putatively radical status as the subject of the first English novel to explicitly represent "female inversion," when she comes to build her house in the avant-garde territory of Paris's Left Bank she reproduces the separation of spheres in the same stylized form she learned from Morton. Stephen clearly understands that the spaces where you dwell can lock you in or liberate you: she passes through a range of transformative spaces in the novel, including the "no-man's-land" of the battlefield, the sexually permissive climate of Orotava, and the anarchy of Parisian gay nightlife. But though she benefits from these new spaces, in her own home she turns her back on the creative use of space and builds in the rigid mold of her upbringing. The realm of separate spheres is, after all, a place where men are men, women are women, and there is no in-between. And that is the place where Stephen has longed to be allowed to live all her life.

Gilbert Scott writes in his *Remarks on Secular and Domestic Architecture* (1857) that "A gentleman's house . . . should protect the womanliness of woman and encourage the manliness of men."[51] For upper-class women, the house *protects*. Architecture offers a physical extension of the proper manly desire to shelter and isolate women, to keep them safe and indoors. For upper-class Victorian men, on the other hand, the house *encourages*. It inspirits them and gives them the resources to go into the world and act; it gives them the privacy that enables and nurtures the public self. The study provides important encouragement to Stephen as an author, keeping her secret, modeling masculinity, and assigning her the privacy necessary to the writer's concentration. Her authorship is also inspired and sanctioned by her father, but she improvises on his example: the father was a reader, but the daughter is a writer; the father's masculinity was inborn, but the daughter crafts hers. Like Colette's father, Sir Philip's pen has grown "rusty" from "long disuse," but Stephen cannot take her claim to masculinity for granted.

Judith Halberstam argues that female masculinity "affords us a glimpse of how masculinity is constructed as masculinity," a claim well illustrated by Stephen's labored and painstaking journey toward manhood.[52] Certainly, theories of social construction take on a refreshing literality in *The Well*'s architectural context. In "Scandal," Irene Adler draws on the spatial prerogatives of masculinity in order to keep her secret safe, while in *The Well* Stephen does so in order to make a man of herself. Each text puts pressure on a portion of the dynamic interplay between authorship, masculinity, and secrecy that circulates within the private environs of the study or its equivalent. In "Scandal," the central term is secrecy; in *The Well*, masculinity. For *A Room of One's Own*, the text with which I conclude this chapter, the focus is on authorship. Woolf attended the obscenity trial for *The Well* and published *A Room of One's Own* in the same year, 1928.[53] In her essay, she pursues explicitly the question implicit in Doyle's and Hall's texts: What can happen when a woman gets a study? Woolf's famous claim that women need money and a room of their own if they are to become writers takes on new meaning when examined in light of the gendered specificity of the writer's room.

"A lock on the door means the power to think for oneself"

In the opening pages of *A Room of One's Own*, Woolf shows how all architectural spaces dedicated to reading and writing—not just the study—have long been men's exclusive territory. Women who attempt to enter the library at Oxbridge University are turned away by a gentleman who informs them that "ladies are only admitted to the library if accompanied by a Fellow of the College."[54] The Round Reading Room of the British Library, where the speaker goes to do research, is a "huge bald forehead . . . splendidly encircled by a band of famous [male] names" (28). Male writers have had rooms of their own in which to write throughout the history of English literature, rooms that are also the site of male privacy. The Oxbridge Library is imagined as a vast repository of secrets, "with all its treasures safe locked within its breast" (10). By contrast, women's attempts to write in private are thwarted by the organization of domestic life. Jane Austen, whose nephew Woolf quotes, "had no separate study to repair to, and most of the work must have been done in the general sitting-room, subject to all kinds of casual interruptions. She was careful that her occupation should not be suspected by servants or visitors or any persons beyond her own family party" (67). Austen craved privacy, concealing her manuscript if anyone entered the room. Woolf also cites the frustration of Florence Nightingale, who fumed over how difficult it was for women to work uninterrupted in the home. Woolf's examples reveal that while male authorship is predicated on privacy and quiet, female authorship is organized by interruption.[55] Yet for all her examples, the most compelling justification of the woman writer's need for a study is provided by the speaker's own experience.

Although an essay, *A Room of One's Own* is structured like a narrative fiction, with a plot and a fictive central character. It is written, the speaker announces early on, "with the liberties and licences of a novelist" (6). The essay loosely narrates the account of how the main character, who is also the narrator, composed the text in response to a request for lectures on the topic, "Women and Fiction." It is divided into six chapters, the first of which is set at Oxbridge, the second in the British Museum and on the streets of London, and the last four in the speaker's home. These shifting locations take the reader on a walking tour of the obstacles to female authorship and finally show that nothing is more essential for women writers than a traditional, masculine study—a somewhat unsettling conclusion for a text committed to the construction of a separate female literary tradition, a text that urges women writers to "think back through [their] mothers" (79).

The opening chapters dramatize the author's claim that women writers cannot fulfill their vocation without private, dedicated work spaces. The speaker is unable to follow through on her ideas when she hatches them in public, even in locations traditionally well disposed to reading, writing, and thoughtful contemplation. An early inspiration sends her walking across the Oxbridge riverbanks, only to be chased off by a Beadle who explains that women are allowed on the grass only if accompanied by a fellow: "The only charge I could bring against the Fellows and Scholars of whatever the college might happen to be was that in protection of their turf, which has been rolled for 300 years in succession, they had sent my little fish into hiding" (8).[56] From the river the speaker makes her way to the Oxbridge Library in search of manuscripts to help develop her emerging theory of literary influence, but again, as an unaccompanied woman, she cannot enter. Not access to the resources of college life but solitary access is at stake here. Privacy continues to elude the speaker as she visits the British Museum, where she can use the books but is distracted by the male student seated next to her. She looks "with envy at the reader next door who was making the neatest abstracts, headed often with an A or a B or a C, while my own notebook rioted with the wildest scribble of contradictory jottings. It was distressing, it was bewildering, it was humiliating" (32). The library's books refuse to serve her purposes; the room itself, shaped like a man's head, denies her the ability to occupy the space. At the same time, as readers, we far prefer her errant scribblings to the tidy banalities of her neighbor.

The closer the speaker draws to her home, the more she settles into a state of reverie and repose conducive to advancing her ideas. Her house, like the colleges of Oxbridge, is also by a river, but here her approach is uncontested: "In my little street . . . domesticity prevailed" (41). The nearby people do not distract her. Rather, they suggest impressions that draw her deeper into her thoughts. The proximity of her home prompts her to an optimistic prediction: "in a hundred years, I thought, reaching my own doorstep, women will have ceased to be the protected sex. Logically they will take part in all the activities and exertions that were once denied them. . . . Anything may happen when womanhood has ceased to be a protected occupation, I thought, opening the door" (41–42). The narrator weaves her homecoming together with her prophecy, as if the former enables the latter, and the home is forecast as a future sanctuary for female authorship instead of a cage for women.

Once inside, the speaker goes into her study, where she can "draw the curtains . . . light the lamp . . . narrow the inquiry" and take her research in a new direction. The scene is one of pure concentration—no more interruptions arise—and the books, which in the British Museum seemed to frustrate all her inquiries, begin to yield up results. If the first two chapters of the essay show the speaker in constant motion—walking, dining, conversing, journeying—once she arrives at her home the "action" abruptly halts. The rest of *A Room of One's Own* consists of a tour of the speaker's private space for reading and writing, the room of the title. Her private library is evidently enormous (her tour of it will last for three chapters), beginning with "the shelf where the histories stand" (43) and going on to broadly investigate the conditions of women's lives. Looking at the bookshelves kept empty to await the writing of more books by women, she enumerates the obstacles to female authorship, beginning with the most important: "In the first place, to have a room of her own, let alone a quiet room or a sound-proof room, was out of the question, unless her parents were exceptionally rich or very noble, even up to the beginning of the nineteenth century" (54). Though her room is full of empty shelves, the speaker does have an extensive library of books by women authors, and she takes them down off the shelves as she reviews them: Lady Bessborough, Lady Winchilsea, Margaret of Newcastle, Dorothy Osborne, and Aphra Behn are early examples; when she comes to the early nineteenth century she has "several shelves given up entirely to the works of women" (66). Lastly she turns to the extensive shelves that hold books by living women and men. And finally, in the last pages of the essay, her reading exhausted, the speaker begins to write: "The very first sentence that I would write here, I said, crossing over to the writing-table and taking up the page headed Women and Fiction, is that it is fatal for anyone who writes to think of their sex" (102). In this deliberate staging of a representative act of female authorship there is a noticeable irony, for how can this writer not think of her sex as she writes?

"It is fatal for anyone who writes to think of their sex." This famous claim seems to go against the grain of much else in *A Room of One's Own*, against the idea of a female sentence and a distinct female literary tradition. How can anyone not think of their sex in a room like the study, a room dedicated to articulating masculinity through its furnishings, accessories, location, and solitude? How can the acquisition of a study make it possible for the woman writer to disengage from the separate spheres of gender that the study was built to secure? In the very room where the speaker makes this pronouncement she herself has grouped the books according to the sex of their authors. Woolf's desire for an androgynous author figure and her desire for an authorial study are incompatible. Yet she reaches for the study because her fantasized scene of writing is bound together with its solitary environs. It is the most private room in the house, a place where the writer can consider the world without being watched by it. Left alone, the writer seemingly dissolves into a universal subjectivity free from self-consciousness. As Woolf instructs, "There must be freedom and there must be peace. Not a wheel must grate, not a light glimmer. The curtains must be close drawn. The writer, I thought, once his experience is over, must lie back and let his mind celebrate its nuptials in darkness" (108). Despite its bedroom overtones, according to Woolf such a scene of authorship can only take place in the study—yet this claim is demonstrably false in the case of Woolf's own primary examples. Shakespeare and Austen, the only two writers Woolf cites as able to transcend their sex through their writing, did not write in studies. Austen wrote in the family sitting room, Shakespeare amid the clatter of theatrical production. Yet both managed to produce Woolf's ideal of androgynous writing.

A Room of One's Own, for all its surface of rhetorical perfection and ease, is riven with contradiction and paradox, much of it generated by Woolf's attraction to the model of authorship she associates with the space of the study. This attraction to "the writer in the study" is so strong that she argues for it in the face of all evidence. Perhaps this is because what the study models for Woolf is not exemplary writing practices but rather privacy and autonomy. The five hundred pounds, in Woolf's account, is also used to purchase autonomy—the ability to follow one's own will and not be coerced into thinking or doing as others prescribe. As Woolf puts it, "a lock on the door means the power to think for oneself" (110). A lock on the door signals that something has been locked in, but the study's history suggests that just as important is what—or who—has been locked out. Though Woolf begins *A Room of One's Own* with scenes of an ambitious woman writer being locked out, she anticipates little difficulty in transforming the woman writer from the excluded figure clamoring at the gates to the sheltered denizen laboring within.

Speaking the text of *A Room of One's Own* to an audience of women university students, Woolf is understandably at pains to strip authorship of its associations with genius and transcendence and anchor it in the material privileges that were newly accessible to educated young women. Authorship devolves not upon being a man, as the denizens of Oxbridge assert, but upon having the money and the study that were the habitual portion of well-to-do Victorian men. Margaret Ezell has argued that, in part because of the influence of *A Room of One's Own*, nineteenth-century notions of female authorship have tended to dominate female literary canon formation; it might be argued that nineteenth-century architectural theories have played an equally disproportionate role.[57] The generative fantasy of *A Room of One's Own*, a fantasy this text shares with many of its contemporaries, *The Well* among them, is that the male space of the Victorian study can become the crucible of an autonomous, potent, and female author figure. Rather than debunk the mystique of the study—as she might have used the example of Austen to do—Woolf wishes only to extend its privileges to women. By making the study one of two preconditions for successful authorship—a claim that her own evidence does not fully support—Woolf attempts to break into the closed circle of masculinity, authorship, and privacy.

But a simple transfer of ownership is hard to manage. Though women writers may claim studies, the effects of the change of ownership register both within and beyond the study doors. In fact, when women acquire rooms of their own and use them for writing, it is masculinity as much as authorship that becomes denatured, a process evident in both "Scandal" and *The Well,* where masculinity attaches to women as readily as to men. Irene Adler must become a man in order to gather the information she needs to outstrip Holmes. Similarly, Stephen Gordon thinks her way into a masculine role in order to become a productive writer. If *A Room of One's Own* sets out to ask the question of how modern women will learn to write "as women write, not as men write" (78), its answer is that women will write as women by writing like men. Further, even as these characters model masculinity to insinuate their way into the study, the study's nature changes. Specifically, the study becomes more transparent, finally yielding up the secrets it was built in part to secure.

"The most secret place in the house"

In its architectural origins the study is inseparable from the closet. The study began as a locked writing desk in the bedroom in fourteenth-century Europe and then was enlarged into a small space directly off the bedroom, called a closet. The *OED* defines the closet as a "place of private study or secluded speculation" and exemplifies this in a 1586 citation: "We doe call the most secret place in the house appropriate unto our owne private studies . . . a Closet."[58] The first closets were studies, and the first studies closets. Even up to the present day, in its form and decor—its traditionally paneled walls—the study has preserved its cabinet origins. Orest Ranum aptly notes that the study "grew from an item of furniture to something like furniture in which one lived."[59] The study and the closet continue to converge in interesting ways in more contemporary times. The closet in its modern form is not its own room but rather acts as a supplement to the single room it adjoins; the objects the closet holds are both in the room it supplements and outside of it. As Henry Urbach notes in his brief history of the closet, "Holding things at the edge of the room, simultaneously concealing and revealing its interior, the closet becomes a carrier of abjection, a site of *interior* exclusion for that which has been deemed dirty."[60] Closets are a way of separating out and hiding something that nevertheless remains integral to the whole.

By the late nineteenth century, studies had not yet ceased to be closets. They retained the closet's elaborate cabinetry, private nature, and use for storage of personal effects. The study, like the closet, held a queer secret: apparently masculinity's stronghold, the study was actually a site of abjection, a place for concealing secrets that offered evidence of the instability of gender identity. Both Adler and Stephen keep secrets in their studies, secrets that offer textual evidence that masculinity and femininity are neither fixed properties nor binary opposites. Adler keeps letters and a photograph that "feminize" the patriarchy and "masculinize" her, while Stephen inherits scientific proof from her father (whose secret it also was) that gender is a continuum, not a binary. The narrator of *A Room of One's Own* fears that men may be hidden in the audience and thus privy to her admission of the existence of desire between women. The secrets that the study holds are the gentleman's most private possession, yet they can undermine the very idea of what being a gentleman means. This secret instability in masculinity's fortress might be described as foundational in the history of the study, rendering the elaborate privacy surrounding the study a careful defense against the exposure of what lies within. If the acknowledged private contents of the study are "family records," the room can actually contain documents that, if they came to light, might destroy the family. When the study does not hold a secret, it still implies secrecy: the ability to keep a secret suggests the existence of the secret.

When women acquire studies, they continue the tradition of keeping secrets inside them; in fact, in all of the texts I have considered, the possession of a secret (a letter, a book, an idea) is the founding possibility of authorship. Yet when women acquire studies, the meaning of the space seems to alter and its secrets become more visible. Sir Philip's secret was ever secure, while Stephen's study—like Adler's—seems to be continually under siege. In both these texts, the study's closeted secrets—homosexuality, sexual inversion, and extramarital sexuality, among others—become open secrets. Even the secretive Stephen gradually loosens her hold on the closet door, dressing exclusively in men's clothing and going to Valerie Seymour's lesbian salon. In the hands of the woman writer, the room becomes less masculinity's fortress and more a space that undermines masculinity's exclusive association with privacy, authority, and authorship. The space retains the advantages of solitude and withdrawal from scrutiny while gradually exposing its secrets to the public view.

Woolf concludes her essay with the claim that women writers can reach the rank of Shakespeare when and if they "escape a little from the common sitting-room and see human beings not always in their relation to each other but in relation to reality" (118). Leave the sitting room and go into the study, the narrator urges her audience, and there you will be able to see things for what they are. The study, in this reading, has become not a place to keep secrets but a place to strip away pretense and disguise, a place where reality is laid open. The woman writer needs a study to write; having got one, she finds her presence changes what this room means. When the doors of the study open to admit the woman writer and the study's secrets are exposed for all to see, the study leaves the closet behind.

5. Interiors

The interior furniture of houses appeared together with the interior furniture of minds.
—John Lukacs

"Phantasmagorias of the interior"

When we imagine the members of the Bloomsbury Group, we see them at home. We can tour Charleston, Vanessa Bell and Duncan Grant's summer house in Sussex, or the nearby home of Virginia and Leonard Woolf, Monk's House, now a National Trust Property. Recent films about Bloomsbury such as *The Hours* (2002) and *Carrington* (1995) depict the Bloomsbury artists and writers sitting in their homes and talking—endlessly, it sometimes seems—about their work, their loves, their thoughts, and their theories. Even the titles of paintings by Bloomsbury artists convey their fascination with their own homes and with scenes of domestic life: Bell's *Conversation at Asheham House* (1912), *Nursery Tea* (1912), *46 Gordon Square* (1911), and *Interior with Duncan Grant* (1934); Dora Carrington's *Kitchen Scene at Tidmarsh Mill* (1922) and *Lytton Strachey and Boris Anrep in the Front Sitting Room at Ham Spray* (1927); Grant's *On the Roof, 38 Brunswick Square* (1912), *Interior at Gordon Square* (1915), and *The Stove, Fitzroy Square* (1936). The rooms seen in these works often became the occasion for an engagement with Post-Impressionism, but they are also important for what they reveal about Bloomsbury's focus on interior space, about the attempt to depict an interiority anchored in the home.

The middle-class home is frequently associated with conformity and tradition, with family and marriage, with leisure and private life. But none of these qualities describe the domestic circumstances envisioned by Bloomsbury artists and writers. They saw the home not as a static backdrop but as the test-ing grounds for a way of living that valued spontaneity, creative work, self-expression, free love, and the affection of friends. It was a site for rebellion against middle-class conventions such as monogamy, heterosexuality, sexism, and social propriety. The coterie of artists, writers, and critics that constitutes "Bloomsbury" did not share a consistent aesthetic, political, or social pro-gram. But their works partook of a common preoccupation with the changing nature of private life. As E. M. Forster recalled, "We deified personal relation-ships and expected them to function outside the appropriate sphere."[1] Private life had political and aesthetic dimensions for Forster and his circle. The Bloomsbury Group set aside Wilde's apolitical aesthetic credo "life is art" in favor of establishing an exchange between the seemingly incommensurate reg-isters of politics, private life, and high art. From the beginning, the organiza-tion and appearance of the domestic interior was the site of their most inten-sive consideration.

Each of the major Bloomsbury artists—Bell, Roger Fry, and Grant—exper-imented extensively with the furnishings of his or her own homes, frequently employing the same Post-Impressionist techniques they were exploring in the fine arts. The connections between the literary, artistic, and decorative experi-ments of Bloomsbury are more than anecdotal; these artists and writers pres-ent a range of shared methodologies and interests that cross disciplines. The synergies range among tradition, technique, and influence to shared ideas about the relation between public and private life, the changing nature of the home, and the role of women in all these controversies. But these synergies, though remarkable, are not my chief subject here. What interests me above all is how Bloomsbury artists and writers participate in the reassessment of interi-ority in British modernism. What I propose here is something like a material history of modernist literary interiority. This history cuts against the fantasy of the severed autotelic self that frequently populates modernist literature and criticism; it substitutes for that vision a sense, in Bill Brown's words, of how "human subjects and material objects constitute one another, and what remains outside the regularities of that constitution that can disrupt the cul-tural memory of modernity and modernism."[2] Rather than emphasize the well-described psychological aspects of modernist literary interiority, I show how it takes its substance from the aesthetic programs of modern art and design.

This chapter is organized around three works of modern fiction: Forster's *Howards End* (1910) and Woolf's *Night and Day* (1919) and *To the Lighthouse* (1927). Each is a domestic novel that portrays the vicissitudes of family life, beyond which the stories appear to overlap very little. Yet I argue that each of these works defines a perceived problem in the organization or conduct of domestic life and devises a potential solution to that problem. Despite the social and dynamic nature of the problems, the solutions tendered by these works are explicitly formalist, often drawing on a technical vocabulary particular to the aesthetic codes of modern art and design. Given the abstract and distanced nature of visual formalism, a formalist resolution to a social dilemma may seem mismatched. More, such a resolution may appear gravely inappropriate, at its worst a kind of retreat from the messiness of the social world into the apparent purity of abstract forms. As will become clear, however, for Forster and more particularly for Woolf, the rhetoric of visual formalism was associated with abstraction and derealization on the one hand and social insurgency on the other. In a sense, this marriage between formalism and the social realm was anticipated by Wilde in *The Picture of Dorian Gray*, since Dorian depends on an aesthetic object—a framed picture—to ensure the continuity of his life in society. For Forster and Woolf the stakes are both more quotidian (no recourse to the supernatural) and more urgent (not a single man's life but the future of the family lies in the balance). To come down to cases, why, in *Howards End*, is the problem of unwed motherhood resolved by having the main characters rearrange the furniture in their new home? To make sense of this apparent non sequitur, I juxtapose my reading of this novel (and the others I analyze) with contemporary Bloomsbury experiments in interior design. The fashioning of modernist literary interiority is tightly bound up with acts like rearranging the furniture, and I explore the implications of this incongruous connection for modernism.

Like the others in this book, this chapter flows from a double meaning in its title. The "interior" is both one's inner nature or being and the inside of a particular space, and my discussion presupposes an essential resemblance or interdependence between these two senses of the word. The former definition is at the heart of literary modernism, the latter considered irrelevant to it. Yet as Walter Benjamin has suggested, the increasing symmetry between these two senses of the interior is part of the advent of modern life, the origin of what he terms "the phantasmagorias of the interior." "For the private individual," he writes, "the private environment represents the universe. In it he gathers remote places and the past. His drawing room is a box in the world theater."[3] As the private environment detaches from the place of work, the individual's inner life aligns with the domestic interior. The phantasmagoria is both a play of optical illusions in an enclosed space and the life of the mind. The phantas-

magoria is the modernist experience of reality and the theater for its performance is the private home.

Interior at Gordon Square

This story begins when Bloomsbury does, in 1904, when Leslie Stephen died
and the Stephen children—Vanessa, Thoby, Virginia, and Adrian—left Hyde
Park Gate to take up residency at Gordon Square in London's Bloomsbury. Literary legend has it that Vanessa chose the new neighborhood by hazard based
on its considerable distance from Kensington, but the intellectual history and
somewhat unique geographical layout of Bloomsbury, organized around
squares in a fashion largely unique to the area, made it an extremely felicitous
choice. Siegfried Giedion, in assessing the plan of Bloomsbury, called it "a dis-
trict which for its human treatment remains unsurpassed to this day . . . a simple and democratic fabric."[4] These are also the values that members of the
Bloomsbury Group sought to bring to domestic life. As Vanessa Bell recalled,
"it was exhilarating . . . to have one's own rooms, be master of one's own time,
have all the things in fact which come as a matter of course to many of the
young today but so seldom then, to young women at least."[5] Simplicity in the
routines of daily life, democracy among household members—that, at any rate,
was their plan.

A group of well-off young people living together in unusually casual circumstances is not the stuff of revolution. But that household did lay the
groundwork for many future ménages, and it also represented a first explo-
ration into the ethics of the everyday, an ethics that found an aesthetic counterpart in Bloomsbury's artistic representations of domesticity. For Woolf,
recalling that time, the move to Bloomsbury authorized a series of social revi-
sions: "We were full of experiments and reforms. We were going to do without
table napkins, we were to have [large supplies of] Bromo instead; we were going
to paint; to write; to have coffee after dinner instead of tea at nine o'clock.
Everything was going to be new; everything was going to be different. Everything was on trial."[6] As with her dream of the kitchen table, Woolf's examples
are drawn from the realm of household minutiae not to show their triviality but
to demonstrate how far they went. Her details mix the artistic (painting and
writing) with the homely (napkins and coffee), the former a staple of revolu-
tionary movements, the latter not. Yet for the Bloomsbury Group, from its
inception in the conversational salons organized by Thoby Stephen at Gordon
Square, the effluvia of domesticity was inseparable from the loftier guiding

principles drawn from the writings of G. E. Moore, the major philosophical influence on Thoby and his friends at Cambridge (among them Leonard Woolf, Lytton Strachey, and Forster).

Sex and sexuality were at the center of the effort to make private life less secret, beginning with Strachey's introduction of semen (in word if not in deed) into the drawing room. In 1907, soon after Vanessa's marriage to Clive Bell, the couple received Strachey while lying in bed. This venture into impropriety stemmed from an impulse, as Bell's biographer Frances Spalding writes, to make sex "part of everyday life."[7] An unchastened Strachey wrote of the incident to Grant,

> The other day I called there (did I tell you?) and went into the room unannounced—fortunately not quite as quickly as I might, so that they just had time to roll off the Louis XV bed, in a very flushed + crumpled condition! I longed to say, "Oh, please don't let me interrupt: if you like, I'll join you!" But I talked of the weather instead.[8]

Strachey returned the favor, as Maynard Keynes described in a letter to Duncan Grant in August of 1908: "Lytton seems to carry on a good deal with his females. He has let Vanessa see his most indecent poems—she is filled with delight, has them by heart, and has made many typewritten copies for Virginia and others."[9] Poetry and promiscuity: from the beginning, Bloomsbury's embrace of sexual freedom ran alongside its creative efforts.

For Leslie Stephen's daughters these altered domestic circumstances seem to have been especially refreshing. University educations had long given well-to-do young men an opportunity for freer living and self-expression, but for young women, kept at home until marriage, such openness about sexuality was unusual—as was their premarital cohabitation with their brother's university friends. Woolf writes with salacious fondness of those years: "We discussed copulation with the same excitement and openness that we had discussed the nature of good."[10] Bell later recalled the importance of the connection between the "lowly" domestic and seemingly more elevated realms: "If you could say what you like about art, sex or religion, you could also talk freely and very likely dully about the ordinary doings of daily life. . . . life was exciting, terrible and amusing and we had to explore it, thankful that one could do so freely."[11] As the doings of daily life attained a new significance, the setting for that life became equally consequential. From the first, Bell and her friends undertook ambitious projects in redecoration. Their bright and open spaces were the design counterpart of the kind of personal exchanges that Bloomsbury valued, and they were spiritually and materially in dialogue with the Victorian interiors so recently left behind. As Christopher Reed notes, "Attempting to imagine ways of living appropriate to determinedly unladylike women and unmanly men, Bloomsbury relied on imaginative recombinations of available conventions."[12] Bell recycled some of the Hyde Park Gate household goods and integrated them into the new decorative scheme, resulting in some odd juxtapositions and a design that Reed characterizes as an instance of "subcultural negotiation."[13] It might be said more simply that despite the best intentions of starting fresh, old things are never easy to dispose of. Forster's novel *Howards End* encapsulates this difficulty with its story of an unconventional family that must try to make shift in an old house. I would like to set the context for examining the role of interior design in *Howards End* by looking at related early Bloomsbury experiments in decoration.

There are broad similarities between the lives of the Stephen children following their father's death and those of the fictional Schlegel children in *Howards End*. Margaret and Helen Schlegel, together with their brother Tibby, are adult orphans living in London on comfortable fixed incomes. Like the Stephens, they have an artistic bent, a decided thirst for intellectual stimulation, and a commitment to the primacy of personal relationships. Moreover, the Schlegels share the Stephens' idiosyncratic twin convictions that houses can determine their inhabitants and that a household unit can be defined by ties of affection as well as by those of blood. Finally, in *Howards End,* as among the Bloomsbury Group, redecoration is seen as central to the reconstruction of private life, and the domestic interior serves as both a mirror and a model for interiority. For the Schlegels, as for the Bloomsbury Group, this means not discarding the old but recycling it into something better suited to the needs of modern life. It was no wonder that Woolf claimed that Forster's books were the only place where she could read about "people like ourselves."[14]

Although he had met some of the future members of the Bloomsbury Group in his earlier days at Cambridge, Forster's close association with the group dates from 1910, the year *Howards End* was published. Woolf remembers him from Bloomsbury's early days as an evanescent figure who moved in and out of their circle: "I used to watch him from behind a hedge as he flitted through Gordon Square, erratic, irregular, with his bag, on his way to catch a train."[15] Forster, like other members of the group, was influenced at Cambridge by the work of G. E. Moore, whose *Principia Ethica* (1903) provided the theoretical basis for Bloomsbury's credo that personal relations supersede all other social claims on the individual. Forster was a member of the Cambridge Apostles, from which

Bloomsbury sprang. Although Forster considered himself a liminal member of the group, he was stimulated by their aesthetic projects. For instance, in a 1911 journal entry, he describes an exciting visit to Fry's house, Durbins, which Fry designed himself, and which he treated as a kind of laboratory for his avant-garde experiments in modern painting and design. Forster wrote of this visit in his diary: "Returned from Fry's yesterday in an exaltation that has not yet subsided. I saw what he was up to—to clean Art of reminiscences. . . . To paint the position of things in space. . . . He and his house always invigorate but never before so strongly. I felt I could do anything and have worked better than usual today."[16] *Howards End* represents another exercise in the cleaning up of reminiscences: like the Stephen children, its characters must literally and figuratively clean house in order to make a future.

"You picked up the pieces and made us a home"

Although the words above are spoken by Helen Schlegel to her sister, Margaret, they apply equally well to Vanessa Bell, who in 1904 had to shepherd her broken family from Kensington to the squares of Bloomsbury. Woolf recalls the energy and violence with which Bell dislodged the old household: "She had sold; she had burnt; she had sorted; she had torn up."[17] The result was less dramatic than it was defiant. "46 Gordon Square could never have meant what it did had not 22 Hyde Park Gate preceded it," Woolf wrote.[18] Bell tried to create a domestic interior that broke with the world of Hyde Park Gate. She sold most of the family furniture to Harrods and decorated the front hall by facing off portraits of Victorian celebrities—Darwin, Tennyson, Browning—with photographs of Julia Stephen taken by eminent photographer and family member Julia Margaret Cameron. Bell also painted all the walls white, a choice that contrasted both with the walls at Hyde Park Gate, which were a typical-for-the-period navy blue and black. Bell had picked up the idea of white walls from painter Charles Furse and his wife, Katharine, in whose home white walls were used to create a backdrop for the display of pictures.[19] She draped the walls and the furniture with Indian shawls in an effort to introduce life and color into what must have seemed a stark interior.

Bell's friends soon joined her foray into interior design. Following Thoby Stephen's death and Clive and Vanessa's marriage, Virginia and Adrian moved to Fitzroy Square, and in 1911, to 38 Brunswick Square, where the unmarried Virginia lived not just with her brother but with other unmarried men: Duncan Grant, Maynard Keynes, and Leonard Woolf. Grant immediately began redecorating some of the rooms.[20] The shutters he designed for Adrian Stephen's room (figs. 14, 15, 16) exhibit figures who are not just nude but freely sensual, even androgynous. Grant's designs went further than Bell's first effort, introducing frankly modern elements into the interior. The erotics of the images are not tied to a heterosexual logic or indeed to any form of coupling. The stylized, brilliantly colored figures seem to fly or swim through space with outstretched limbs either seeking embrace or displaying a self-contained sensuality. Also in Adrian Stephen's rooms, and perhaps with his aid, Grant executed a large mural of tennis players in a Post-Impressionist style (fig. 17). The only surviving photograph of the mural is in black and white, but the mural was bright red and yellow. The tennis players share with the shutter decorations an exuberant nudity and a preference for scenes drawn from the ordinary life of the body. If Victorian interiors seemed in some ways to be organized around a denial of embodiment, Grant used the bones of the house to reintegrate the body into the domestic interior. Although he and his friends were only renting the house and perhaps never intended an extended stay, he applied his images to fixed parts of the interior, leaving an aesthetic record for future occupants.

Grant's early decorative work focused on the intimate life of the body and its pleasures. He seemed to enjoy painting with his current lover in the rooms where their coupling took place. This spirited approach to design went public in 1913 when he, Vanessa Bell, and Roger Fry founded the Omega Workshops, a professional studio for the production and sale of artist-decorated home furnishings. The Omega collective sought to transform the look of the modern home, from walls to floor and furnishings. Like the Hogarth Press founded by the Woolfs, the Omega was a homegrown Bloomsbury business that both furthered creative experimentation and publicly disseminated the products of that experimentation to a wider audience. Over its seven-year life span, a broad range of artists worked for the Omega—including Wyndham Lewis, Edward Wadsworth, Paul Nash, Henri Gaudier-Brzeska, and Nina Hamnett—though in the spirit of the collective, most works were unsigned. The wares produced or decorated included textiles, pottery, murals, painted furniture, clothing, and more.

The Omega approach to interior design upheld a belief that, in Reed's words, "the objects of daily life reveal and perpetuate the social and moral conditions of their creation,"[21] a conviction that draws on the ideas of William Morris, but to very different ends than his. Working out of a building on Fitzroy Square, the Omega artists quickly acquired a notorious reputation for

Figures 14 and 15. Duncan Grant, designs for shutters at 38 Brunswick Square, 1912. ©1978 Estate of Duncan Grant, courtesy Henrietta Garnett and the Courtauld Institute Galleries, Fry Bequest.

Figure 16. Duncan Grant, designs for shutters at 38 Brunswick Square, 1912. ©1978 Estate of Duncan Grant, courtesy Henrietta Garnett and the Courtauld Institute Galleries, Fry Bequest.

Figure 17. Duncan Grant, mural at 38 Brunswick Square, 1912. ©1978 Estate of Duncan Grant, courtesy Henrietta Garnett and the Tate Gallery, London, Vanessa Bell Photographic Collection.

producing goods that suggested questionable morality. Winifred Gill, in a letter written to Duncan Grant recalling her days working at the Omega, tells the following story:

> One morning after our opening, two ladies came into the showroom. I was rung for and came down to see what they wanted. They wished to see furniture. I showed them what we had. They were not satisfied. I had not shown them everything. I took them to the back showroom upstairs where there was some unfinished work. No. That was not what they came for. Hadn't we some furniture that we didn't show to everyone? There was some as yet unpainted furniture in the cellar. They inspected this. "What's in here?" exclaimed one of them, suspiciously opening the door of a shallow shelved cupboard in the showroom. At last they rather shamefacedly said that they had heard that our furniture was "immoral" and they wanted to see some. "O," said I, "that's only because we paint our chairs scarlet." It was I think the Morning Post that said that. Was that all, they said, rather disappointed. "We couldn't think what immoral furniture would be like." "Yes," interrupted the other, "all we could think of was a sort of armchair and commode combined."[22]

The visitors' invention of an armchair/commode pointed to the source of the Omega's scandal—that the workshop's designs incorporated all sorts of improper positions and functions of the body. Like Grant's work at Brunswick Place, many Omega designs represented the human body as unclothed, androgynous, and rapturous. In Arnold Bennett's novel *The Pretty Lady* (1918), he described the effect of walking into an Omega interior:

> The footman left G. J. alone in a room designated the boudoir. G. J. resented the boudoir, because it was like nothing that he had ever witnessed. The walls were irregularly covered with rhombuses, rhomboids, lozenges, diamonds, triangles, and parallelograms; the carpet was treated likewise, and also the upholstery and the cushions. The colourings of the scene in their excessive brightness, crudity and variety surpassed G. J.'s conception of the possible. . . . He was as disturbed as he might have been disturbed by drinking a liqueur on the top of a cocktail. On the front of the mantelpiece were perversely but brilliantly depicted, with a high degree of finish, two nude, crouching women who gazed longingly at each other across the impassable semicircular abyss of the fireplace.[23]

Though Bennett's satire is broad, he identifies some elements central to Omega design: abstraction, color, geometric patterning, and an emphasis on innovation through surface decoration. Wholesale redesign was integral to the Omega goal of the total transformation of domestic space. In rooms designed by the Omega, as would be the case at Charleston, every surface—from walls to floor to furnishings—is covered with colorful designs. One of the group's early prominent commissions was a room designed for the Ideal Home exhibition in 1913, titled the "Post-Impressionist Room" (fig. 18). The room is energized by its contrasts, juxtaposing the strict and angular shapes of the central table, cane-backed chairs (topped with the Omega logo), and rugs with the more vivid and complex geometrical patterning of the textiles, murals, and the inlaid motif of the desk. As Richard Cork writes, the "Post-Impressionist Room" "demonstrates [Fry's] readiness to bring this variety together in one space, even though he ran the risk of producing an indigestible stylistic mixture."[24]

The room's most noticeable feature is its murals, six-foot-tall abstract nudes reminiscent of Matisse. The exhibition catalog description, likely written by Fry, describes the walls as "decorated in distemper by various artists working together on the general theme of designs based on the movements of the dance."[25] This description takes in the stylization of the figures in the murals, but just as prominent is the bright coloration (red, orange, and acid green), ecstatic posturing, and sensuality of form. The bodies of the dancers became formal elements of a design based on flow and lines of motion, turning twisting bodies in intimate, mirroring relations with one another. The addition of large-scale nudity brings sex into the drawing room in a manner that still seems forthright. In a fashion related to Whistler's exhibitions and Wilde's drawing room, these murals play with the distinction between the artistic and the decorative, between the gallery and the domestic interior. For Fry such murals were an ideal way to create an organic and useful role for art in the home; in 1917 he wondered in *Colour* magazine whether "the artist might not compete, and compete successfully, with the house painter."[26]

The furnishings in the "Post-Impressionist Room" have simplified, modern lines, and their casual and lightweight nature encourages a flexible use of the space. It speaks for the radical appearance of the "Post-Impressionist Room" that it was singled out at the exhibition by members of the royal family who declared it a "perfect example of how not to decorate a sitting-room."[27] Other entries in the exhibition were similarly fanciful—including a Moonlight Sonata Room—but it was the Omega entry that became "a popular focal point for laughter and abuse" at the exhibition.[28] Other reviews of the room accused the

Figure 18. Omega Workshops, "Post-Impressionist Room," Ideal Home Exhibition, 1913. Courtesy of the *Illustrated London News* Picture Library.

Omega of abandoning all traditions of the decorative arts: "One might almost say that [the Omega] has set itself the colossal task of trying to discover how man might express himself in decorative pattern if he possessed no knowledge of what had hitherto been done in that direction."[29] Omega decorations were seen not as a bold leap forward but as a return to the prehistoric. This rhetoric coincides with the accusations of degeneracy directed at Post-Impressionist painting that I will discuss later, but in the domestic context the design seemed to undercut the English way of life. When imported into the home by British artists, Post-Impressionism seemed to propose spontaneity, lawlessness, and sensuality—for both a room and its inhabitants.

In *Howards End* none of the characters are artists, and the redecoration that takes place involves only a reworking of existing elements. There are no over-sized nudes or Post-Impressionist flourishes, yet the novel centers on issues similar to those that stimulated Bloomsbury's experiments in interior design. The title of Forster's novel refers to a house, the ownership of which is tied to a debate about changing sexual mores, as exemplified in the relations between two families. The Wilcoxes (father, mother, and children; conventional, wealthy, and patriarchal) are the house's residents at the story's opening; the Schlegels (two sisters and a brother; half-German, bohemian, and moderately well off) will eventually possess it. The house Howards End plays a pivotal role in sorting out the fates and fortunes of these characters, solving the problem of housing those who break away from the approved standards of sexual conduct. If the traditional home was built to support marriage and patriarchal lines of inheritance, can an unmarried woman and her child find accommodation and patrimony in the heart of England? The novel begins with a description of the house, written by the younger sister, Helen Schlegel, to the older, Margaret, on the occasion of Helen's first visit to the house.

> Dearest Meg,
> It isn't going to be what we expected. It is old and little, and altogether delightful—red brick. . . . From hall you go right or left into dining-room or drawing-room. Hall itself is practically a room. You open another door in it, and there are the stairs going up in a sort of tunnel to the first-floor. Three bedrooms in a row there, and three attics in a row above.[30]

Helen initially finds the house unexpected because she had anticipated that the Wilcoxes would favor a more grandiose setting, but the house will become even more unexpected by the end of the story, as it seems to assert its own will to become the property of the Schlegels.

To bring the two families together—a goal implicit in Forster's epigraph "Only Connect"—would represent a move beyond the era of gender-segregated domesticity. As Margaret tells Helen, the Schlegels' home at the novel's opening is "irrevocably feminine," while Howards End, under the Wilcoxes' ownership, is "irrevocably masculine" (34). The Wilcoxes' London home on Ducie Street is equally manly, "as if a motor-car had spawned" (118). At the Schlegels', conversations center on the arts and women's rights, while at the Wilcoxes' the talk is of finances and empire, if there is talk at all; "We never discuss anything at Howards End" (58), Mrs. Wilcox says. Margaret dislikes this code of "ladies sheltering behind men, men sheltering behind servants" (153), and she criticizes the design of Howards End, where the drawing room beams have been matchboarded because "the facts of life must be concealed from ladies" (144). But the novel asserts that traditional English domesticity cannot assimilate modern sexuality.

In spite of Howards End's design defect, the house becomes a crucible in which the problem of sheltering sexual transgressors can be resolved. Although Meg dislikes the hypocritical matchboarding, she looks through it to discern the house's underlying architectural identity: "Drawing-room, dining-room, and hall—how petty the names sounded! Here were simply three rooms where children could play and friends could shelter from the rain. Yes, and they were beautiful" (144). Meg sees the house in abstract terms, stripping away the labels and furbelows placed on the domestic space to reveal the essential function of architecture: shelter. In fact, the classy labels on the rooms are a superficial overlay likely not intended by the house's original owners. The Howards did not have the kind of landed gentry status to which businessmen like the Wilcoxes lately aspired. Rather, the house had begun as a small working farm of thirty acres, with the property now reduced through sales over the years. The genteel hall that forms the current entrance is a latter-day innovation introduced by Mr. Wilcox. Before the renovation, the front room of the house was the kitchen, now relegated to the servant quarters in the back of the house. This history suggests that the matchboarding introduced by Mr. Wilcox is indeed superficial and that the house upholds an older moral code that does not stand on ceremonies of birth. Forster continually associates Howards End with fecundity and a healing property that is part of his pastoral, perhaps romanticized, ideal: "In these English farms, if anywhere, one might see life steadily and see it whole, group in one vision its transitoriness and its eternal youth, connect" (191). The ancient wych elm in front of the house is another symbol of fertility, another incarnation of a value system that is older than the Wilcox line.

"House and tree transcended any similes of sex" (148), Margaret observes. Only redecoration is needed to realize the house's inner identity. In Margaret's vision of the house, architecture loses its social function as a guardian of gender difference and recaptures its original purpose of nurturing people bound together by ties of either blood or affection.

If Howards End unsettles conventional notions of gender, it has a similar effect on conventional notions of property, as indicated by the possessive apostrophe that is missing in the house's name. Ownership of the house is contested after Mrs. Wilcox, the house's owner as the last of the Howard line, dies suddenly and surprises her family by writing a casual, extralegal will that bequeaths the house to Margaret. In one of the narrator's asides, he or she asserts that in bequeathing the house to Margaret, Mrs. Wilcox is challenging the system of blood inheritance and instituting one of affection: "she sought a spiritual heir" (73). And though Mr. Wilcox sets aside his wife's wishes, his subsequent marriage to Margaret restores them. Against instructions, the local caretaker Miss Avery redecorates Howards End with the Schlegels' household goods as though the family were in residence. When Margaret comes down to reverse Miss Avery's actions, Miss Avery tells her, "You are living here now," and Margaret concedes that "The furniture fitted extraordinarily well" (194).

Margaret tells Miss Avery that she and Mr. Wilcox will never live at Howards End, but subsequent events alter her outlook. The unmarried Helen becomes pregnant, a condition she conceals until tricked into meeting Margaret at Howards End. The architectural response to unwed motherhood at the time was a variant of eviction: a woman would be sent far from home at least until after the birth—Helen has been hiding out in Germany. But Margaret has a different notion of the function of the domestic interior, as she explains to her husband and a doctor. " 'It all turns on affection now,' said Margaret. 'Affection. Don't you see?' Resuming her usual methods, she wrote the word on the house with her finger. 'Surely you see. I like Helen very much. . . . And affection, when reciprocated, gives rights' " (207). Inscribing her credo on the house is Margaret's first act of redecoration. Many homes at the time bore mottoes for conduct on their walls, often in the form of quotations or slogans. At 22 Hyde Park Gate, a motto in the entryway began "What is it to be a gentleman?" and continued by outlining a high Victorian standard of behavior. The word "affection," written on Howards End, opens the house to a new code of conduct based not on law but on the rights of affection, the sort of bond that drew the Bloomsbury Group into a variety of domestic partnerships. It might be pointed out that Margaret is only writing in dust, redecorating the house in a fashion even more superficial than Mr. Wilcox. But her theory of inheritance seems more attuned to the house's own essential spirit, one symbolized by the house's relationship to the great wych elm that relates to the house as "a comrade, bending over the house" (148).

Affection decrees that property should pass along lines determined by comradeship; the Wilcox mind-set sees bloodlines and marriage as more valid conduits. Mr. Wilcox tells his eldest son: " 'The house is mine—and, Charles, it will be yours—and when I say that no one is to live there, I mean that no one is to live there. I won't have it. . . . To my mind this question is connected with something far greater, the rights of property itself' " (231). Helen's pregnancy means that she is no longer entitled to the shelter of the domestic interior. Mr. Wilcox refuses the pregnant Helen even a night's shelter at Howards End, and the neighboring farm initially refuses her too, as the owners "did not see why they should receive the offscourings of Howards End" (234). Offscourings are dirt that must be expelled from the domestic interior in order to preserve its value and identity. Helen can be considered dirty from a number of viewpoints: she is sexually impure by dint of her extramarital promiscuity and indiscreet in allowing her condition to be known; further, her pregnancy places her in a threshold or transitional state such as is commonly associated with uncleanness. Despite her femaleness—and hence attachment to the domestic—Helen is seen as antithetical to all that domesticity represents. When Margaret sarcastically asks her husband, "Will Helen's condition depreciate the property?" (218), the answer is yes.

Accommodating Helen requires redefining the clean and the dirty, and Margaret takes an initial step in that process when she posts her motto in the dust on the walls, redecorating in dirt. This is only the first step in remaking Howards End. No sooner has Margaret turned to face the pregnant Helen for the first time than the two sisters automatically turn to the work of redecoration, of creating a home to house what convention would evict. They move chairs, discuss the need for a rug, and notice how their furnishings suit the house. As Helen observes, "The hall seems more alive even than in the old days, when it held the Wilcoxes' own things" (209). Rather than imposing their own vision on Howards End, Helen and Margaret's redecoration is restorative, uncovering the house's original spirit in an act of what the narrator calls "the past sanctifying the present" (212). Helen and Margaret conclude through their work that Howards End "has wonderful powers," that "it kills what is dreadful and makes what is beautiful live" (213), suggesting that the house has a purifying force that is partly aesthetic (nurturing beauty) and partly moral (destroying dreadfulness). The fusion of these properties is the key to the house's agency, mingling the physical with the spiritual, the decorative with the profound, and domestic interiority with interior life. Their efforts are always in the vein of bringing out the house's own powerful character, as opposed to imposing their own vision: "They opened window after window, till the inside, too, was rustling to the spring. Curtains blew, picture-frames tapped cheerfully. Helen uttered cries of excitement as she found this bed obviously in its right place, that in its wrong one" (213). This is not modernist design, but it does lead to modernization—and it certainly marks a change from the Wilcoxes' tenure. It seems relevant that the Wilcoxes and the Schlegels meet for the first time at the cathedral at Speyer, a structure that has been ruined by improper restoration. The relationship between the two families culminates in the proper restoration undertaken by Helen and Margaret.

Despite the prohibition against their visit, in the chaos that ensues after Charles Wilcox is removed to prison Margaret brings her sister and husband together and settles them at Howards End. Helen observes in retrospect, "You picked up the pieces and made us a home," an action she dubs "heroic" (240). The grounds for the continuity of this new domesticity are laid in the novel's final scene, in which Henry Wilcox announces to his family his intent to bequeath Howards End to his wife, from whom it will pass to Helen's son.[31] Robert K. Martin argues that the resolution of the novel lies in its creation of a feminine household; as he asserts, "The union, or connection, at the heart of *Howards End*, is that between Helen and Margaret, and it is they who, acting on behalf of Ruth [the first Mrs. Wilcox], can form a female sacred family assuring continuity." The final disposition of Howards End seems more nearly to represent a fusion of masculine and feminine spaces, with Mr. Wilcox in residence, and the house itself slated to pass to a male.[32] Margaret's homemaking depends on her alchemical ability to mix disparate elements, proper with improper, old with new, Wilcox with Schlegel.[33] The redecoration of the Wilcox/Howard home with Schlegel furniture is the central symbol of this amalgam.

Although Howards End is an old house, reminiscent of agrarian traditions, Margaret comes to feel by the end of the novel that the house "is the future as well as the past" (240). In its new incarnation the house has provided a solution to the problem of providing a future for a family that would normally be excluded from patrimony. Margaret and Helen's redecoration allows them to imaginatively possess the house and prepare for their legal possession of it. Their redesign is rudimentary and haphazard, not unlike Vanessa Bell's rough-and-ready reuse of Hyde Park Gate's furnishings for Gordon Square. In many ways, *Howards End* presents the least saturated version of the dynamic I am tracing in this chapter, something as simple as: Want a modern life? Start moving furniture. Forster's formula is an ingenuous "design produces change." But in his work—and much more so in Woolf's—particular kinds of design are geared to produce particular kinds of change. For instance, when Margaret and Helen are arranging their furniture at Howards End, they find that the caretaker has set the chairs in the dining room in partners. They shift them "so that anyone sitting will see the lawn" (211), taking the emphasis away from coupling and placing it on contemplation and the outdoor life. Indeed, the lawn itself challenges the drawing room's primacy as a social space; the narrator describes it as "one of those open-air drawing-rooms" (195). The overriding principle for design at Howards End is one of connection across difference.

Howards End also represents a fusion of urban and rural England; as Paul Wilcox points out, "it's not really the country, and it's not the town" (241). The final scene of the novel, in which the hay crop is harvested, seems to indicate the triumph of the rural idyll, but in fact the plot of the novel relies on the nature of city life. Forster depends heavily on the coincidences caused by the mingling of different types and classes of people in the city. Helen, for instance, first encounters her future lover when they are seated by each other at a public concert. Although the Wilcoxes and Schlegels meet while abroad, their relationship only continues because they are neighbors in London. And an important meeting between Margaret and Henry occurs when they unexpectedly encounter one another on Chelsea Embankment. In the country, Wilcoxes and Schlegels alike stay at home or motor through the country at speeds that preclude surprise meetings. But the social space of the city streets impinges upon the domestic interior when characters encounter each other in the street and then adjourn to each others' homes. Forster also relies on the city to help define his characters, who suffer from the rootlessness endemic to modern urbanism. Howards End offers a stability and a natural routine that Forster sees as both eminently desirable and unavailable to city inhabitants. Moving on from Forster's domestic sanctuary set in a semi-rural hideaway, I turn now to the influence of the city on modernist interiors, to the colors, rhythms, and sensations of city life that informed Bloomsbury design and literature.

"Along all the broad pavements of the city"

The city street, commonly understood to be the central arena of modernist creativity and self-expression, is personified by the flaneur. The flaneur observes with pleasure the spectacular and ordinary rites of urban life and is the avatar of the modernist artist. As Benjamin has it, the flaneur "surrounds the approaching desolation of city life with a propitiatory luster."[34] For the flaneur, even the most depraved aspects of the city have a romance. The city seduces, entertains, and inspires the urban subject, but it can also overwhelm him. Georg Simmel is perhaps the best-known chronicler of the psychological dangers of urban life; his 1903 essay "The Metropolis and Mental Life" was among the first to outline the effects of urban living on the individual psyche. For Simmel, the stimulations of the city ultimately had a debilitating effect on the urban subject. "Through the rapidity and contradictoriness of [nervous] changes," he writes, "more harmless impressions force such violent responses, tearing the nerves so brutally hither and thither that their last reserves of strength are spent."[35] For Simmel, the danger of city life lies in its shocking, percussive nature, in the tumult of sensation which, though exciting, can also be traumatic.

The home offers a possible antidote or counterbalance to the dangers of the street; it extends a sheltering retreat from the shock and dissonance of urban life. Benjamin notes that "The de-realized individual creates a place for himself in the private home"; if the street threatens to turn the individual into another anonymous man of the crowd, the home restores individuality: "the traces of the occupant . . . leave their impression on the interior."[36] For Benjamin, the urban subject is a collector who tries through the expression of taste to create a private world that emanates from his own seeming uniqueness. This appeal to singularity is an attempt to counteract the dehumanizing power of the urban environment. Simmel argues that the urban subject "summon[s] the utmost in uniqueness and particularization, in order to preserve his most personal core. He has to exaggerate this personal element in order to remain audible even to himself."[37] It is no coincidence that at the time of his writing the home was becoming a more personalized sphere, expected to reflect the taste of its owner rather than simply conform to social expectations. The home was a place where the individual could shore up his resources before going out to face the beguiling but disorienting world of the street. In James Joyce's *Ulysses*, Leopold Bloom walks the city streets all day and all night, but home is still the place where he returns with the expectation of finding comfort after his dizzying foray into Nighttown.

Women fit uneasily into the role of the flaneur, one molded according to the experiences and habits of male city dwellers who circulate in the public sphere.[38] If the flaneur was very much at home on the city street, for middle-class women the street was often not a zone of comfort but one of potential danger. The relative invisibility of the flaneur, who looks at others but is not himself an object of the gaze, is unavailable to women, who also could not venture into all parts of the city at any hour. The dynamic outlined by Benjamin and Simmel does not square with women's experience of the city, but women did derive tremendous pleasure from the modern city. Specifically, in Woolf's work women seem to find the city street, despite its dangers, not traumatizing but curative, a welcome counterbalance to what for them was often a stale and limiting domestic environment. Helen and Margaret's attempt to open the Howards End drawing room onto the outdoors bespeaks a deeper problem with the insularity of nineteenth-century domestic spaces. The home could seem like a dungeon for middle-class women—dark, encircling, and escapable only under carefully controlled circumstances. For women who lived in the city, the problem was especially acute. Women's egress to the city streets was quite restricted, putatively for reasons of reputation and personal safety but more acutely because of their close identification with home and hearth. As Woolf puts it in *A Room of One's Own*, "women have sat indoors all these millions of years."[39] Her work defines the problem of the claustrophobic home and depicts women as grateful for the release afforded by the city rather than overwhelmed by it. Generally, Woolf offers portraits of domesticity that emphasize its cloistered nature, but her early novel *Night and Day* articulates a design solution to the problem of women's captivity in the home, one that involves opening up the spaces of private life to the stimulating aesthetics of the public city street. This solution, as I will show, is mirrored by a group of murals by the Omega Workshops that upend the tradition of the flaneur by placing women in control of the public sphere.

Woolf's Clarissa Dalloway provides an example of how women used the stimulation of the city to counter the deadening stasis of the home. *Mrs. Dalloway* (1925) famously opens with its heroine venturing forth into the city: "Mrs. Dalloway said she would buy the flowers herself." The task is a pretext: delight in the urban scene is what motivates her journey. Clarissa finds on the city streets a refreshing energy and a wealth of stimuli: "In people's eyes, in the swing, tramp, and trudge; in the bellow and the uproar; the carriages, motor cars, omnibuses, vans, sandwich men shuffling and swinging; brass bands; barrel organs; in the triumph and the jingle and the strange high singing of some aeroplane overhead was what she loved; life; London; this moment of June."[40] Clarissa is drawn to forward motion above all else—the pace of pedestrians, the progress of vehicles on the land and in the air—but is she herself actually making measurable headway? Like all the other female characters in the novel, Clarissa goes out into the city only to shop; having accomplished her errand she returns home immediately, and by the same route as before. Her path through the city is the shortest of any character except the shell-shocked Septimus Smith. By contrast, male characters in the novel (with the exception of Septimus) wander freely all over the city, never taking the same route twice, deciding as they meander which way to turn their steps. Clarissa finds her urban stroll gratifying, but in many ways hers is the pleasure of a dog on a leash. Clarissa's daughter Elizabeth, by contrast, ventures with her governess into parts of the city that no other character in the novel explores. However, she too retraces her path on the return home.[41]

Compared to the excitement of the street, with its attendant pleasures of accomplishment and continuous movement, Clarissa's home is a space of repetition and stillness. Her mood alters completely as she crosses the threshold: "The hall of the house was as cool as a vault. Mrs. Dalloway raised her hand to her eyes, and, as the maid shut the door to, and she heard the swish of Lucy's skirts, she felt like a nun who has left the world and feels fold round her the familiar veils and the response to old devotions" (29). Like a nun, Clarissa has a domestic life built around routines, hierarchy, and silence, and although she enjoys it, there is a gulf between the routinized feminine domestic interior and the masculine realm of the street—which, for all the restrictions she endures, affords her spontaneous experience. Clarissa is a consummate hostess and an accomplished homemaker, and so it may seem specious to claim that her pleasures of the domestic interior mean little when compared to those of the street. Yet at the moment of her greatest social triumph in the novel, as she escorts the prime minister through the throngs at her party, her victory seems empty to her: "though she loved it and felt it tingle and sting, still these semblances, these triumphs (dear old Peter, for example, thinking her so brilliant), had a hollowness; at arm's length they were, not in the heart" (190). Shortly afterward she drifts out of the room and goes to a window to stare at the sky and the houses opposite.[42] Clarissa makes the most of her portion, but she is always happy to set aside domestic duties and go out into the city.

Clarissa frequently associates interior spaces with death, a response that causes her moments of unprovoked panic throughout the day. While talking to Peter at home, "It was all over for her. The sheet was stretched and the bed narrow. She had gone up into the tower alone and left them blackberrying in the sun." Or while laying a brooch on a table, "she had a sudden spasm, as if, while she mused, the icy claws had had the chance to fix in her." At her party, "there was in the depths of her heart an awful fear" (49, 38, 202). For Anthony Vidler, Clarissa exemplifies "phobic modernism." He diagnoses Clarissa with "modernist urban phobia," a condition characterized by "necessary interiority, either mental or physical, or both; hence the ascription agora- or claustrophobia. Its forms are those of stream of consciousness, of entrapment, of intolerable closure, of space without exit, of, finally breakdown and often suicide."[43] Vidler suggests that despite modernism's universalist pretensions, it is in part founded on women's fear.[44] Clarissa's claustrophobia seems to be provoked not by fear of urban space but by the confinements of women's domestic life. "Narrower and narrower would her bed be," she thinks as she takes a medically prescribed rest in her solitary attic room (32). This etiology is confirmed by the manner of suicide selected by her alter ego in the novel, Septimus Smith. Smith hurls himself from the window in order to escape the rest cure about to be imposed by his physician, the aptly named Dr. Holmes. The "cure" that awaits him is only a more extreme form of the enforced rest, silence, and confinement that is Clarissa's lot.

The contrast between the expansive joy of the street and the encircling domestic sphere is similarly on display in Woolf's essay "Street-Haunting: A London Adventure" (1930), frequently cited as a key text of female flânerie.[45] In "Street-Haunting" the anonymous speaker sets out on an errand to purchase a pencil, but as in the case of *Mrs. Dalloway*, female consumerism provides camouflage, "an excuse for walking half across London between tea and dinner," and with it access to an experience that the speaker calls "the greatest pleasure of town life." Drinking in the sights of the city, the speaker becomes an all-seeing eye, absorbing the lives of others in the spirit of the flaneuse. Returning to her flat after the novelty and exhilaration of the street, she describes the home as a place of habit and refuge, where "the old possessions, the old prejudices, fold us round; and the self, which has been blown about at so many street corners . . . sheltered and enclosed."[46] Woolf's description of the domestic interior is tinged with a claustrophobia that is simultaneously comforting and suffocating. Modernist urban phobia is provoked by the disparity between exterior and interior, suggesting that the flaneuse will pay a price for her urban pleasures so long as she is subject to the pain of recontainment in a domesticity that, while cozy, is also confining. But Woolf suggests that if the flaneuse could return home to a space more continuous with the street she might sidestep the spatial pathology so frequently associated with women in the city and discover a roomier interior life.

In Woolf's work we find this combination of circumstances in what might seem an unlikely place, her second novel *Night and Day* (1919). *Mrs. Dalloway* is frequently considered Woolf's most innovative city novel, where she pioneered modernist literary techniques that captured the complex rhythms of city life and the distinctive mentality of modern urbanism. But while *Mrs. Dalloway* is more formally experimental than *Night and Day*, the later novel retreats from *Night and Day*'s optimism about the impact that life in the city can have on women's public and private lives. If the city is a welcome distraction for Clarissa, for the female characters in *Night and Day* it is much more—a sphere of power and pleasure that can either accentuate the constraints of the home or dissolve them. *Night and Day* shares this notion of a female urban modernism with a set of murals painted three years before its publication by members of the Omega Workshops in the Berkeley Street house of the art dealer Arthur Ruck. Woolf does not mention these murals in her letters or diary, but it is hard to imagine that she was unfamiliar with them. In 1916 Ruck's house was a significant commission for the Omega, and the entire project was overseen and in part executed by Fry, one of Woolf's closest friends, who often talked with her about his work. Work began in the spring of 1916, and in June *Colour* magazine devoted an extensive spread to the rooms; these images are the only surviving record of the installation. Looking at the novel in conjunction with these murals provides an illuminating and integrating context for *Night and Day*; it further identifies Woolf's work as taking part in a cross-disciplinary dialogue about women, the city, and aesthetics. Moreover, the murals seem to have provided Woolf with a kind of visual vocabulary for describing the transformative impact of the aesthetics of urban life on the home.

The painters of the Berkeley Street murals and Woolf shared the experience of living and working in London at a strange and anomalous time, in the midst of World War I, when among many other changes the number of men on the city streets was temporarily diminished. Their works cope with the impact of the war by almost entirely effacing it; neither *Night and Day* nor the murals reference the war at all. What makes these works legible as artifacts of the war is their joint representation of a city where women find themselves in the majority on the street. The women depicted in these works take to the street with an authority that would be difficult to sustain under peacetime conditions.

The commission Ruck gave the Omega was for the design of two rooms. Vanessa Bell was originally invited to design a stained-glass window and paint one of the walls, but her absence from London meant that Fry had to enlist the aid of other Omega members; his collaborators were Nina Hamnett, Roald Kristian, and Dolores Courtney. Women artists were more readily available than men, many of whom had either joined the army or, in the case of declared pacifists (and the Omega included several), been assigned to compensatory wartime service. Fry designed a carpet and some inlaid tables for the rooms, but the dominant feature of the design was the murals, collectively titled "Scenes from Contemporary London Life" (fig. 19).[47] Their overall mood was one of color and energy, as Mrs. L. Gordon-Staples wrote for *Colour,* "the first effect upon entering this room is comparable to that produced by the first sea-bath of the season—a sort of spasmodic transition to a fresh artistic temperature accompanied by a violent bracing-up of the artistic perceptions."[48] The murals shocked the observer with their novelty, brightness, and exuberance.

The first panel, by Roger Fry, primarily depicts a well-to-do woman emerging from a tube station. She is carefully and expensively dressed in a flowing purple skirt and a rose-colored jacket trimmed with fur, finished off with a yellow feathered hat. Richard Cork comments: "Fry makes sure that the lady's festive colours enliven her surroundings as well."[49] The woman's clothes flow out and around her, splashing colorful reflections on the whole scene, which is cut with swaths of yellow and pink, picking up the colors of the clothing. By contrast, the male newsstand worker's drab attire is carried over into the dark border that surrounds his stand. The woman dominates the scene: she is the only complete figure since the other pedestrians are fragmented by the mural's borders. Even the lettering of the "Underground" sign is only partially visible, making it more of a formal design element than a text; the bottom of the final and initial letters, for instance, mirror the forms of the balustrade. Finally, the gaze of the dog in the foreground further directs our attention to the woman. But she does not seem aware of herself as an object of attention; she is withdrawn, lost in thought, perhaps a little somber. The street is not a place that requires her attentive vigilance; rather it moves her to introspection and permits her free passage through space. Unlike the confined newspaper man, the woman can travel by train or by foot. Her garb, though fashionable and vivid, does not hamper her movements.

The centrality of women in the city is carried over into the second panel, a set of street scenes by Dolores Courtney. In part by virtue of the fragmenting montage, Courtney's work seems more abstract than Fry's, full of expressive color, strong geometric shapes like the tree in the last image, and conveying the impression that the city itself is an artwork for the women to look upon. In Courtney's work, gaily dressed women and girls stroll, gaze, shop, play, and read, on the street and in the park, in a modified form of flânerie. The women are neither prostitutes nor passive consumers; they are modestly but fashion-

Figure 19. Omega Workshops, "Scenes from Contemporary London Life," Berkeley Street, London, 1916.

ably dressed and interact with each other. They are also positioned as interpreters of their world, studying the posters, shapes, and books that dot the cityscape. By presenting a series of juxtaposed scenes, Courtney creates a montage that seems to transmit a view from everywhere, as though a Post-Impressionist lens hovered over London, capturing random images, all of which happen to contain only women. In both Fry's and Courtney's works, women have managed more than the right to share the streets with men; they have taken over.[50]

The "Scenes from Contemporary London Life" depict a city of women, a city brought into being by the war that has taken away most of the men but left almost all of the women behind. In a survey of European paintings by men of city streets, 1913–15, Janet Wolff found that "the masculine depiction of modernity produced a skewed account, in which the only women visible (apart from at home in the family) were 'marginal' women or women involved in less than respectable occupations."[51] It was the war that transformed the status of women in the city for the Omega muralists in 1916, the war that, as Sandra Gilbert and Susan Gubar have argued, "transform[ed] 'All Man's Land' into Herland."[52] The only man in either mural, the newsstand worker, is noticeably shrunken and emaciated compared to the robust figures of the women; he alone is depicted in a sitting position; he appears cramped and meager, imprisoned in the door frame that Fry incorporated into his design as the outline of the kiosk. The worker's long, bony fingers trail over his wares as he reads a newspaper, and his dark brown jacket and dark blue cap seem to blur into the blackness of the background. It might be said that the woman pedestrian has contributed to his enervation by drawing all the light, color, and space from the scene into her domain. The war functions as a similarly invisible presence in *Night and Day*, which is set just before the war. The text shows how access to the city streets can transform the lives of middle-class women by offering an alternative to the dead end of domestic routine. As in Fry's and Courtney's murals, the women of Woolf's novel come alive on the streets, where their ambitions are stimulated and their senses gratified. Despite claims that prolonged exposure to city streets would lead to nervous overstimulation, these women find on the streets a space of introspection and enrichment.

Night and Day contrasts the lives of two young women, Katharine Hilbery, who lives with her parents and is helping her mother to write a biography of Katharine's famous grandfather, and Mary Datchet, who lives alone and works for a suffrage organization. Although she is the wealthier of the two girls, Katharine has very little freedom compared to Mary. Her parents are friendly, tolerant people, but Katharine finds her home life stultifying; the house itself is dark, heavy, and even foggy. Far more so than in "Street-Haunting" or *Mrs. Dalloway*, Woolf depicts the domestic interior in *Night and Day* as a claustro-phobic, backward-looking environment. Ralph Denham, who enters the Hilberry's drawing room as the novel opens, is struck by the contrast with the street he has left behind:

> A fine mist, the etherealized essence of the fog, hung visibly in the wide and rather empty space of the drawing-room, all silver where the candles were grouped on the tea-table, and ruddy again in the firelight. With the omnibuses and cabs still running in his head, and his body still tingling with his quick walk along the streets and in and out of traffic and foot-passengers, this drawing-room seemed very remote and still; and the faces of the elderly people were mellowed, at some distance from each other, and had a bloom on them owing to the fact that the air in the drawing-room was thickened by blue grains of mist.[53]

Compared to the sharpness of the street, the Hilberry drawing room seems very out of touch; compared to the youth of the city the drawing room strikes a geri-atric note. The indoor weather influences behavior as well: in the dank spaces of her home, Katharine can only repeat old ideas and behavior, speaking "as if she knew what she had to say by heart" (15). Katharine has a secret passion for mathematics that she only dares to pursue early in the morning or late at night in her own room: "Her actions when thus engaged were furtive and secretive, like those of some nocturnal animal. Steps had only to sound on the staircase, and she slipped her paper between the leaves of a great Greek dictionary which she had purloined from her father's room for this purpose" (45). Like Clarissa Dalloway, who goes up to a room at the top of her house to dream of her child-hood love Sally Seton and sleep in a narrow, sexless bed, Katharine's pursuit of mathematics is pushed to the domestic margins. Like Woolf's account of Jane Austen concealing her work-in-progress from public view, Katharine must deny the existence of her vocation.

On the other hand, Katharine's experience of the city is joyous; her flânerie allows her a measure of freedom unavailable at home. She takes long city walks throughout the novel, and though she feels most free when she is on the street the men who sometimes accompany her seem to feel constrained. When Katharine is walking along the embankment at night with her suitor William Rodney, he raises objections: " 'You may laugh, Katharine, but I can tell you that if any of your friends saw us together at this time of night they would talk about it, and I should find that very disagreeable' " (68). Katharine does laugh at his objection and says when they part that she would prefer to walk home alone. Rodney is scandalized that she refuses a cab, and "with a despotic gesture" and a plea " 'Don't let the man [the cab driver] see us struggling, for God's sake!' " (68), he forces her into the waiting taxi. Rodney is far more intimidated by the city than Katharine.

With Ralph, another suitor, Katharine frequently walks in the street, and at the climax of the novel she feels compelled to rush out into the city in search of him. In a strange turn for a novel that generally pursues a marriage plot, once she is in the street she finds that the excitement of the city overcomes even her passion for romance.

> She stood fascinated at the corner. The deep roar filled her ears; the changing tumult had the inexpressible fascination of varied life pouring ceaselessly with a purpose which . . . filled her with at least a temporary exaltation. The blend of daylight and of lamplight made her an invisible spectator, just as it gave the people who passed her a semi-transparent quality, and left the faces pale ivory ovals in which the eyes alone were dark. They tended the enormous rush of the current—the great flow, the deep stream, the unquenchable tide. She stood unobserved and absorbed, glorying openly in the rapture that had run subterraneously all day. Suddenly she was clutched, unwilling, from the outside, by the recollection of her purpose in coming there. She had come to find Ralph Denham.
>
> (439)

The fading light gives Katharine access to the aspect of flânerie most commonly denied to women, the ability to be an "invisible spectator" of life. Katharine sees the city as an abstract painter might, as lines of movement and force dotted with significant forms. For a moment it seems as if she is more in love with the city than she is with Ralph, that her search for him is almost as much a pretext for urban strolling as Clarissa's flowers or the "Street-Haunting" narrator's pencil. What appeals to Katharine in particular about the city scene is its limitlessness; the city is as uncontrollable and uncontainable as the sea and provides an apt antidote for the claustrophobia of home life. She pursues Ralph all over the city and finally finds that he has been waiting for her at her home—the home, not the city, is the physical seat of marriage, after all.

If Katharine, like Clarissa, can catch only moments of urban pleasure, Mary Datchet's way of life provides a more continuous response to the problem of the restrictive drawing room. Mary creates her home in the image of the streets in order to change the drawing room from a foggy tomb to a flexible space for political and cultural activity. As in the Omega designs for Arthur Ruck, Mary has brought the colors, sounds, and stimuli of the street into her flat, and thrives on them. Like the street, Mary's home is full of noise, activity, and random meetings between strangers. She provides accommodation for the "fortnightly meeting of a society for the free discussion of everything" that invariably involves "a great deal of moving, and pulling, and ranging of furniture against the wall, and placing of breakable and precious things in safe places" (47). Katharine's home seems physically calcified by its dedication to ancestor worship, while the exchange of ideas that Mary's flat accommodates finds a parallel in the free disposition of the furniture and household accoutrements. When Mary pulls a mattress onto the floor for additional seating, she treats her possessions in a style that mirrors the casual, variable state of the city and of her life. This spontaneity was characteristic of Bloomsbury interiors and marked a break from the heavy furnishings of the previous generation. On her first visit to the flat, Katharine observes: "The whole aspect of the place . . . struck her as enviably free; in such a room one could work—one could have a life of one's own" (272). Anticipating Woolf's claim in *A Room of One's Own*, Katharine intuits that the ability to control the domestic interior is central to women's creative expression.

Mary's room is also reminiscent of Bloomsbury interior style in its liberal use of light and color, qualities its owner cherishes: "High in the air as her flat was, some beams from the morning sun reached her even in November, striking straight at curtain, chair, and carpet, and painting there three bright, true spaces of green, blue, and purple, upon which the eye rested with a pleasure which gave physical warmth to the body" (77). In comparison with the generally prosaic narrative style of *Night and Day*, this description is lyrical and alliterative ("striking straight," "curtain, chair, and carpet," "there three"), using sound to create a chiasmus that enacts the phrase's emotional content. Mary's enjoyment of the sun in the flat is explicitly compared to the experience of viewing an abstract picture ("painting there three bright true spaces of green, blue, and purple, upon which the eye rested with a pleasure"). The city light turns Mary's flat into an aesthetic object. Visual abstraction seems to serve the same purpose in the Omega murals as it does at Mary's: transmuting the familiar objects and scenes of the everyday into colorful tokens of the possibilities and pleasures of urban life. Abstraction has the effect of purging reminiscence, stripping the home of its memorial qualities and replacing them with spontaneity. In Katharine's home, every object is irreplaceable by dint of its history.

In Mary's, the rooms can be and are turned upside down to suit the occasion. If the traditional home claimed to sustain the occupants with its cozy surrounds, Woolf has substituted the nurturing power of aesthetic experience which can also give "physical warmth to the body." Unlike the urban subject described by Simmel, she does not need to define the space of private life in opposition to those of the city in order to forestall breakdown; rather, the contiguity of the two is what satisfies her most.

Mary is determined to enjoy her freedom to the fullest; she thinks: "What was the good, after all, of being a woman if one didn't keep fresh, and cram one's life with all sorts of views and experiments?" (79). For Mary, the spheres of home and work are symbiotic: "to have sat there [in her room] all day long, in the enjoyment of leisure would have been intolerable" (78). She leaves her flat in the morning, rides the tube, looks in shop windows, and mingles with the army of workers on the streets of London. The office of the suffrage society where she works is in Bloomsbury, "at the top of one of the large Russell Square houses, which had once been lived in by a great city merchant and his family, and was now let out in slices to a number of societies . . . disseminating their views upon the protection of native races, or the value of cereals as foodstuffs" (79–80). In the late nineteenth century, Bloomsbury was a favored location for many organizations dedicated to women's rights, a choice that, as Lynne Walker has argued, had the effect of undermining the traditional role of women in the domestic sphere: "feminists . . . adapted their family homes for meetings and other events associated with women's rights, while the offices of related projects for women's organisations, clubs and restaurants were located within walking distance of their homes in Marylebone and Bloomsbury. . . . This juxtaposition of home and work made the home a political space in which social initiatives germinated and developed."[54]

Woolf's choice of the private home of a wealthy plutocrat, renovated to serve liberal causes, adds to the politics of this address by calling attention to the history of the home as a site of women's work. Mary's home is a place where she works, and her place of work was formerly a home. Katharine is also engaged in work at her home, helping her mother prepare a biography of Katherine's dead grandfather, but this is not paid work. Worse, in the befogged atmosphere of her home, the project has stalled, and Katharine doubts it will ever be finished. Katharine's flânerie grows out of a need to escape her stifling home and find a diversion, but for Mary the city is a part of her home and as a result her interior life is co-extensive from work to the street to her house. As she sits in her flat working, the noises of the city fill her ears: a paperboy shouts his rounds, a bus grinds to a stop and moves on, a fog arises with its own indefinable sound (267). Walking toward the Strand while considering her feelings toward Ralph, Mary finds the city shaping her thoughts: her self-reflections "seemed even to take their color from the street she happened to be in. Thus the vision of humanity appeared to be in some way connected with Bloomsbury, and faded distinctly by the time she crossed the main road; then a belated organ-grinder in Holborn set her thoughts dancing incongruously" (171). Vision and hearing, both invoked in this passage, are the two senses most activated by the city in Woolf's work. Mary's interior life flows into her experience of the city with none of the predicted loss of individuality or trauma. The different locations she visits create the channels in which her thoughts circulate. Unlike Mrs. Dalloway or the narrator in "Street-Haunting," who must devise pretexts for their urban ventures, or Katharine, who needs the city to help her escape the claustrophobia of her life, Mary simply goes in to the city—and at the same time finds that the city comes into her.

At the end of *Night and Day*, Katharine is engaged to be married while Mary's brief romance is over. After recovering from what she calls the "tyranny of love" (449), Mary decides to go home and work on a scheme for social reform. In the last pages of the novel, Katharine and her fiancé stand under Mary's window, late at night, where a light is still burning, and Katharine asks: " 'Is she alone, working at this time of night? What is she working at? . . . Why should we interrupt her?' she asked passionately. 'What have we got to give her? She's happy too,' she added. 'She has her work' " (505). Katharine has wealth and romance, but she envies Mary's independence. Mary's work seems to present an alternative resolution that undercuts Katharine's traditional one. Susan Merrill Squier argues that the "utopian" resolution to Mary's story is made possible only by the novel's London location, that this perfect combination of privacy and meaningful work is an exclusively urban formulation for women.[55] It might be said that the flexibility of Mary's flat gives it a narrative quality that can compete with the inexorable marriage plot.

Mary's home is both private and public, a place of solitary refuge and a meeting ground for urban intellectuals. At the same time, her workplace has many traditional features of a home—she and her coworkers cozily take tea together every day and banish work talk, and friends drop by to pass the time. Unlike most of Woolf's other female characters, her flânerie is not propelled by a modernist urban phobia but by a desire for stimulation and a change of scene. Yet there is a melancholy to the final image of Mary, working alone with the lights burning in her window: she has a room of her own and the right to be left alone there—and she *is* left alone. Her life is filled with people, at work and in her home, but she is still alone. The women in the Berkeley Street murals convey a similar isolation: they are rapt in their own thoughts, or transfixed by the urban landscape, but they do not connect with each other. This aspect of flânerie is bedrock for modernist subjectivity, as if the very complexity of interior life precluded any meaningful meeting of minds, or as if Simmel would have it, as if the overstimulation of the city has nudged its dwellers into mental isolation.

Like the Berkeley Street murals, Mary's flat is resonant as a site of abstraction in two senses. It is both a place that encourages its occupant to abstract, to think and reflect, and one that resembles an abstract artwork. The double meaning of "abstraction" is closely related to the two senses of "interior" that are crosshatched in Bloomsbury modernism. Just as the domestic interior is related to interior life, the painterly process of abstraction is linked to the mental process of abstraction. To take one example, Mary exits the novel walking "slowly and thoughtfully up the street alone," thinking of "a point distant as a low star upon the horizon of the dark" (452–53). The abstract sights of the city give rise to her thoughts. This latter conjunction may seem far less intuitive than the former, yet it is at the center of Woolf's later novel *To the Lighthouse*, in which painter Lily Briscoe draws on the Post-Impressionist language of visual abstraction to craft a new way of thinking about the domestic interior. Woolf associated visual abstraction with great potency, and she tied a revolution in painting to interior life. Perhaps she was drawn to abstraction because of the way it clears the decks. As Forster suggests, it offers a way "to clean Art of reminiscences." By draining its subject of personal history and substituting the artist's formal vision, abstraction converts the ambivalent, overdetermined nature of any social encounter into a set of forms that can be bent to the artist's concept of the subject. In other words, at least in the realm of aesthetics, visual abstraction suggested to Woolf a way she could begin to remake the world according to her own liking.

"She would move the tree to the middle, and need never marry anybody"

Post-Impressionism offered Bloomsbury painters a new means of thinking about representation in painting in which the artist's formal vision outweighed the need for fidelity to the subject. Moral opprobrium was heaped on Post-Impressionism upon its English debut, just as public derision underlay the suspicion and scorn often accorded the products of the Omega Workshops. But

Woolf, whose closest friends were the central English proponents of the new style, recognized a different kind of import in what she saw at the Post-Impressionist exhibitions. No wonder she wrote to her sister that she felt they were living in a "Post-Impressionist age." *To the Lighthouse* draws expressly on the visual language of Post-Impressionist abstraction to resolve the social dilemma around which the novel turns, a dilemma the character Mrs. Ramsay takes as her credo: "people must marry, people must have children."

"Post-Impressionism" was a term first coined by Roger Fry when in 1910, he, Desmond MacCarthy, and Clive Bell mounted the first large-scale exhibition in England of paintings by a number of European artists, featuring most prominently Cézanne, Matisse, Picasso, Gaugin, and Van Gogh. The show was hastily put together, but it contained an astonishing array of pictures, many of which are now considered icons of modern art, including Van Gogh's *Crows in the Wheatfield* and *Dr Gachet.* The exhibition exposed British audiences to a generation of mostly French painters not previously seen in England. From the beginning the show created a sensation and was at the center of a controversy that drew more and more visitors; over the course of its run it was attended by an impressive twenty-five thousand people, each of whom paid a shilling to get in.[56]

Although a critical minority welcomed the innovative new style, many responses to the exhibition were stridently derisive: writing for the *Morning Post*, Robert Ross compared the Post-Impressionist movement to "the rat plague in Suffolk" and hoped it would be exterminated as soon as possible.[57] Wilfred Blunt, a Tory MP, recorded in his diary that he had been "half ashamed to be seen in such a pornographic show."[58] Post-Impressionism was seen by some as a kind of sexual invasion, and possibly a contagious one. The sexuality of the art commingled with its apparently dangerous politics. As Hermione Lee has noted, the rhetoric directed at the Post-Impressionist exhibition was very similar in content and tone to that aimed at the women's suffrage movement.[59] Those who favored both Post-Impressionism and suffragism also saw connections between the movements. Christina Walshe, writing in the *Daily Herald*, proclaimed Post-Impressionists and suffragists "dangerous and determined rebels against the dead, rotten laws of a humanity without art."[60] Post-Impressionism was considered by many a harbinger of social and sexual degeneracy. J. B. Bullen notes that in the public reception of the exhibition, Post-Impressionism was frequently associated with "anarchy, revolution, social and psychological disturbance," in part because of frequent British press reports about anarchist activities in France, the movement's home.[61]

As Ross had feared, British artists, including those of the Bloomsbury Group, proved highly susceptible to Post-Impressionism. The effects of the new art actually did turn out to be contagious: only two years later, when Fry organized a second Post-Impressionist exhibition with the aid of Leonard Woolf, he was able to include the work of a substantial number of British artists, who by then were experimenting with the new style. For the Bloomsbury artists seeing Post-Impressionist paintings substantially displayed for the first time, the effect was electric and inspiring. Duncan Grant remembered: "We were wildly excited about the exhibition."[62] Vanessa Bell wrote of the show:

> It is impossible I think that any other single exhibition can ever have had so much effect as did that on the rising generation . . . here was a sudden pointing to a possible path, a sudden liberation and encouragement to feel for oneself, which were absolutely overwhelming. . . . it was as if at last one might say things one had always felt instead of trying to say things that other people told one to feel. Freedom was given one to be oneself and that to the young is the most exciting thing that can happen.[63]

For Bell, as for Woolf, a large part of what the show represented was freedom to be true to one's own instincts and ideas. Though Bell was far more influenced by the new art, both sisters took up Post-Impressionism as a banner of rebellion—in the winter of 1911, for instance, they appeared with friends at a costume ball dressed as figures from a Gaugin painting.[64] The show seemed to communicate a permission to undo tradition that must have seemed especially meaningful to the sisters who had just left behind the stifling atmosphere of Hyde Park Gate and set out to break with convention in their personal lives. Now a space for the same kind of nonconformity seemed to open in the arena of work. And yet the moment of separation between these spheres was brief. If the Omega had a radical content, it lay in taking the aesthetic innovations of the Post-Impressionist exhibition and bringing them into the home, finding in the French avant-garde a critique of traditional English domesticity.

The first Post-Impressionist exhibition was one of the main events Woolf had in mind when she declared December 1910 the watershed moment for British modernism in "Mr. Bennett and Mrs. Brown."[65] In her biography of Roger Fry, Woolf places great emphasis on the exhibition as a cultural marker that launched new ways of thinking about design, aesthetics, and the function of art across disciplines. The show was significant not only for its introduction of its new concepts and techniques but for its invitation to set tradition aside.[66] Representation itself took on a new meaning in Post-Impressionism: color, form, perspective, line—all were rethought. Abstraction was the purest distillation of artistic expression. Particularly in the early years, the Post-Impressionist painter appeared to be in a position to remake the world. Post-Impressionism, as Simon Watney argues, "became the *dernier cri* of anti-Edwardianism. . . . [It] challenged the totality of cultural ideology in [England] by articulating a sharp denial to the validity of one relatively small part."[67] Watney's analysis is a fair description of the task that Post-Impressionist painter Lily Briscoe assumes in *To the Lighthouse*. The subject of the painting she works on for a good portion of the novel is traditional—a mother and child—but her method is modern. She uses the vocabulary of Post-Impressionism to describe the changes in meaning and conduct of domestic life that she has witnessed as a summer guest of the Ramsay family. Using abstraction to distance herself from convention, Lily ponders the scope of women's interior lives.

To the Lighthouse is set in a house modeled after Talland House, the remote Cornish home where Virginia Woolf spent her childhood summers. Woolf later called these summers "the best beginning to life conceivable,"[68] but the portrait of the Ramsay family that she composes in *To the Lighthouse* is hardly idyllic. The Ramsays' domestic life is depicted by Woolf as dilapidated and pressured by modernity. The three sections of the novel narrate the emergence of a new kind of domestic interior: in the first, the old way of living is anatomized in a day in the life of the Ramsay family; the second section of the novel demolishes this model, and the third formulates a new domestic one. Woolf considered this book an elegy for her parents, on whom the characters of Mr. and Mrs. Ramsay are based, but it is also an elegy for a whole way of life.[69] Like any elegy, *To the Lighthouse* lingers lovingly and reverently on its subjects and then completes the work of mourning by imagining life without them. The social problems of *Howards End* and *Night and Day* are problems of the domestic interior: how to house an unmarried woman and her illegitimate child, how to open up the drawing room to the world around it. *To the Lighthouse* seems to have moved beyond such concerns—the house is symbolically demolished in book 2 of the novel, and the house cannot hold Lily, the protagonist, who is outdoors more than in. But even as she roams about doing her painting, she worries over Mrs. Ramsay's command: "people must marry, people must have children." Is there a way around that "must"? That is the problem Lily sets out to solve with her painting.

The Ramsays' summer home is hardly the scene of the strict decorum and heavy furniture and oils Woolf recalled from her London childhood. Set in a wild and out-of-the-way location, the house is in a state of blowsy decline in spite of the servants employed by the Ramsays to maintain it. Mrs. Ramsay thinks regretfully: "The mat was fading; the wall-paper was flapping. You couldn't tell any more that those were roses on it."[70] The house is full of decrepit relics; more than merely shabby, the summer furnishings are imagined by the house's inhabitants as sick, dying, or dead beings: "[The chairs'] entrails . . . were all over the floor. . . . Mats, camp beds, crazy ghosts of chairs and tables whose London life of service was done—they did well enough here" (43). The house is a hospice for furniture, where old household items go to finish their lives. These comparisons render the house sentient, a theme Woolf expands in the second part of the novel, when the house and its furnishings take over the narrative.

The dying and ghostly furniture suggests that the way of life the house accommodates is also waning. The Ramsays appear to be a large, robust family, but their fragility is suggested by the decrepit surroundings. The cause of the decline, according to Mrs. Ramsay, is that the inhabitants refuse to respect the boundaries of the domestic space. She works to maintain the proper spatial integrity of the house: "That windows should be open, and doors shut—simple as it was, could none of them remember it?" (44) Mrs. Ramsay's dictum is drawn directly from the writings of Florence Nightingale and suggests Victorian principles of hygiene and regimentation.[71] This doctrine articulates Mrs. Ramsay's desire for uniformity and hierarchy not just in domestic objects but also in domestic relations, in the conduct of the inhabitants. Windows open, doors shut: this credo is predicated on two interrelated oppositions, the first of which mandates a distinction between interior and exterior, between the private life of the home and the public life beyond; the second distinction, between open and closed, regulates how the external may be assimilated into the interior. Together, these oppositions are meant to elevate and safeguard the domestic sphere—but none of the family can remember them.

Like Coventry Patmore's Angel in the House, Mrs. Ramsay protects and sanctifies the domestic realm, creating an umbrella of nurture for her guests and family members and most of all for her husband. The angel of the Ramsay family is a beautiful, compelling figure, but she manipulates family members and friends to perpetuate the reproduction of her own domestic style with a second refrain that echoes "windows open, doors shut"—"people must marry, people must have children." On the first day we spend with the family, Mrs. Ramsay is encouraging two unwilling women to marry: Minta, a tomboy, is to marry Paul Rayley and Lily Briscoe, a spinster artist, is to marry the widowed Mr. Bankes. Mrs. Ramsay concedes that her drive to marry people off has complicated motivations:

And here she was, she reflected, making life rather sinister again, making Minta marry Paul Rayley; because . . . she was driven on, too quickly she knew, almost as if it were an escape for her too, to say that people must marry; people must have children.

(92–93)

Does the house support Mrs. Ramsay's drive to reproduce the family, or does Mrs. Ramsay support the house's drive to remain intact and inhabited? Mrs. Ramsay's compulsion to propagate marriage is inseparable from her role as guardian of the domestic interior. The house, despite its shabbiness, has a weight and a presence that is comparable to Mrs. Ramsay's own.

The picture Lily paints in the first section of the novel is an abstract rendering of Mrs. Ramsay and her philosophy. Lily has set the scene to paint Mrs. Ramsay and her young son James sitting in the garden, but as Mr. Bankes observes, no human shape is discernable among the lines and colors on her canvas: "[T]he picture was not of them, she said. Or, not in his sense. . . . It was a question, she remembered, how to connect this mass on the right hand with that on the left. She might do it by bringing the line of the branch across so; or break the vacancy in the foreground by an object (James perhaps) so" (81–83). Critics have speculated widely about the significance of Lily's painting.[72] Some have read it as offering a parallel to Woolf's writing process, while others have seen in it an ironic resolution of the characters of Mr. and Mrs. Ramsay,[73] or a moment of feminist triumph.[74] Richard Shone's comment that "the lighthouse of [Woolf's] novel has been made to stand for almost anything" seems to apply equally well to the variety of interpretations directed at the painting.[75] But if the symbolic content of the painting is undecidable, its method is reasonably clear.

Unlike the picture that hangs in Mr. Bankes's drawing room, which faithfully represents "the cherry trees in blossom on the banks of the Kennet," Lily's picture is not mimetic. Rather, in the words Roger Fry used to describe the Post-Impressionist movement in *Vision and Design*, her work "dispense[s] once and for all with the idea of likeness to Nature, of correctness or incorrectness as a test, and consider[s] only whether the emotional elements inherent in natural form are adequately discovered."[76] Lily's name alludes to the flower that was the central symbol of Aestheticism, and her commitment to the autonomy of the work of art also harks back to this philosophy. Creating its own visual language, the picture privileges its spatial composition over fidelity to her models, which become not "objects of . . . veneration" (as Mr. Bankes calls them) but rather the means by which the painter creates a formal unity.

Fry's position is stated even more simply by Woolf herself, writing in her diary in 1918, after having been to see a work by Cézanne at Gordon Square with Fry and Bell: "There are 6 apples in the Cézanne picture. What can 6 apples *not* be? I began to wonder. There's their relationship to each other, & their colour, & their solidity."[77]

Lily's debt to Fry's Post-Impressionist aesthetics is unmistakable, as is Woolf's; she told Fry that she would have dedicated *To the Lighthouse* to him if she had thought it good enough.[78] Yet the first time Lily tries to paint her picture, she has trouble following her avant-garde aesthetic program. Some sense of responsibility to her subject constrains the range of her expression, and she continues to believe that "a picture must be a tribute" and that a monumental subject such as a mother and child deserves "reverence" (81). She cannot integrate the implications of her assumptions about reverencing her subject with her modernist aesthetics. Reverencing her subject means reverencing a way of life that would rather see her married and mothering than outdoors squinting at an easel. Lily struggles to balance the masses in her painting just as she struggles to balance her attachment to her unconventional way of life with her respect and love for Mrs. Ramsay and her home. The first time she tries to paint the picture, she cannot square these masses, perhaps because abstraction and reverence (mimeticism) are so at odds with each other.

However, as foreshadowed by the anthropomorphic decline of the furnishings, in "Time Passes" Mrs. Ramsay's system collapses in tandem with the deterioration of the house: "Nothing, it seemed, could survive the flood, the profusion of darkness which, creeping in at keyholes and crevices, stole round window blinds, came in bedrooms, swallowed up here a jug and basin, there a bowl of red and yellow dahlias, there the sharp edges and firm bulk of a chest of drawers" (189–90). Night falls, and the gender differences that structure the domestic interior evaporate: "Not only was furniture confounded; there was scarcely anything left of body or mind by which one could say, 'This is he' or 'This is she' " (190). With the confusion of the furniture, the gender differences that organize both the house and its occupants are readily effaced. Moreover, as the night with which "Time Passes" begins extends into many nights and to the death of Mrs. Ramsay (relegated to a parenthetical aside), the disintegration that Mrs. Ramsay had forestalled commences in earnest. It is after her textually inconsequential death that the house begins to deteriorate physically, abandoned by the family for ten years. Moisture from the sea attacks its walls, and plant life works its way in through cracks, blurring the crucial boundary between the protected interior and the outside world: "A thistle thrust itself between the tiles in the larder. The swallows nested in the drawing-room; the floor was strewn with straw; the plaster fell in shovelfuls" (207). The concurrent damage to the house and to Mrs. Ramsay indicates how they share a vulnerability to the passage of time.

The story of "Time Passes"—if such dreamy writing can be said to have a story—is that of the summer house during the years the family is absent. Woolf substitutes the story of the house itself for the story of her characters, emphasizing the close interrelationship between the space and its departed inhabitants. As we learn in brief asides scattered across the narrative of the house's ruin, the seemingly sturdy structure of domestic life is as fragile as the house itself. The marriage between Minta and Paul Rayley that Mrs. Ramsay engineered turns out to be a failure. Andrew Ramsay dies in World War I, and Prue, the most beautiful of the Ramsay children, described by her mother as a "perfect angel" (90) and thus Mrs. Ramsay's natural successor, dies in childbirth. The Rayleys' estrangement and the deaths of Prue and Andrew are offered as a backdrop to the intermingling of inside and outside that transforms the house and as the physical tokens of more subtle atmospheric changes, of a new influence in the air. This is an "extraordinary stimulus to range hither and thither in search of some absolute good, some crystal of intensity, remote from the known pleasures and familiar virtues, something alien to the processes of domestic life, single, hard, bright, like a diamond in the sand" (199). With its hints of exile, spiritual questing, reinvention of tradition, and anti-domesticity, the new stimulus sounds a great deal like modernity knocking at the door. At the end of "Time Passes," when two women, hired by the Ramsays to clean the house, discuss the family's likely reaction to the house's appearance, the cleaners agree that "They'd find it changed" (212). Changed—but not eradicated. The house, for all the damage it has sustained, still stands. And despite Mrs. Ramsay's death and the failure of her plans, Lily is left to grapple with her sturdy legacy.

The first section of the novel opens with the words of Mrs. Ramsay; the third ("The Lighthouse") begins with those of Lily. In spite of the return of Lily, the remaining Ramsays, and their other guests, Mrs. Ramsay's death instills a palpable absence at the house's center. It is a fissure that affects Lily's painting, which she has taken up again. As she works on her painting outside, she becomes vividly aware of how the house is altered by Mrs. Ramsay's death: "Oh! Mrs Ramsay! she called out silently. . . . Suddenly, the empty drawing-room steps, the frill of the chair inside, the puppy tumbling on the terrace, the whole wave and whisper of the garden became like curves and arabesques flourishing round a centre of complete emptiness" (266). With her painterly eye, Lily abstracts the domestic scene into a series of curves and flourishes, but the composition she envisions lacks an essential stabilizing component. Without Mrs. Ramsay, the household has lost its logic, retaining only its forms, which are meaningless in the absence of the domestic program Mrs. Ramsay maintained.

Empty forms, however, are precisely Lily's province; her use of abstraction strips objects of their history and imbues them with formal meaning. With Mrs. Ramsay gone, Lily can more clearly see the flaws in her domestic system. Thinking of the failure of the Rayleys' marriage, Lily fantasizes a conversation she would like to have now with Mrs. Ramsay:

> She would feel a little triumphant, telling Mrs. Ramsay that the marriage had not been a success. . . . Mrs. Ramsay has faded and gone, she thought. We can over-ride her wishes, improve away her limited, old-fashioned ideas. . . . And one would have to say to her, It has all gone against your wishes. They're happy like that; I'm happy like this. Life has changed completely.
>
> (260)

The war and the changing times have weakened Mrs. Ramsay's influence and have also helped to dissipate Lily's "reverence." Remembering Mrs. Ramsay's homogenizing system, Lily thinks about different successful households while she paints. The Rayleys, no longer in love with each other, still share an affectionate and companionate partnership that satisfies them both. Mr. Carmichael (another of the Ramsays' summer visitors) refuses to participate in social relations and is happy to need very little from other people, in spite of Mrs. Ramsay's many attempts to involve him. Lily also thinks of her own friendship with William Bankes, "one of the pleasures of her life" (263), which she reflects would have been ruined by marriage. These diverse domestic arrangements, overshadowed in "The Window" by the dominance of the Ramsay family life, come to the fore in "The Lighthouse" as beacons themselves, contented lives led outside the mainstream. For Lily, painting makes it possible. Focusing on the compositional problems presented by the landscape, she justifies her way of life with her art: "She had been looking at the table-cloth, and it had flashed upon her that she would move the tree to the middle, and need never marry anybody, and she had felt an enormous exultation" (262). Art removes her from the marriage plot; art and life intertwine so that events in Lily's painting have consequences for the structure of her life. In other words, the seeming atemporality of abstract painting takes on a narrative quality because, as Lily shifts the forms on the canvas, she also writes the story of and justification for her way of life.

By finishing the painting she left incomplete in "The Window," Lily resolves the problem she has contended with throughout the novel: how to sidestep Mrs. Ramsay's command. The lives of the people around her have provided her with one answer, but the final resolution of the problem is rendered in a formal vocabulary, not a social one. On her return to the Ramsays' house ten years after the events of "The Window," she restates the dilemma: "There was the wall; the hedge; the tree. The question was of some relation between those masses. She had borne it in her mind all these years. It seemed as if the solution had come to her: she knew now what she wanted to do" (221). On her original attempt, Lily had considered using the figure of James to unify the work. But now the human figures have dropped out of the scene, and the abstract problem of balancing the masses is presented solely in terms of the elements of the landscape. Lily's problem concerns both relations between masses and relations among individuals. Confronting the blank center of the canvas, Lily is grateful to find it empty: "Heaven be praised for it, the problem of space remained, she thought, taking up her brush again. It glared at her. The whole mass of the picture was posed upon that weight" (255). Without pausing to "reverence" her subject, Lily is free to solve "the problem of space" formally instead of figuratively. She is also free because Mr. Ramsay, who sails to the lighthouse while Lily paints, has landed, and the obligation she feels to tend to him in Mrs. Ramsay's absence has vanished. Looking at the steps where Mrs. Ramsay had once posed for her but which now are empty, she sees the way: "With a sudden intensity, as if she saw it clear for a second, she drew a line there, in the centre. It was done; it was finished. Yes, she thought, laying down her brush in extreme fatigue, I have had my vision" (310). Mrs. Ramsay's absence allows Lily to see on two levels, both visualizing her subject and experiencing a "vision," an artistic view of the interior. Lily's gaze transcends the literal plane of the subject and weaves an abstract resolution out of line and color.

The final line restores a sense of balance to the polarized relations that structure the Ramsays' lives. This ability to use the center to find balance is one that may be traced to Fry's aesthetic program: "One chief aspect of order in a work of art is unity . . . this unity is due to a balancing of the attractions of the eye about the central line of the picture."[79] Although Lily's line balances her picture as Fry describes, this line has implications that transcend the formal. The painting turns on finding a new relationship between competing forces, in this case a symbolic set of abstract masses, but the concrete result is that of authorizing the narrative she has chosen for her life: "she would move the tree to the middle, and need never marry anybody."

Even as Lily creates a work of aesthetics, she is sensitive to her painting as an object in the material world. Twice as she works on the painting she contemplates its future: "it would be hung in the attics, she thought; it would be rolled up and flung under a sofa; yet even so, even of a picture like that, it was true" (267). Lily's fear is that her work will be swallowed up by the traditional domestic interior because Mrs. Ramsay and her ilk can decide how and if the painting will be displayed. The house too might be said to exercise some say in the painting's future, potentially subjecting it to mold and decay. Lily fears her work may be vulnerable to the judgment of the very conventions she paints against, and the only mental defense she can marshal is the long view: "One might say, even of this scrawl, not of that actual picture, perhaps, but of what it attempted, that it 'remained for ever,' she was going to say, or, for the words spoken sounded even to herself, too boastful, to hint, wordlessly; when, looking at the picture, she was surprised to find that she could not see it" (267). Lily cannot see her painting because she is crying, mourning Mrs. Ramsay, but few people mourn forever, and Lily's response suggests that the best defense against her adversary is time. The house falls apart; Mrs. Ramsay dies; but Lily's painting—or the idea of Lily's painting—may endure. If one generation stores it under the sofa, the next may hang it in a museum. In a book preoccupied with the transitory nature of life, only one class of objects offers the promise of immortality, and that is art. In the novel's last lines, Lily again returns to the thought of her painting's neglect: "There it was—her picture. Yes, with all its greens and blues, its lines running up and across, its attempt at something. It would be hung in the attics, she thought; it would be destroyed. But what did that matter? she asked herself, taking up her brush again" (309–10). Secure in her belief that the artist's vision is indestructible, Lily completes her work.

For Lily, painterly abstraction goes hand in hand with mental abstraction, and "significant form" is the container that gives shape to the flow of thought. This near-pun on abstraction is one I have imposed on Lily. In a sense, what I have attempted here and throughout this chapter is a deliberate abuse of the elasticity of the words "abstract" and "interior." These words carry ranges of meanings that are unrelated: "abstract" (as a noun) refers to nonrepresentational art; as a verb, it refers to a habit of thought. "Interior" comfortably accommodates both the notion of being inside, within boundaries, as well as that which pertains to mental life. I have relied on these double meanings primarily to make a point about the elasticity of modernist representations of thought and to relate such representations to important changes in the worlds of both the fine and the applied arts. But perhaps Lily is guilty of using formalism to fulfill a role it cannot serve. If she seeks a weapon with which to ward off Mrs. Ramsay, if what she wants is social reform, then why is her implement a paintbrush and not a soapbox? Why, of all things, did Bloomsbury turn to interior design and avant-garde art to craft a new kind of private life? I have already sketched one answer: Post-Impressionism came to Bloomsbury trailing clouds of French radicalism and sexuality that were played up by the British press. Its outré status made it a perfect vehicle of rebellion. But it was Bloomsbury that took Post-Impressionism off the wall and put it into the objects of everyday life. This gesture raises the stakes of the aesthetic encounter by suggesting that the new art will meet you not just in the lofty space of the museum or gallery but also where you live.

Why does Lily think that the right formalist gesture can dislodge social convention? A staunch faith in the power of interior design pervades all the work I have discussed. Margaret Schlegel reaches the heights of idealism as she shifts the furnishings at Howards End in the hopes of creating a domestic setting that will accommodate her scandalously unwed pregnant sister. Mary Datchet's bohemian London flat is presented to the reader as a satisfactory substitute for love. And then there's Lily, who sees moving the tree to the middle as a way to sidestep the fetters of marriage. Critics have argued that Woolf's later work moved away from the formalist resolution offered in *To the Lighthouse* precisely because that resolution precluded art's claim to social relevance.[80] But Lily's picture fuses formalism with social intervention on a number of levels. First, her central line symbolically resolves the difficulties she has faced in finding a proportionate response to Mrs. Ramsay and her dictum: "people must marry, people must have children." Next, her ability to complete the painting affirms Lily's belief in her own artistic ability, an ability that, to her mind at least, justifies her unconventional and resolutely non-marital lifestyle. Finally, Woolf instills Lily's painting with narrative properties, both by telling the story of its production and by imbuing the canvas with its own interior. Lily is "tunnelling her way into her picture, into the past" (258). As she "[dips] into the blue paint, she dipped too into the past there" (256). Lily's painting is replete with interiority in spite of its two dimensionality and reliance on abstract forms.

Formalism was described by critics including Fry as a self-referential doctrine of aesthetic autonomy, but it need not be interpreted that way. Form and social reform are what Forster might call the warp and woof of Bloomsbury literature, art and design.[81] For Bloomsbury, formalism is not a retreat from the social world but an attempt to use the artist's vision to organize and redefine that world. This interpretation—or misuse—of formalist doctrine is certainly flavored with a literary sensibility, since narrative is one of the tools used to knit together the formal and the social. Bringing together interior design and reform was not, however, an act that originated with Bloomsbury. While Gordon Square and its successors broke with family tradition, these spaces kept faith with English design tradition. Bloomsbury interiors partook of the distinctively nineteenth-century idea that the designed objects of everyday life have a social and moral content, that the conditions of their making determine the felicity of their use, and that good design should be available to everyone. These ideas would have been familiar to Ruskin and Morris, and they found a different kind of proponent in the writings of Marx. That the domestic interior molds the individual was already the consensus position; Bloomsbury reshaped the mold—with alacrity and originality.

One week in 2002, the comic strip "Biff," which runs in London's *Guardian*, attempted to capture the spirit of Bloomsbury domesticity (fig. 20). In it, Woolf puffs on a cigarette and waves a paint-covered hand at Roger, complaining, "Bloody 'ell, Roger—this chaise longue's covered in wet bloody *paint*! Why do you have to go round *painting* everything? Fireplaces . . . furniture . . . I couldn't even find the *bathroom door* this morning—covered in bloody naiads and satyrs!!" and Fry answers, "Ah, yes . . . I was moved to create a mural after hearing Duncan playing 'Prelude a l'Apres-Midi d'un Faune' on his mouth organ" (original italics). Spontaneous art, spontaneous life, and a decorative scheme that embodies and enables both—those are the familiar ingredients of the Bloomsbury interior. Moreover, as cartoonists Chris Garratt and Mick Kidd suggest, the bathroom is ever the representative site of Bloomsbury experimentation. As in household memoirs, the bathroom stands for the invasion of improper into the proper, for the unavoidable messiness of daily life, for the simple fact that the home is the place where bodies are tended, disciplined, and pleasured. An art that remakes the bathroom has gone as far as it can go in claiming the spaces of private life as its territory.

Yet if Garratt and Kidd faithfully represent the style and tenor of Bloomsbury interior design, their version of the relationship of Bloomsbury's writers and designers is less accurate. In the strip, far from being an admirer of Fry's handiwork, Woolf is critical of it. It is interesting that both Woolf and Strachey are depicted with hands that are prominent but idle. The panels bristle with the

Figure 20. Chris Garratt and Mick Kidd, "Biff," 2002. © Biff Products.

atmosphere of work being done: Keynes crafting his political critique, Fry painting on the furniture, Quentin Bell reading *Ulysses*. Vanessa Bell, drawn in a Post-Impressionist style, seems to have turned herself into an artwork. But the writers do not labor: though Strachey's hand is clean and unemployed, he refuses to use it to make tea; Woolf's hand also seems useless to her. With wet paint glistening on it, she cannot turn to her own creative endeavors. Even Forster, sketched in the background between Fry and Strachey, evidently has time on his hands. The writers cannot or will not work, but why? Woolf's dilemma can perhaps speak for all: rather than being inspired by her friend's visual creations, she is victimized by them. Fry's work makes hers impossible. But such, I have argued, was far from being the actual state of affairs. Rather, the art, design, and literature of the Bloomsbury Group intermingled, producing an exchange of ideas, vocabularies, and aesthetic forms across different expressive media.

Garratt and Kidd call attention to another important aspect of Bloomsbury design culture: the way it bears the imprint (literally, in the case of Woolf's hand) of everyday life and cannot avoid sharing in whatever fate comes to the spaces it transforms. Although Charleston has now become a museum, Bloomsbury design was in some ways not meant to last. It was supposed to reflect the transitory, to provide a domestic interior geared to the current desires and dispositions of the inhabitants and was designed to change along with those inhabitants. Ironically, then, it is perhaps a fitting testimony to the Omega's philosophy that so few of its decorative interiors have survived intact. Most of the spaces I have described—the "Scenes from Contemporary London Life," the "Post-Impressionist Room," the Omega nursery—no longer exist. The design of these interiors was of a piece with the process of their creation, a collaborative, provisional process that was necessarily ephemeral.

This emphasis on process speaks to the unusually narrative qualities of Bloomsbury interiors. In any number of ways, these works called attention to the process of their own creation and their propensity to change over time. Permanent works in progress, they depicted fanciful or abstract images, but the emphasis on process nodded to a temporal structure of making, unmaking, and remaking. The furniture that filled these interiors was of a light and flexible nature—think of Mary Datchet's flat or the posable animals in the Omega nursery—able to be transformed through use. Thus these interiors unfolded in time as well as space, imparting another kind of chronological structure to the normally repetitive temporality of domestic life. This infusion of what might have been static spaces with a temporal dimension bespoke a commitment to experimentation in both visual and social terms.

Like Wilde before her, Woolf seems to balk at the narrative limitations of art. Wilde overcame these limitations by imagining a painting that physically changed over time and told its story through those changes. Woolf focused on process, making the story of Lily's work on her painting more important than the finished product. When the painting is done, the story is over. *To the Lighthouse* juxtaposes the time experience of reading and writing with that of painting, and it privileges the temporality of the artistic process over the finished work of art. In other words, Lily's experience of creation is as important, perhaps more important than what she creates. Her painting may be stored in the attic, but the story of its making, the narrative of discovery and development, becomes the stuff of literature.

1. Kitchen Table Modernism

1. Judith Kegan Gardiner offers a sensitive, extended reading of this passage in her "Good Morning, Midnight; Good Night, Modernism," *Boundary 2* 11 (1983): 233–51.

2. Jean Rhys, *Good Morning, Midnight* (1939, reprint, London: Penguin, 1969), 33.

3. Virginia Woolf, "Mr. Bennett and Mrs. Brown," *Collected Essays*, vol. 1 (New York: Harcourt, Brace, 1925), 319–37; quotation at 320.

4. For a full account of the year's events in relation to modernism, see Peter Stansky, *On or About December 1910: Early Bloomsbury and Its Intimate World* (Cambridge, MA: Harvard University Press, 1996).

5. Woolf, "Mr. Bennett and Mrs. Brown," 320.

6. Ibid., 320–21.

7. Virginia Woolf, *To the Lighthouse* (1927: reprint, San Diego: Harvest/HBJ, 1955), 38.

8. The import of this philosophy for Lily and for Woolf's work has been explored by Ann Banfield in *The Phantom Table: Woolf, Fry, Russell and the Epistemology of Modernism* (Cambridge: Cambridge University Press, 2000).

9. Woolf, *To the Lighthouse*, 81–82.

10. Reed's sociological approach to Bloomsbury visual culture has been very influential for my own thinking. See Christopher Reed, Introduction to *Not at Home: The Suppression of Domesticity in Modernist Art and Architecture*, ed. Reed, 7–17 (London: Thames and Hudson, 1996), quote on 15. Also see his essay in the same volume, " 'A Room of One's Own': The Bloomsbury Group's Creation of a Modernist Domesticity," 147–60.

11. Antoine Prost, Introduction to *A History of Private Life*, vol. 5, *Riddles of Identity in Modern Times*, ed. Prost and Gérard Vincent, trans. Arthur Goldhammer (Cambridge: Harvard University Press, 1991), 3.

12. Hannah Arendt, "The Public Realm and the Private Realm," in *The Hannah Arendt Reader*, ed. Peter Baehr (New York: Penguin, 2000), 182–231, quote on 212.

13. Virginia Nicholson, *Among the Bohemians: Experiments in Living, 1900–1939* (London: Viking, 2002), xv.

14. There is an extensive critical literature linking the New Woman novel to the critique of the Victorian home. See, for instance, Ann L. Ardis, *New Women, New Novels: Feminism and Early Modernism* (New Brunswick, NJ: Rutgers University Press, 1990); Elizabeth Langland, *Nobody's Angels: Middle-Class Women and Domestic Ideology in Victorian Culture* (Ithaca, NY: Cornell University Press, 1995); Sally Ledger, *The New Woman: Fiction and Feminism at the Fin De Siècle* (Manchester: Manchester University Press, 1997); Jane Eldridge Miller, *Rebel Women* (London: Virago, 1994); and Elaine Showalter, *A Literature of Their Own: British Women Novelists from Brontë to Lessing* (Princeton, NJ: Princeton University Press, 1977).

15. Thomas Hardy, *A Laodicean* (1881; reprint, New York: Oxford, 1981), 41.

16. Paula is a precursor of *Jude the Obscure*'s Sue Bridehead, another woman who cannot easily find a home to accommodate her and her family. As Millgate notes, "Paula in her combination of fastidiousness, Hellenism, and rather aggressive modernism strikingly anticipates [Sue Bridehead]" (*Thomas Hardy: His Career as a Novelist* [New York: Random House, 1971], 173).

17. Hardy, *A Laodicean*, 140–41, 431.

18. George Gissing, *The Odd Women* (1893; New York: Norton, 1977), 248.

19. Talia Schaffer, *The Forgotten Female Aesthetes: Literary Culture in Late-Victorian England* (Charlottesville: University Press of Virginia, 2000), 101. For a broader account of women's roles in design reform, see Isabelle Anscombe, *A Woman's Touch: Women in Design from 1860 to the Present Day* (New York: Elizabeth Sifton Books/Viking, 1984).

20. John Tosh has characterized the period as marked by a "flight from domesticity," a decline in men's preoccupation with traditional views of home and hearth. See *A Man's Place: Masculinity and the Middle-Class Home in Victorian England* (New Haven, CT: Yale University Press, 1999), 171.

21. Leonore Davidoff, "The Family in Britain," in *The Cambridge Social History of Britain 1750–1950*, vol. 2, *People and Their Environment*, ed. F. M. L. Thompson (Cambridge: Cambridge University Press, 1990), 71–130.

22. See Siegfried Giedion, *Mechanization Takes Command: A Contribution to Anonymous History* (New York: Norton, 1969), 512–609.

23. For accounts of the ideological work of domesticity in the Victorian middle-class home, see Nancy Armstrong, *Desire and Domestic Fiction: A Political History of the Novel* (New York: Oxford University Press, 1989); Patricia Branca, *Silent Sisterhood: Middle-Class Women in the Victorian Home* (London: Croom Helm, 1975); Monica Cohen, *Professional Domesticity in the Victorian Novel: Women, Work, and Home* (Cambridge: Cambridge University Press, 1998); Leonore Davidoff and Catherine Hall, *Family Fortunes: Men and Women of the English Middle Class, 1750–1850* (Chicago: University of Chicago Press, 1987); Mary Poovey, *Uneven Developments: The Ideological Work of Gender in Mid-Victorian England* (Chicago: University of Chicago Press, 1988). Also see Mark Girouard, *The Victorian Country House*, rev. ed. (New Haven, CT: Yale University Press, 1979).

24. Richard Weston, *Modernism* (London: Phaidon Press, 1996), 174.

25. Aldous Huxley, *Crome Yellow* (1921; reprint, Chicago: Dalkey Archive Press, 2001), 48.

26. Radclyffe Hall, *The Well of Loneliness* (1928; reprint, New York: Anchor, 1990).

27. Doris Lessing, *The Grass Is Singing* (1950; reprint, New York: Plume, 1978).

28. Critics have discussed the representation of the home in British literature; see Ellen Eve Frank, *Literary Architecture, Essays Toward a Tradition: Walter Pater, Gerard Manley Hopkins, Marcel Proust, Henry James* (Berkeley: University of California Press, 1983); Richard Gill, *Happy Rural Seat: The English Country House and the Literary Imagination* (New Haven, CT: Yale University Press, 1972); Warren Hunting Smith, *Architecture in English Fiction* (New Haven, CT: Yale University Press, 1934); and Philippa Tristram, *Living Space in Fact and Fiction* (London: Routledge, 1989).

29. There is a more substantial critical tradition in the American context, where the utopian architectural theories of writers such as Charlotte Perkins Gilman and Catherine Beecher have long attracted attention. For a history of nineteenth-century American feminist architectural innovations, see Dolores Hayden, *The Grand Domestic Revolution: A History of Feminist Designs for American Homes, Neighborhoods, and Cities* (Cambridge: MIT Press, 1981) and Leslie Kanes Weisman, *Discrimination By Design: A Feminist Critique of the Man-Made Environment* (Urbana: University of Illinois Press, 1992). For interesting critical discussions of nineteenth- and twentieth-century American literature in relation to architecture, see Polly Wynn Allen, *Building Domestic Liberty: Charlotte Perkins Gilman's Architectural Feminism* (Amherst: University of Massachusetts Press, 1988); Marilyn Chandler, *Dwelling in the Text: Houses in American Fiction* (Berkeley: University of California Press, 1991); Judith Fryer, *Felicitous Space: The Imaginative Structures of Edith Wharton and Willa Cather* (Chapel Hill: University of North Carolina Press, 1986); and Diana Fuss, "Interior Chambers: The Emily Dickinson Homestead," *differences* 10, no. 3 (1998): 1–46.

30. Karen Chase and Michael Levenson, *The Spectacle of Intimacy: A Public Life for the Victorian Family* (Princeton, NJ: Princeton University Press, 2000), 143.

31. Sharon Marcus, *Apartment Stories: City and Home in Nineteenth-Century Paris and London* (Berkeley: University of California Press, 1999). Also see Steve Dillon, "Victorian Interior," *MLQ* 62, no. 2 (2001): 83–115.

32. Raymond Williams, *Culture and Society, 1780–1950* (New York: Harper, 1958), 30.

33. Qtd. in Fiona MacCarthy, *British Design since 1880* (London: Lund Humphries, 1982), 43.

34. See Francesco Dal Co, *Figures of Architecture and Thought, 1880–1920* (New York: Rizzoli, 1990) and Frederic J. Schwartz, *The Werkbund: Design Theory and Mass Culture before the First World War* (New Haven, CT: Yale University Press, 1996).

35. Roger Fry, "Preface to the Omega Workshops Catalog," in *The Roger Fry Reader*, ed. Christopher Reed (Chicago: University of Chicago Press, 1996), 201.

36. Another important aspect of design reform emerged in fashion. In England, at the Glasgow School, and elsewhere in Europe, theories of reform or "rational dress," especially for women, were tied to critiques of the domestic interior. See Mary McLeod, "Undressing Architecture: Fashion, Gender, and Modernity," in *Architecture: In Fashion*, ed. Deborah Fausch et al. (New York: Princeton Architectural Press, 1994), 38–123.

37. One of the best documented of these links is the relationship between Woolf and Bell, which has been addressed in two full-length studies: Jane Dunn's *A Very Close Conspiracy: Vanessa Bell and Virginia Woolf* (London: J. Cape, 1990), which is biographical in

nature, and Diane Filby Gillespie's *The Sisters' Arts: The Writing and Painting of Virginia Woolf and Vanessa Bell* (Syracuse, NY: Syracuse University Press, 1988), which discusses more fully with the relationship between the literary and visual arts. Other works that deal in part with connections between modernist design and modernist literature include Mary Ann Caws, *Women of Bloomsbury: Virginia, Vanessa, and Carrington* (New York: Routledge, 1990) and Jane Goldman, *The Feminist Aesthetics of Virginia Woolf: Modernism, Post-Impressionism, and the Politics of the Visual* (Cambridge: Cambridge University Press, 1998). Tyrus Miller's *Late Modernism: Politics, Fiction, and the Arts between the World Wars* (Berkeley: University of California Press, 1999) briefly discusses Mina Loy's literary production in relationship to her work as a lampshade designer.

38. Astradur Eysteinsson, *The Concept of Modernism* (Ithaca, NY: Cornell University Press, 1990), 27.

39. Marcel Proust, *Remembrance of Things Past: The Past Recaptured*, trans. Andreas Mayor (1927; reprint, New York: Random House, 1981), 950.

40. See Bill Brown, "The Secret Life of Things (Virginia Woolf and the Matter of Modernism)," *Modernism/Modernity* 6 (1999): 1–28; Bill Brown, *A Sense of Things: The Object Matter of American Literature* (Chicago: University of Chicago Press, 2003); Jonathan Crary, *Suspensions of Perception: Attention, Spectacle, and Modern Culture* (Cambridge: MIT Press, 2001); Douglas Mao, *Solid Objects: Modernism and the Test of Production* (Princeton, NJ: Princeton University Press, 1998); Jeffrey Schnapp, "Crash (Speed as Engine of Individuation)," *Modernism/Modernity* 6 (1999): 1–49.

41. The role of women and, more broadly, gender issues in modernism has been explored by many critics, but some of the key texts are Shari Benstock, *Women of the Left Bank: Paris 1900–1940* (Austin: University of Texas Press, 1986); Marianne DeKoven, *Rich and Strange: Gender, History, Modernism* (Princeton, NJ: Princeton University Press, 1991); Rita Felski, *The Gender of Modernity* (Cambridge: Harvard University Press, 1995); Sandra M. Gilbert and Susan Gubar, *No Man's Land: The Place of the Woman Writer in the Twentieth Century*, 3 vols. (New Haven, CT: Yale University Press, 1988–89); Jane Marcus, *Virginia Woolf and the Languages of Patriarchy* (Bloomington: Indiana University Press, 1987); Bonnie Kime Scott, ed. *The Gender of Modernism* (Bloomington: Indiana University Press, 1990); and Bonnie Kime Scott, *Refiguring Modernism*, vol. 1: *The Women of 1928* (Bloomington: Indiana University Press, 1995).

42. Reed, Introduction to *Not at Home*, 7.

43. Jessica Feldman, *Victorian Modernism: Pragmatism and the Varieties of Aesthetic Experience* (Cambridge: Cambridge University Press, 2002), 115.

44. Thomas Foster, *Transformations of Domesticity in Modern Women's Writing: Homelessness at Home* (New York: Palgrave Macmillan, 2002), 3.

45. Also see *Unmanning Modernism: Gendered Re-Readings*, ed. Elizabeth Jane Harrison and Shirley Peterson (Knoxville: University of Tennessee Press, 1997).

46. In architecture, this new wave of scholarship was initiated in large part by the 1992 publication of *Sexuality and Space*, a collection of essays edited by Beatriz Colomina (New York: Princeton Architectural Press, 1992). For further references, including an account of the first wave of feminist architectural scholarship, see Joan Rothschild and Victoria Rosner, "Feminism and Design: Review Essay" in *Design and Feminism: Revisioning Spaces, Places, and Everyday Things*, ed. Rothschild et al. (New Brunswick, NJ: Rutgers University Press, 1999), 7–33.

47. Alice T. Friedman, *Woman and the Making of the Modern House: A Social and Architectural History* (New York: Harry N. Abrams, 1998), 16.

48. Anthony Vidler, *Warped Space: Art, Architecture, and Anxiety in Modern Culture* (Cambridge, MA and London: MIT Press, 2000), 12.

49. Virginia Woolf, "A Sketch of the Past," *Moments of Being*, 2nd ed., ed. Jeanne Schulkind (San Diego: Harcourt Brace Jovanovich, 1985), 124.

50. Virginia Woolf, *A Room of One's Own* (1928; reprint, New York: Harcourt Brace and World, 1945), 92.

51. Virginia Woolf, *Three Guineas* (1938; reprint, San Diego; Harvest/HBJ, 1966), 33–34.

52. Richard Cork, *Art Beyond the Gallery in Early Twentieth Century England* (New Haven, CT: Yale University Press, 1985), 154.

53. P. G. Konody, "Post Impressionism in the Home," *Observer*, 14 Dec 1913, 8.

54. "Would You Let a Child Play in This Nursery?" *Daily Sketch*, 20 Dec 1913, 9. See also Reed, "A Room of One's Own," 156.

55. "Nurse Lugton's Curtain," *The Complete Shorter Fiction of Virginia Woolf*, ed. Susan Dick, 2nd ed. (San Diego: Harvest Books, 1989), 160–61. This story cannot be dated with any accuracy, since it was not published and was found among Woolf's papers after her death. The fact that the manuscript was found with papers relating to *Mrs. Dalloway* suggests that the date of composition may be circa 1924.

56. Ibid., 160.

57. Ibid., 161.

58. Although she reaches different conclusions than I do, Jane Goldman has also recently argued for joint interpretations of Bell's and Woolf's work. She writes: "Woolf shares her sister's aesthetic preoccupations: they both try to show non-physical experiences as formal realities, at the same time emphasizing and illuminating feminine experience. Both show communication between people as material events. Both relate this to colour" (*Feminist Aesthetics of Virginia Woolf*, 150).

2. Frames

1. Oscar Wilde, *The Picture of Dorian Gray*, ed. Donard L. Lawler (1891; New York: Norton, 1988), 25, 170. Further references to this work are given in the text.

2. Eva Mendgen, Introduction, in *In Perfect Harmony: Picture and Frame 1850–1920*, ed. Eva Mendgen and trans. Rachel Esner (Amsterdam: Van Gogh Museum, 1995), 9.

3. *The Complete Letters of Oscar Wilde*, ed. Merlin Holland and Rupert Hart-Davies (London: Fourth Estate, 2000), 436.

4. "The Soul of Man Under Socialism," in Robert Ross, ed., *The Collected Works of Oscar Wilde* (London: Routledge/Thoemmes Press, 1993), 8: 321.

5. Charlotte Gere, *The House Beautiful: Oscar Wilde and the Aesthetic Interior* (Hampshire: Lund Humphries in association with the Geffrye Museum, 2000), 11, 12.

6. John Ruskin, "Modern Manufacture and Design," in *The Genius of John Ruskin*, ed. John D. Rosenberg (Boston: Routledge and Kegan Paul, 1979), 226.

7. See Fiona MacCarthy, *British Design since 1880* (London: Lund Humphries, 1982), 7–32.

8. Qtd. in Deanna Marohn Bendix, *Diabolical Designs: Paintings, Interiors, and Exhibitions of James McNeill Whistler* (Washington, DC: Smithsonian Institution Press, 1995), 80.

9. Any citation of Wilde's lectures must acknowledge the instability of the source text. Wilde's lectures changed each time he gave them, and for several of his lectures, including "The House Beautiful," no manuscript survives at all and we must rely on newspaper accounts. In an appendix to his book *Oscar Wilde in Canada: An Apostle for the Arts* (Toronto: Personal Library, 1982), Kevin O'Brien explains the genesis of this lecture (151, 153), which Wilde first presented in 1882 under the title "Interior and Exterior House Decoration," and offers texts of Wilde's lectures based on a greater range of sources than that used by Ross in his *Collected Works of Oscar Wilde*.

10. O'Brien, *Oscar Wilde in Canada*, 177.

11. "L'Envoi" (Introduction to *Rose Leaf and Apple Leaf* by Rennell Rodd), in Ross, *Collected Works of Oscar Wilde*, 14: 32.

12. Oscar Wilde, "The English Renaissance of Art," in Ross, *Collected Works of Oscar Wilde*, 14: 270.

13. Oscar Wilde, *The Importance of Being Earnest*, in Ross, *Collected Works of Oscar Wilde*, 6: 117.

14. Talia Schaffer, *The Forgotten Female Aesthetes: Literary Culture in Late-Victorian England* (Charlottesville: University Press of Virginia, 2000), 73.

15. For a discussion of personal collections in relation to the nineteenth-century domestic interior, see Didier Maleuvre, *Museum Memories: History, Technology, Art* (Stanford: Stanford University Press, 1999), 113–87.

16. E. R. Pennell and J. Pennell, *The Life of James McNeill Whistler* (Philadelphia: J. Lippincott, 1909), 2: 13.

17. For an excellent account of the different artist-designers in late-nineteenth-century London, see Bendix, *Diabolical Designs*, esp. chapter 3.

18. Qtd. in Pennell and Pennell, *The Life of James McNeill Whistler*, 2: 219.

19. Qtd. in Gere, *The House Beautiful*, 72.

20. José Ortega y Gasset, "Meditations on the Frame," trans. Andrea L. Bell. In *The Art of the Edge: European Frames, 1300–1900*, ed. Richard Brettell and Steven Starling (Chicago: Art Institute of Chicago, 1986), 22.

21. Meyer Schapiro, "On Some Problems in the Semiotics of Visual Art: Field and Vehicle in Image-Signs," *Semiotica* 1, no. 3 (1969): 227.

22. Jacques Derrida, *The Truth in Painting*, trans. Geoff Bennington and Ian McLeod (Chicago: University of Chicago Press, 1987), 69.

23. Charles L. Eastlake, *Hints on Household Taste*, 3rd ed. (London: Longmans, Green, 1872), 195.

24. An extensive catalog of Pre-Raphaelite framing techniques can be found in Lynn Roberts, "Nineteenth Century English Picture Frames. I: The Pre-Raphaelites," *International Journal of Museum Management and Curatorship* 4 (1985): 155–72.

25. Ira M. Horowitz, "Whistler's Frames," *Art Journal* 39, no. 2 (1979–80): 124.

26. J. Mathey, "The Letters of James McNeill Whistler to George A. Lucas," *The Art Bulletin* 49 (1967): 253.

27. Dudley Harbron, *The Conscious Stone: The Life of Edward William Godwin* (London: Latimer House, 1949), 114.

28. Bendix, *Diabolical Designs*, 251–52.

29. Pennell and Pennell, *The Life of James McNeill Whistler*, 1: 126.

30. Edgar Munhall, *Whistler and Montesquiou: The Butterfly and the Bat* (New York: Frick Collection; Paris: Flammarion, 1995), 66–67.

31. Bendix, *Diabolical Designs*, 104–6.

32. For a full account of Whistler's exhibition designs, see David Park Curry, "Total Control: Whistler at an Exhibition," in *Studies in the History of Art*, vol. 19, *James McNeill Whistler: A Reexamination*, ed. Ruth E. Fine (Hanover, NH: University Press of New England, 1987), 67–84.

33. James McNeill Whistler, "To Waldo Story, 5 February 1883. 'Arrangement in White and Yellow' at the Fine Art Society," in *Whistler on Art: Selected Letters and Writings of James McNeill Whistler*, ed. Nigel Thorpe (Washington, DC: Smithsonian Institution Press, 1994), 75.

34. Kenneth John Myers, *Mr. Whistler's Gallery: Pictures at an 1884 Exhibition* (London: Freer Gallery of Art and Scala; Washington, DC: Smithsonian Institution, 2003), 11.

35. Oscar Wilde, *The Letters of Oscar Wilde*, ed. Rupert Hart-Davies (New York: Harcourt, Brace and World, 1962), 135.

36. John Forbes-Robertson quoted in Bendix, *Diabolical Designs*, 228.

37. A number of critics have drawn parallels between Whistler's paintings and Wilde's poems. No explicit link is usually claimed for "Symphony in Yellow." Birgit Borelius argues that this is because the poem was written in 1889, after the Whistler/Wilde friendship had collapsed into enmity, accusations, and vitriolic correspondence carried on in the newspapers. Borelius writes: "Reading the first stanza of the poem, could any contemporary who was familiar with Whistler and his signature help associating it with the painter who was generally called The Butterfly?" (*Oscar Wilde, Whistler and Colours* [Lund: Gleerup, 1968], 21).

38. Henry Heydenryk, *The Art and History of Frames* (New York: James H. Heineman, 1963), 91.

39. O'Brien, *Oscar Wilde in Canada*, 176.

40. Susan Weber Soros's recent work has given Godwin by far the most considered and extensive appraisal he has yet received. My understanding of Godwin is largely due to her two volumes: Soros, *The Secular Furniture of E. W. Godwin* (New York: Bard Graduate Center and Yale University Press, 1999) and Soros, ed., *E. W. Godwin, Aesthetic Movement Architect and Designer* (New York: Bard Graduate Center and Yale University Press, 1999).

41. Lionel Lambourne, *The Aesthetic Movement* (London: Phaidon Press, 1996), 154.

42. William Watt, *Art Furniture From Designs by E. W. Godwin, F. S. A., and Others* (London: B. T. Batsford, 1877), iv.

43. MacCarthy, *British Design since 1880*, 53.

44. Richard Ellman, *Oscar Wilde* (New York: Vintage, 1987), 256.

45. Qtd. in Montgomery Hyde, *Cases That Changed the Law* (London: William Heinemann, 1951), 151.

46. Though the Whistler etchings were installed as planned, I have not found later sources that reference the Burne-Jones series. Vyvyan Holland refers to "Etchings, several of them by Whistler, who had given them to my father, [lining] a great part of the walls." The sale catalog for the household contents (a notoriously flawed document) mentions

works by Whistler but not by Burne-Jones. Holland, *Son of Oscar Wilde* (London: Rupert Hart-Davies, 1954), 43.

47. Qtd. in *Reading Wilde*, exhibition catalog, Fales Library, New York University (New York: NYU Press, 1995), 61.

48. H. Montgomery Hyde, "Oscar Wilde and His Architect," *Architectural Review* 109 (March 1951): 176.

49. Walter Benjamin, "Paris, Capital of the Nineteenth Century," in *Reflections: Essays, Aphorisms, Autobiographical Writing*, ed. Peter Demetz and trans. Edmund Jephcott (New York: Schocken, 1986), 155.

50. "Art and the Handicraftsman (Fragments of Lecture Notes c. 1882)," in Ross, *The Collected Works of Oscar Wilde*, 14: 301.

51. Eve Kosofsky Sedgwick, *Epistemology of the Closet* (Berkeley: University of California Press, 1990), 172.

52. Alan Sinfield, *The Wilde Century: Effeminacy, Oscar Wilde and the Queer Moment* (London: Cassell, 1994), 102.

53. Jeff Nunokawa, "The Importance of Being Bored: The Dividends of Ennui in *The Picture of Dorian Gray*," in *Novel-Gazing: Queer Readings in Fiction*, ed. Eve Kosofsky Sedgwick (Durham, NC: Duke University Press, 1997), 151.

54. Elaine Showalter, *Sexual Anarchy: Gender and Culture at the Fin-de-Siècle* (New York: Viking, 1990), 118.

55. Sedgwick also pairs *Dorian Gray* with *Jekyll and Hyde*, in *Epistemology of the Closet*, 172.

56. As Tamar Katz has recently observed, a central ideology of Victorian culture is "an equation between the private sphere and the privatized subject" (*Impressionist Subjects: Gender, Interiority, and Modernist Fiction in England* [Urbana: University of Illinois Press, 2000], 7).

57. In giving the painting the responsibility for keeping his secret, Dorian confers a heightened power upon it that is suggested by his obsessive protection of the room where it is concealed. Julia Prewitt Brown observes: "In *The Picture of Dorian Gray*, the tendency to keep the painting private, to own it, even to hide it, suggests a sacralizing and fetishizing power from which we can never fully protect ourselves, just as Dorian cannot resist returning to the locked room where the painting is hidden" (*Cosmopolitan Criticism: Oscar Wilde's Philosophy of Art* [Charlottesville: University Press of Virginia, 1997], 77–78.

58. Coulson Kernahan, *In Good Company* (1917; reprint, Freeport, NY: Books for Libraries Press, 1968), 212–13.

59. Jacob Simon, *The Art of the Picture Frame: Artists, Patrons and the Framing of Portraits in Britain* (London: National Portrait Gallery, 1996), 134–44.

60. My quotations throughout are taken from the 1891 version of the novel, which incorporates the changes Wilde made when he prepared the manuscript for publication as a book. The sentence that describes the destruction of the portrait is altered: in the 1890 edition, it reads, "He seized it, and stabbed the canvas with it, ripping the thing right up from top to bottom" (280). The 1891 version runs as follows: "He seized the thing, and stabbed the picture with it" (169).

61. Mary Ann Caws, *Reading Frames in Modern Fiction* (Princeton, NJ: Princeton University Press, 1985), 262–63.

3. Thresholds

1. Lytton Strachey, "Lancaster Gate," in *Lytton Strachey by Himself*, ed. Michael Holroyd (New York: Holt, Rinehart and Winston, 1971), quote on 17. Further references to "Lancaster Gate" are given in the text and are drawn from this edition.

2. Strachey and Woolf's memoirs are the only works I will consider in this chapter, although other Bloomsbury figures wrote in a similar vein. E. M. Forster, for instance, composed several memoirs about his childhood home Rooksnest, one a fragment written for the Memoir Club in which he claimed that if his family had not been made to leave Rooksnest, he "should have become a different person, married, and fought in the war" (qtd. in S. P. Rosenbaum, *Victorian Bloomsbury: The Early Literary History of the Bloomsbury Group*, vol. 1 [New York: St. Martin's, 1987], 71.) Another of Forster's Rooksnest memoirs, written in 1894 when he was fifteen, is among his earliest surviving pieces of writing; he returned to continue this memoir in 1901, and again in 1947. Other members of the club also offered recollections of their early home lives, including Vanessa Bell, who supplemented her sister's essays with her own, "Notes on Bloomsbury" and "Notes on Virginia's Childhood." Both essays are collected in *Sketches in Pen and Ink*, ed. Lia Giachero (London: Hogarth, 1997). Woolf's essays "Old Bloomsbury," "A Sketch of the Past," and "22 Hyde Park Gate," can be found in her *Moments of Being*, ed. Jeanne Schulkind, 2nd ed. (San Diego: Harcourt Brace Jovanovich, 1985), 179–201, 61–159, and 164–77, respectively. These will be hereafter cited parenthetically.

3. The genre of the "household memoir," in which an autobiography is organized around and extensively anatomizes the subject's home, is a small but recognizable subset of English autobiography that extends beyond the Bloomsbury Group. A catalog of household memoirs written about or during the late nineteenth and early twentieth centuries in England would include, for instance, Walter Pater's essay "The Child in the House" (first published in *Macmillan's* in 1878 and republished in Pater's 1895 *Miscellaneous Studies*); Ursula Bloom's *Sixty Years of Home* (London: Hurst and Blackett, 1960); Mary Butts's *The Crystal Cabinet: My Childhood at Salterns* (1937; reprint, Boston: Beacon, 1988), Leslie Lewis's *The Private Life of a Country House, 1912–1939* (1980; reprint, Phoenix Hill: Sutton, 1992); Angela Thirkell's *Three Houses* (London: Oxford University Press, 1931); and Kathleen Woodward's *Jipping Street; Childhood in a London Slum* (New York: Harper, 1928). Of a slightly different variety are Vita Sackville-West's *Knole and the Sackvilles* (London: W. Heinemann, 1923) and Elizabeth Bowen's *Bowen's Court* (London: Longmans, Green, 1942), both of which tell the story of their respective family histories in conjunction with the history of the home that was the family seat for many generations.

4. Holroyd, Introduction to *Lytton Strachey by Himself*, 9.

5. Mary Ann Caws, *The Metapoetics of the Passage* (Hanover, NH: University Press of New England, 1981), 14.

6. Although I restrict my discussion to autobiography and biography, C. Ruth Miller has discussed the prevalent motif of the threshold in Woolf's fiction; for instance, she observes that a number of Woolf's novels end with the image of the main character standing at a threshold. See C. Ruth Miller, *Virginia Woolf: The Frames of Art and Life* (Hampshire: Macmillan, 1988), 87–92.

7. Stefan Muthesius, *The English Terraced House* (New Haven, CT: Yale University Press, 1982), 45.

8. Robert Kerr, *The Gentleman's House* (New York: Johnson Reprint, 1972), 67. Facsimile reprint edition of the 1871 revised edition.

9. Mrs. Eustace Miles, *The Ideal Home and Its Problems* (London: Methuen, 1911), 4.

10. Mark Girouard, *The Victorian Country House*, rev. ed. (1971; reprint, New Haven, CT: Yale University Press, 1979), 34.

11. Karen Chase and Michael Levenson observe: "It is a fragile machine, this gentleman's house, which builds walls against the inferior orders and then hires them to cook and clean and nurse; which brings together men and women, children and adults, and then pursues distance at close quarters; which gathers enough people to constitute a small community and then arranges them to further the cause of privacy" (*The Spectacle of Intimacy: A Public Life for the Victorian Family* [Princeton, NJ: Princeton University Press, 2000], 170).

12. Robin Evans, "Figures, Doors, and Passages," *Architectural Design* 48, no. 4 (1978): 274.

13. Kerr, *The Gentleman's House*, 117.

14. "Secret" comes from the Latin *secretus*, which is the past participle of the verb *secernere*, meaning to separate or divide. This etymology, and the role of secrets in modern life, is discussed in Gérard Vincent's "A History of Secrets?" in *A History of Private Life*, vol. 5, *Riddles of Identity in Modern Times*, ed. Antoine Prost and Vincent, trans. Arthur Goldhammer (Cambridge: Harvard University Press, 1991), 145–281.

15. Kerr, *The Gentleman's House*, 115.

16. Mary Douglas, *Purity and Danger: An Analysis of the Concepts of Pollution and Taboo*, 2nd ed. (London: Routledge, 1966), 97.

17. Annmarie Adams, *Architecture in the Family Way: Doctors, Houses, and Women, 1870–1900* (Montreal: McGill-Queen's University Press, 1996), 164.

18. Douglas, *Purity and Danger*, 97.

19. Dominique Laporte, *History of Shit*, trans. Nadia Benhabib and Rodolphe el-Khoury (Cambridge: MIT Press, 2000), 28.

20. Anne McClintock, *Imperial Leather: Race, Gender, and Sexuality in the Colonial Contest* (New York: Routledge, 1995), 154.

21. Woolf's number would bring the total of the house's inhabitants to eighteen. This figure is controverted by the London census records for 1891, in which Leslie Stephen entered the names of only five servants: Sophie Firron, a cook; Suzette Stutz and Josephine Grosvallet, both nurses; Ellen Eldridge, a housemaid; and Elizabeth Searle, a parlor maid. There may, however, have been others who worked in the house, but did not live in. F. H. W. Sheppard, ed., *The Survey of London*, vol. 38, *The Museums Area of South Kensington and Westminster*, City of Westminster (London: Athlone Press and University of London, 1975).

22. Woolf reports that Julia Stephen made the initial design for the renovation in the interests of economy: "My mother, I believe, sketched what she wanted on a sheet of notepaper to save the architect's fees" ("Bloomsbury" 182).

23. Sheppard, *Survey of London*, 38, 22. Hyde Park Gate retains its original facade (along with a Blue Plaque commemorating Leslie Stephen), but the interior has been carved into individual flats.

24. The plans for the addition, together with correspondence related to the acquisition and maintenance of the building, can be found at the Kensington and Chelsea Public

Libraries in London, where they were deposited as a gift from Professor and Mrs. Quentin Bell in 1987. Choosing anachronism over inconsistency, I refer to Virginia Woolf, née Stephen, as "Woolf" throughout this work.

25. Geoffrey Scott, *The Architecture of Humanism: A Study in the History of Taste*, 2nd ed. (1914; reprint, Gloucester: Peter Smith, 1965), 159, 177.

26. The thrust of this comparison accords with Gaston Bachelard's phenomenological treatment of shells in *The Poetics of Space*, where he writes that "wherever life seeks to shelter, protect, cover or hide itself, the imagination sympathizes with the being that inhabits the protected space." But where Bachelard imagines a ready identification between inhabitant and shell, Woolf feels simultaneously overwhelmed and diminished by her relationship to the scale of 22 Hyde Park Gate. See Gaston Bachelard, *The Poetics of Space* (1958; reprint, Boston: Beacon, 1994), 152.

27. Adams, *Architecture in the Family Way*, 102.

28. Ellen Lupton and J. Abbott Miller remark that the design of the bathroom is "crucial to intimate body experience, helping to form an individual's sense of cleanliness and filth, taste and distaste, pleasure and shame, as well as his or her expectations about gender and the conduct of domestic duties" (*The Bathroom, The Kitchen, and The Aesthetics of Waste: A Process of Elimination* [New York: Princeton Architectural Press, 1992], 11).

29. Mike Hepworth, "Privacy, Security and Respectability: The Ideal Victorian Home," in *Ideal Homes? Social Change and Domestic Life*, ed. Tony Chapman and Jenny Hockey (London: Routledge, 1999), 17–29, quote on 23.

30. J. J. Stevenson, *House Architecture*, vol. 2, *House-Planning* (London: Macmillan, 1880), 62.

31. Kerr, *The Gentleman's House*, 115.

32. Bridget Cherry and Nikolaus Pevsner, *The Buildings of England, London 3: North West* (London: Penguin, 1991), 688.

33. Anthony Vidler, *The Architectural Uncanny* (Cambridge: MIT Press, 1992), 8.

34. Leonore Davidoff writes: "Nineteenth-century cleanliness really had more to do with tidying and polishing—sparkling glasses, gleaming silver, brass, copper and polished wood—than our notions of dirt control. Tidiness was seen to be as much a moral as a physical attribute" ("The Rationalisation of Housework," in *Sexual Divisions Revisited*, ed. Diana Leonard and Sheila Allen [New York: St. Martin's Press, 1991], 59–94, quote on 67).

35. James B. Twitchell, *Forbidden Partners: The Incest Taboo in Modern Culture* (New York: Columbia University Press, 1987), 98.

36. A full account of this relationship is given in Louise DeSalvo, *Virginia Woolf: The Impact of Childhood Sexual Abuse on Her Life and Work* (New York: Ballantine, 1989).

37. According to Miles, incest was among the most popular themes of Victorian pornography, and one that contained an element of social critique. See Henry Miles, *Forbidden Fruit: A Study of the Incest Theme in Erotic Literature* (London: Luxor Press, 1973), 9. Qtd. in Twitchell, *Forbidden Partners*, 176.

38. Mary Poovey, *Uneven Developments: The Ideological Work of Gender in Mid-Victorian England* (Chicago: University of Chicago Press, 1988), 10.

39. Trev Lynn Broughton characterizes the relation between separate spheres and Victorian life writing as one of reciprocity: "Certain discursive spaces—the club, the professional father's study and *biography itself*—exist precisely to adjudicate the boundaries of,

and hence themselves help to construct, the so-called separate spheres enjoined by compulsory heterosexuality. In this way Victorian Life-Writing produces, even as it discredits, the privacies it purports to protect" (*Men of Letters, Writing Lives: Masculinity and Literary Auto/Biography in the Late Victorian Period* [London: Routledge, 1999], 20). Italics in original.

40. Regenia Gagnier, *Subjectivities: A History of Self-Representation in Britain, 1832–1920* (New York: Oxford University Press, 1991), 39.

41. Qtd. in Trev Lynn Broughton, *Men of Letters, Writing Lives*, 22.

42. As Martin A. Danahay notes, "Nineteenth-century masculine autobiographers inscribe themselves within their texts as autonomous subjects free from the constraints of any social context" (*A Community of One: Masculine Autobiography and Autonomy in Nineteenth-Century Britain* [Albany: State University of New York Press, 1993], 7). This is, of course, not the only tradition in Victorian life writing.

43. Christopher C. Dahl discusses similarities between Woolf's life writing and her father's in his essay "Virginia Woolf's Moments of Being and the Autobiographical Tradition in the Stephen Family," *Journal of Modern Literature* 10, no. 2 (1983): 175–96.

44. Leslie Stephen, *The Mausoleum Book* (1895 Oxford: Oxford University Press, 1977), 4.

45. Ibid., 22, 44, 88, 96.

46. Virginia Woolf, "The New Biography," in *Granite and Rainbow* (New York: Harcourt Brace, 1958), 150.

47. Virginia Woolf, *Roger Fry* (San Diego: Harvest/HBJ, 1940). Thanks to Deborah Nelson for our conversations about privacy.

48. Lytton Strachey, "Monday June 26th 1916," in *Lytton Strachey by Himself*, 139.

49. Virginia Woolf, "The Art of Biography," in *The Death of the Moth and Other Essays* (San Diego: Harvest/HBJ, 1970), 188.

50. Ibid., 189, 194

51. Lytton Strachey, *Eminent Victorians* (Harmondsworth, UK: Penguin, 1948), ix. As Holroyd notes in *Lytton Strachey by Himself*, many critics assumed this to be a quotation from Voltaire; in fact, Strachey invented the phrase (420).

52. Strachey, *Eminent Victorians*, 135.

4. Studies

1. Colette, *My Mother's House* and *Sido*, trans. Una Vicenzo Troubridge and Enid McLeod (1922, 1929; reprint, New York: Farrar, Straus and Giroux, 1953), 196. The first translator of this volume will be recognized as Radclyffe Hall's longtime partner and biographer.

2. Walter Benjamin, "Paris, Capital of the Nineteenth Century," in *Reflections*, ed. Peter Demetz and trans. Edmund Jephcott (New York: Schocken, 1986) 154.

3. As John Tosh points out, doctors, lawyers, and members of the clergy also sometimes conducted some business from the home. He argues that the study conformed to the separation of spheres by separating itself off from the rest of the household. See his *A Man's Place: Masculinity and the Middle-Class Home in Victorian England* (New Haven, CT: Yale University Press, 1999), 17, 60.

4. Sandra M. Gilbert and Susan Gubar discuss the woman writer's struggle to define and lay claim to female authorship in an argument that centers on the psychological conflicts of the woman writer in her quest to affiliate with a literary tradition. See their "Forward into

the Past: The Female Affiliation Complex," *No Man's Land: The Place of the Woman Writer in the Twentieth Century*, vol. 1, *The War of the Words* (New Haven, CT: Yale University Press, 1988), 165–226. Also see Susan Sniader Lanser, who has explored female authorship through attention to the formation of narrative voice in *Fictions of Authority: Women Writers and Narrative Voice* (Ithaca, NY: Cornell University Press, 1992).

5. "Study," *Oxford English Dictionary*, 2nd ed.

6. Ibid.

7. Trans. John Bourchier and Lord Berners (1533). Quoted in Alan Stewart, *Close Readers: Humanism and Sodomy in Early Modern England* (Princeton, NJ: Princeton University Press, 1997), 165.

8. See Heidi Brayman Hackel, "The 'Great Variety' of Readers and Early Modern Reading Practices," *A Companion to Shakespeare*, ed. David Scott Kastan (Oxford: Blackwell, 1999), 147. Also see Lawrence Stone, *The Family, Sex, and Marriage in England, 1500–1800* (New York: Harper, 1979), 154.

9. Lena Cowen Orlin, *Private Matters and Public Culture in Post-Reformation England* (Ithaca, NY: Cornell University Press, 1994), 186.

10. Jacqueline Pearson, *Women's Reading in Britain, 1750–1835: A Dangerous Recreation* (Cambridge: Cambridge University Press, 1999), 155. See also Patricia Howell Michaelson, *Speaking Volumes: Women, Reading, and Speech in the Age of Austen* (Stanford: Stanford University Press, 2002).

11. It is impossible to make a hard-and-fast distinction between the study and the private library, since these terms are sometimes used interchangeably. Where a distinction is intended, the study is often associated more with writing and the library with reading; the study is more typically a room for one person alone and the library more often open to other household members.

12. See James Raven, "From Promotion to Proscription: Arrangements for Reading in Eighteenth-Century Libraries," in *The Practice and Representation of Reading in England*, ed. James Raven, Helen Small, and Naomi Tadmor (Cambridge: Cambridge University Press, 1996), 175–201.

13. Mark Girouard, *Life in the English Country House* (New Haven, CT: Yale University Press, 1978) 180.

14. The library also accommodated the growing interest in reading aloud in groups, an activity often cast in feminine terms (Roger Chartier, "The Practical Impact of Writing," in *A History of Private Life*, vol. 3, *Passions of the Renaissance*, ed. Roger Chartier and trans. Arthur Goldhammer [Cambridge: Harvard University Press, 1989]), 147.

15. Kate Flint, *The Woman Reader, 1837–1914* (Oxford: Clarendon, 1993), 100. Italics in the original.

16. Peter Thornton, *Authentic Decor: The Domestic Interior, 1620–1920* (London: Weidenfeld and Nicolson, 1984), 150.

17. Jill Franklin, *The Gentleman's Country House and Its Plan, 1835–1914* (London: Routledge and Kegan Paul, 1981), 39.

18. Similarly, John Gloag notes that "in nearly every type of home, furniture was unmistakably masculine or feminine" (*Victorian Comfort* [New York: St. Martin's Press, 1973], 60).

19. Mark Girouard, *The Victorian Country House*, rev. ed. (1971; New Haven, CT: Yale University Press, 1979), 34.

20. Robert Kerr, *The Gentleman's House*, rev. ed. (New York: Johnson Reprint, 1972), 115.

21. George Eliot, *Daniel Deronda* (1876; reprint, Harmondsworth, UK: Penguin, 1967), 505.

22. Sarah Grand, *The Heavenly Twins* (1893; reprint, Ann Arbor: University of Michigan Press, 1992), 475.

23. Kerr, *The Gentleman's House*, 116.

24. Quoted in John Marshall and Ian Willox, *The Victorian House* (London: Sidgwick and Jackson, 1986), 86.

25. Raymond Irwin, *The Heritage of the English Library* (New York: Hafner, 1964), 262.

26. Kerr, *The Gentleman's House*, 123.

27. John Gloag and Leslie Mansfield, *The House We Ought to Live In* (London: Duckworth, 1923). Illustrations by A. B. Read.

28. Robert W. Edis, *Decoration and Furniture of Town Houses* (London: C. Kegan Paul, 1881), 189.

29. R. A. Briggs, *The Essentials of a Country House* (London: B. T. Batsford, 1911), 41.

30. Emily Apter has discussed the related phenomenon of cabinet collections, eroticized spaces that held fetishized objects. For Apter, the lure of the cabinet arose in part from the disjunctive combination of the "bourgeois notion of 'home' " and the "morally tainted connotations of 'closet' sexuality" ("Cabinet Secrets: Fetishism, Prostitution, and the Fin de Siècle Interior," *Assemblage* 9 [1989]: 8).

31. Mary Haweis, *The Art of Housekeeping*, qtd. in John Tosh, *A Man's Place*, 182.

32. Arthur Conan Doyle, "A Scandal in Bohemia," in *The Adventures of Sherlock Holmes*, ed. Richard Lancelyn Green (New York: Oxford University Press, 1993). Further references to this work are given in the text.

33. As Joseph A. Kestner discusses, it is notable that Adler is represented as having a stronger sexual drive than Holmes does, as demonstrated by her affairs with both the King of Bohemia and Godfrey Norton. See his *Sherlock's Men: Masculinity, Conan Doyle, and Cultural History* (Aldershot, UK: Ashgate, 1997), 77.

34. Kerr, *The Gentleman's House*, 121.

35. Ibid., 123.

36. Briggs, *The Essentials of a Country House*, 41.

37. Remembering Freud's Dora, another secretive woman who reached for her jewel box under threat of fire, it seems that Holmes may slyly be indicating that an unmarried woman's most valuable asset is her genitals. William A. Cohen has discussed why the need for this substitution carried such urgency; he states: "Though it hardly seems to warrant the scrupulous attention of detectives as eminent as Holmes and Freud, the symbolic substitution of female genitals with receptacles for valuables nonetheless requires constant proof" ("Trollope's Trollop," *Novel* 28 [spring 1995]: 235).

38. In *Feminine Sentences: Essays on Women and Culture* (Cambridge: Polity Press, 1990), Janet Wolff argues that Adler's behavior is less than radical, because it only reaffirms women's exclusion from the street. But Laurie Langbauer affirms that Adler's performance "not only points up how such identities are performed, it also suggests the different practices that can operate within a space that seems already settled" ("The City, the Everyday, and Boredom: The Case of Sherlock Holmes," *differences* 5, no. 3 [1993]: 98).

39. Doyle may have picked up this technique from reading Poe's "The Purloined Letter" (1844), a story that shares many elements with "Scandal," including a monarch threatened

by sexual scandal, a masterful detective, a diversion created outside a window, and a sham letter substituted for a scandalous one. The study also figures prominently in the story: it opens in the "little back library, or book-closet" of Detective Dupin and this room is also the place he secretes the letter once he has recovered it. In his seminar on "The Purloined Letter," Lacan shows how the main characters of the story exchange roles whenever the letter changes hands: "The minister is in what had been the Queen's position, the police are in that of the King, of this degenerate King who believes only in the real, and who sees nothing. The step-wise displacement of the characters is perfect" ("The Purloined Letter," in *The Seminar of Jacques Lacan. Book 2: The Ego in Freud's Theory and in the Technique of Psychoanalysis, 1954–1955*, trans. Sylvana Tomaselli [New York: Norton, 1988], 203). The characters in "Scandal," including the degenerate king of the realm, perform similar displacements all through the story. See Edgar Allan Poe, "The Purloined Letter," in *The Short Fiction of Edgar Allan Poe*, ed. Stuart Levine and Susan Levine (Urbana: University of Illinois Press, 1976), 225–35.

40. *The Well* has long been read by critics as a lesbian novel—as *the* lesbian novel; indeed, the cover of my edition dubs it "A 1920s Classic of Lesbian Fiction." However, Jay Prosser offers a compelling reading of *The Well* as a transsexual narrative. As Prosser states, "*The Well* comes into focus as not only not a lesbian novel, not only our first and most canonical transsexual novel, but a narrative that itself contributed to the formalization of transsexual subjectivity" (*Second Skins: The Body Narratives of Transsexuality* [New York: Columbia University Press, 1998], 140), For Prosser, Stephen Gordon's persistent male identification, her failed lesbian relations, and her yearning for a man's body all place the narrative squarely in a transsexual context—before that term was invented. (The word "lesbian" is also absent from the text.) For the purposes of my discussion, I will use the terminology the book itself relies on, that of the "invert."

41. Esther Newton, "The Mythic Mannish Lesbian: Radclyffe Hall and the New Woman," *Signs* 9, no. 4 (1984): 568.

42. Although Morton has many conventional aspects, it seems unlikely that Hall referred to an actual house in her depiction of it. While *The Well* is in some ways an autobiographical novel, Stephen's aristocratic childhood was not Radclyffe Hall's. Upton-on-Severn, the town named by Hall, has no major country house, according to Nikolaus Pevsner's definitive catalog, *The Buildings of England: Worcestershire* (London: Penguin, 1968). Pevsner does list a Morton Hall in another part of Worcestershire, and a Great Moreton Hall, even further from the Malvern Hills.

43. According to Jean Radford, Hall's depiction of Morton also conformed to the conventions of romantic fiction in the period. For Radford, the house is part of a classic representation of aristocracy, replete with topical allusions to, for instance, the society portraitist Millais, who paints Stephen and her mother. See "An Inverted Romance: *The Well of Loneliness* and Sexual Ideology," in *The Progress of Romance: The Politics of Popular Fiction*, ed. Jean Radford (London: Routledge and Kegan Paul, 1986), 97–112.

44. Radclyffe Hall, *The Well of Loneliness* (1928; reprint, New York: Anchor, 1990), 11. Further references to this work are given in the text.

45. Kerr, *The Gentleman's House*, 68.

46. See Sonja Ruehl's interesting discussion about the important connections between sexuality and class in *The Well* in "Inverts and Experts: Radclyffe Hall and the Lesbian Identity," in *Feminist Criticism and Social Change: Sex, Class, and Race in Literature and Culture*, ed. Judith Newton and Deborah Rosenfelt (New York: Methuen, 1985), 165–80, esp. 170–74.

47. Newton, "The Mythic Mannish Lesbian," 569.

48. Terry Castle has analyzed this scene for its spectral elements, arguing convincingly that Stephen is haunted by her lesbian self. For Castle, Stephen faces Sir Philip's ghost, and with it, herself. See Castle's *The Apparitional Lesbian: Female Homosexuality and Modern Culture* (New York: Columbia University Press, 1993).

49. As D. A. Miller notes, "the social function of secrecy . . . is not to conceal knowledge, so much as to conceal the knowledge of the knowledge" (*The Novel and the Police* [Berkeley: University of California Press, 1988], 206).

50. Siegfried Giedion, *Mechanization Takes Command: A Contribution to Anonymous History* (New York: Norton, 1969), 329.

51. Gilbert Scott, *Remarks on Secular and Domestic Architecture, Present and Futures* (London: J. Murray, 1857).

52. Judith Halberstam, *Female Masculinity* (Durham: Duke University Press, 1998), 1.

53. See Bonnie Kime Scott, *Refiguring Modernism*, vol. 1, *The Women of 1928* (Bloomington: Indiana University Press, 1995) and Jane Marcus, "Sapphistory: The Woolf and the Well," in *Lesbian Texts and Contexts: Radical Revision*, ed. Karla Jay, Joanne Glasgow, and Catharine R. Stimpson (New York: New York University Press, 1990), 164–79.

54. Virginia Woolf, *A Room of One's Own* (1928; reprint, London: Penguin, 1945), 9. Further references to this work are given in the text.

55. See Peggy Kamuf, "Penelope at Work: Interruptions in *A Room of One's Own*," *Novel: A Forum on Fiction* 16, no. 1 (1982): 3–18.

56. Mary Jacobus writes: "Woolf's satire, in delineating the confines within which women must walk ('This was the turf; there was the path') traverses and exposes them. . . . At once within this culture and outside it, the woman writer experiences not only exclusion, but an internalized split" (*Reading Women: Essays in Feminist Criticism* [New York: Columbia University Press, 1986], 38).

57. Margaret J. M. Ezell, *Writing Women's Literary History* (Baltimore: Johns Hopkins University Press, 1993), 38.

58. "Study," *Oxford English Dictionary*, 2nd ed.

59. Annik Pardailhé-Galabrun sees the growing popularity of the study in the homes of wealthy Parisians in the eighteenth century as the combined product of a trend toward specialization of rooms and a concomitant increase in the number of rooms dedicated to private uses. She quotes the *Dictionnaire de l'Académie Française*, which defines the "cabinet" as "a withdrawn place for working or for conversing privately, or for arranging papers, books or some other thing" (*The Birth of Intimacy*, trans. Jocelyn Phelps [Philadelphia: University of Pennsylvania Press, 1991], 63). See Orest Ranum, "The Refuges of Intimacy," in *A History of Private Life*, 3: 227.

60. Henry Urbach, "Closets, Clothes, disClosure," in *Desiring Practices: Architecture, Gender and the Interdisciplinary*, ed. Katerina Rüedi, Sarah Wigglesworth, and Duncan McCorquodale (London: Black Dog, 1996), 253. Italics in the original.

5. Interiors

1. E. M. Forster, "Three Generations," E.M. Forster Papers, Kings College Archives, Cambridge University. Paper delivered to political discussion group at University College, Nottingham, 28 January 1939.

2. Bill Brown, "The Secret Life of Things (Virginia Woolf and the Matter of Modernism)," *Modernism/Modernity* 6 (1999): 5.

3. Walter Benjamin, "Paris, Capital of the Nineteenth Century," in *Reflections*, ed. Peter Demetz and trans. Edmund Jephcott (New York: Schocken, 1986), 154.

4. Siegfried Giedion, *Space, Time and Architecture: The Growth of a New Tradition*, 5th rev. ed. (Cambridge: Harvard University Press, 1982), 764.

5. Vanessa Bell, "Notes on Bloomsbury," in *Sketches in Pen and Ink*, ed. Lia Giachero (London: Hogarth, 1997), 99. In the interest of consistency, I refer to Vanessa and Virginia with their married names throughout.

6. Virginia Woolf, "Bloomsbury," in *Moments of Being*, ed. Jeanne Schulkind, 2nd ed. (San Diego: Harcourt Brace Jovanovich, 1985), 185.

7. Frances Spalding, *Vanessa Bell* (New Haven, CT: Ticknor and Fields, 1983), 63.

8. Lytton Strachey, letter to Duncan Grant, 2 June 1907, British Library Archives.

9. Qtd. in Quentin Bell, *Virginia Woolf* (San Diego: Harcourt Brace, 1972), 124n.

10. Woolf, "Bloomsbury," 196.

11. Bell, "Notes on Bloomsbury," 105.

12. Christopher Reed, " 'A Room of One's Own': The Bloomsbury Group's Creation of a Modernist Domesticity," in *Not at Home: The Suppression of Domesticity in Modern Art and Architecture*, ed. Christopher Reed (London: Thames and Hudson, 1996), 149.

13. Ibid.

14. Woolf, "Bloomsbury," 198.

15. Ibid.

16. E. M. Forster, Confidential Journal 1909–67, vol. 4/4, 24 November 1911, King's College Archives, Cambridge University.

17. Woolf, "Bloomsbury,"184.

18. Ibid., 182.

19. Bell, *Virginia Woolf*, 95.

20. In some of the work he was assisted by Vera Waddington (Frances Spalding, *Duncan Grant* [London: Pimlico, 1998], 114).

21. Christopher Reed, "Architecture and the Decorative Arts," in *A Roger Fry Reader*, ed. Reed (Chicago: University of Chicago Press, 1996), 169.

22. Winifred Gill, "Memoir of the Omega," June 1966, Tate Gallery Archives, London.

23. Arnold Bennett, *The Pretty Lady* (London: Cassell, 1918), 169–70.

24. Richard Cork, *Art Beyond the Gallery in Early-Twentieth Century England* (New Haven: Yale University Press, 1985), 143.

25. Ibid., 144.

26. Fry, "The Artist as Decorator," in *A Roger Fry Reader*, ed. Christopher Reed (Chicago: University of Chicago Press, 1996), 207.

27. Judith Collins, *The Omega Workshops* (Chicago: University of Chicago Press, 1984), 60.

28. Richard Shone, *Bloomsbury Portraits: Vanessa Bell, Duncan Grant and Their Circle*, rev. ed. (London: Phaidon, 1993), 111.

29. *Journal of the Royal Society of Arts*, 17 October 1913, 1042.

30. E. M. Forster, *Howards End* (New York: Norton, 1998), 5. Further page references given parenthetically.

31. Charu Malik imaginatively suggests that the relationship between Helen's son and

Tom Avery, Miss Avery's grand-nephew, who is depicted as an attentive and loving babysitter for Helen's child, suggests a future union of homosexual comradeship across class boundaries. Could Forster have seen this relationship, like that of Maurice and Alec in *Maurice*, as the next step in the evolution of a domesticity based on tolerance and affection? ("To Express the Subject of Friendship: Masculine Desire and Colonialism in *A Passage to India*," in *Queer Forster*, ed. Robert K. Martin and George Piggford [Chicago: University of Chicago Press, 1997], 230).

32. Robert K. Martin, " 'It Must Have Been the Umbrella": Forster's Queer Begetting," in *Queer Forster*, ed. Robert K. Martin and George Piggford, 270.

33. Elizabeth Langland writes: "Through Margaret Schlegel, the traditional terms of masculinity and femininity are scrutinized and subjected to the demands of higher integration" ("Gesturing Toward an Open Space: Gender, Form, and Language in E. M. Forster's *Howards End*," in *Out of Bounds: Male Writers and Gender(ed) Criticism*, ed. Laura Claridge and Elizabeth Langland [Amherst: University of Massachusetts Press, 1990], 252–67.

34. Benjamin, "Paris," 156.

35. Georg Simmel, "The Metropolis and Mental Life," in *The Sociology of Georg Simmel*, ed. Kurt Wolff (New York: Free Press, 1964), 414.

36. Benjamin, "Paris," 155.

37. Simmel, "The Metropolis and Mental Life," 422.

38. No small amount of critical commentary has accreted around the flaneuse, the flaneur's female counterpart who, according to who you ask, may be a prostitute, a shopper, a moviegoer, or who may not exist at all except in the critical imagination. See, in particular, Deborah Epstein Nord, *Walking the Victorian Streets: Women, Representation, and the City* (Ithaca, NY: Cornell University Press, 1995); Griselda Pollock, "Modernity and the Spaces of Femininity," in *Vision and Difference: Femininity, Feminism, and Histories of Art* (London: Routledge, 1988), 50–90; and Judith Walkowitz, *City of Dreadful Delight: Narratives of Sexual Danger in Late-Victorian London* (Chicago: University of Chicago Press, 1992). See also Rachel Bowlby, *Still Crazy After All These Years: Women Writing and Psychoanalysis* (London: Routledge, 1992); Anke Gleber, *The Art of Taking A Walk: Flanerie, Literature, and Film in Weimar Culture* (Princeton, NJ: Princeton University Press, 1999); Sally R. Munt, *Heroic Desire: Lesbian Identity and Cultural Space* (New York: New York University Press, 1998); Mica Nava, "Modernity Disavowed: Women, the City, and the Department Store," in *Modern Times: Reflections on a Century of English Modernity*, ed. Mica Nava and Alan O'Shea (London: Routledge, 1996); Deborah Parsons, *Women and the City: Streetwalking in the Metropolis* (Oxford, UK: Oxford University Press, 2000); Elizabeth Wilson in *The Sphinx in the City: Urban Life, the Control of Disorder, and Women* (Berkeley: University of California Press: 1991); as well as Janet Wolff, "The Invisible Flaneuse: Women and the Literature of Modernity," *Theory, Culture, and Society* 2, no. 3 (1985): 37–46.

39. Virginia Woolf, *A Room of One's Own* (1928; reprint, New York: Harcourt, 1945), 91.

40. Virginia Woolf, *Mrs. Dalloway* (1925; reprint, San Diego: Harvest/HBJ, 1997), 2–3. Further references given parenthetically in the text.

41. See David Dowling's maps of the characters' paths in his *Virginia Woolf: Mapping Streams of Consciousness* (Boston: Twayne, 1991).

42. Clarissa's daughter Elizabeth feels even less ambivalence about her preference for

the street's unenclosed spaces; riding a bus through the middle of the center "she was delighted to be free. The fresh air was so delicious. It had been so stuffy in the Army and Navy Stores" (147).

43. Anthony Vidler, "Bodies in Space/Subjects in the City," *differences* 5, no. 3 (1993): 45.

44. As Esther Da Costa Meyer points out, agoraphobia, typically a condition that afflicts white, middle-class women, comes into being simultaneously with the rise of the metropolis. See Da Costa Meyer, "La Donna è Mobile: Agoraphobia, Women, and Urban Space," in *The Sex of Architecture*, ed. Diana Agrest, Patricia Conway, and Leslie Kanes Weisman (New York: Harry N. Abrams, 1996), 147.

45. Virginia Woolf, "Street Haunting: A London Adventure," in *Collected Essays, Vol. 4* (New York: Harcourt Brace and World, 1967), 155–66.

46. Woolf, "Street Haunting," 155, 166.

47. Mrs. L. Gordon-Staples, "On Painting and Decorative Painting," *Colour Magazine*, June 1916, 187–88.

48. Gordon-Staples, "On Painting," 188. Although I will concentrate on the murals, a complete descriptive account of the other furnishings, the artists involved, and the history of the project can be found in Collins's definitive work, *The Omega Workshops*, 131–36. Of the other two murals, Dolores Courtney recalled in the 1970s that they represented "a part of London's industrial area," with darker color schemes (qtd. in ibid, 133).

49. Cork, *Art Beyond the Gallery*, 164.

50. As Sally Ledger notes: "The New Woman, to put it bluntly, wanted the streets of the metropolis to herself, free of the constraints imposed by the impropriety associated with the appearance of unaccompanied women in the public spaces of the city" (*The New Woman: Fiction and Feminism at the Fin de Siècle* [Manchester: Manchester University Press, 1997], 154).

51. Janet Wolff, *Feminine Sentences: Essays on Women and Culture* (Berkeley: University of California Press, 1990), 59.

52. Sandra M. Gilbert and Susan Gubar, *No Man's Land: The Place of the Woman Writer in the Twentieth Century*, vol. 2, *Sexchanges* (New Haven, CT: Yale University Press, 1989), 272.

53. Virginia Woolf, *Night and Day* (1919; New York: Harvest/HBJ, 1948), 10. Further references to this work given parenthetically in the text.

54. Interestingly, one major activist for women's rights whom Woolf knew well actually lived at the location of Mary Datchet's place of employ, on Russell Square. Mary (Mrs. Humphrey) Ward later became a pronounced enemy of women's suffrage, but she had previously worked extensively for the cause of women's higher education (Lynne Walker, "Home and Away: The Feminist Remapping of Public and Private Space in Victorian London," in *New Frontiers of Space, Bodies, and Gender*, ed. Rosa Ainley [London: Routledge, 1998], 66). Anna Snaith explores the relationship between public and private in Woolf's work in *Virginia Woolf: Public and Private Negotiations* (Hampshire: Palgrave Macmillan, 2000).

55. Susan Merrill Squier, "Tradition and Revision: The Classic City Novel and Virginia Woolf's *Night and Day*," in *Women Writers and the City: Essays in Feminist Literary Criticism*, ed. Susan Merrill Squier (Knoxville: University of Tennessee Press, 1984), 129.

56. Peter Stansky, *On or About December 1910: Early Bloomsbury and Its Intimate World* (Cambridge: Harvard University Press, 1996), 210.

57. Robert Ross, "The Post-Impressionists at the Grafton: the Twilight of the Idols," *Morning Post*, 7 Nov 1910, 3 (reprinted in *Post-Impressionists in England: The Critical Reception*, ed. J. B. Bullen [London: Routledge, 1988], 104).

58. Qtd. in Stansky, *On or About December 1910*, 205.

59. Hermione Lee, *Virginia Woolf* (New York: Knopf, 1997), 287.

60. Christina Walshe, "Post-Impressionism and Suffrage," *Daily Herald*, 25 March 1913.

61. Bullen, *Post Impressionists in England*, 15, 35.

62. Qtd. in Ian Dunlop, *The Shock of the New: Seven Historic Exhibitions of Modern Art* (London: Weidenfeld and Nicolson, 1972), 158. Of course, as Dunlop relates, not every member of Bloomsbury took to the exhibition. Neither E. M. Forster nor Lytton Strachey cared for the new art. Forster called the paintings, "too much for me" (158).

63. Bell, "Memories of Roger Fry," in *Sketches in Pen and Ink*, 129–30.

64. Ibid., 134.

65. See Peter Stansky, *On or About December 1910*, 188–236.

66. As Robins writes, "the exhibition . . . became both a radical cultural arena and a free marketplace—an institutionalized space and time of apparent freedom from the insidious forms of Victorian convention and control where dramatic and compelling artefacts of modernity, perceived by some as indicators of both aesthetic and social change, were exhibited in great numbers and variety before an English audience" (Anna Gruetzner Robins, *Modern Art in Britain 1910–1914* [London: Merrell Holberton in association with the Barbican Art Gallery, 1997], 16.)

67. Simon Watney, *English Post-Impressionism* (London: Studio Vista, 1980), 9.

68. Woolf, "A Sketch of the Past," in *Moments of Being*, 128.

69. Virginia Woolf, *Diary*, vol. 3, ed. Anne Olivier Bell (San Diego: Harcourt, 1980), 208.

70. Virginia Woolf, *To the Lighthouse* (1927; San Diego: Harvest/HBJ, 1955), 44. Further page references given parenthetically.

71. Florence Nightingale, *Notes on Nursing for Labouring Classes* (London: Harrison, 1860), 15, quoted in Karen Chase and Michael Levenson, *The Spectacle of Intimacy: A Public Life for the Victorian Family* (Princeton, NJ: Princeton University Press, 2000), 143.

72. See, for instance, David Dowling, *Bloomsbury Aesthetics and the Novels of Forster and Woolf* (London: Macmillan, 1985); Henry Harrington, "The Central Line down the Middle," *Contemporary Literature* 21 (1980): 363–82; Keith May, "The Symbol of Painting in Virginia Woolf's *To the Lighthouse*," *Review of English Literature* 8, no. 2 (1967): 91–98; Jack Stewart, "A 'Need of Distance and Blue': Space, Color, and Creativity in *To the Lighthouse*," *Twentieth Century Literature* 46, no. 1 (2000): 78–99.

73. Jane Fisher argues that, "Since Lily's 'line there, in the centre,' completes her composition by formally dividing it, her painting only achieves an ironic sort of closure or unity. This closure by division effectively combines Mrs. Ramsay's emphasis on unity with Mr. Ramsay's principles of linearity" (" 'Silent as the Grave': Painting, Narrative, and the Reader in *Night and Day* and *To the Lighthouse*," in *The Multiple Muses of Virginia Woolf*, ed. Diane F. Gillespie [Columbia: University of Missouri Press, 1993], 106). S. P. Rosenbaum also argues that Lily's final triumph is the uniting of Mr. and Mrs. Ramsay's philosophies in his *Aspects of Bloomsbury: Studies in Modern English Literary and Intellectual History* (London: Macmillan, 1998), 27.

74. Nancy Topping Bazin argues, for instance, that "Lily Briscoe creates a symbolic vision of the androgynous work of art" (*Virginia Woolf and the Androgynous Vision* [New Brunswick, NJ: Rutgers University Press, 1973], 46). An alternative feminist reading of the painting is articulated by Jane Goldman, who argues that it "is to be understood as prismatic feminist elegiacs" (*The Feminist Aesthetics of Virginia Woolf: Modernism, Post-Impressionism, and the Politics of the Visual* [Cambridge: Cambridge University Press, 1998], 170).

75. Richard Shone, *The Art of Bloomsbury: Roger Fry, Vanessa Bell and Duncan Grant* (London: Tate Gallery, 1999), 12.

76. Roger Fry, *Vision and Design*, ed. J. B. Bullen (Mineola: Dover, 1998), 27.

77. Virginia Woolf, *Diary*, 1: 140.

78. Virginia Woolf, *Letters*, vol. 3, ed. Nigel Nicolson and Joanne Trautman, 27 May 1927 (New York: Harcourt Brace Jovanovich, 1977), 385.

79. Fry, *Vision and Design*, 22.

80. Christopher Reed, "Through Formalism: Feminism and Virginia Woolf's Relation to Bloomsbury Aesthetics," *Twentieth Century Literature* 38 (1992): 20–43. Reed tracks Woolf's changing views on formalism throughout her career.

81. In her insistence on a symbolic (and thus not purely formal) reading of Vanessa Bell's great 1912 painting *Studland Beach*, Lisa Tickner insists that "It is a defective sensibility that insists on the autonomy of form and on the absolute severing of the emotions of 'life' from those of 'art,' which bears their impress, always." Lisa Tickner, *Modern Life and Modern Subjects: British Art in the Early Twentieth Century* (New Haven, CT: Yale University Press, 2000), 141.

Works Cited

Adams, Annmarie. *Architecture in the Family Way: Doctors, Houses and Women, 1870–1900*. Montreal: McGill-Queen's University Press, 1996.

Allen, Polly Wynn. *Building Domestic Liberty: Charlotte Perkins Gilman's Architectural Feminism*. Amherst: University of Massachusetts Press, 1988.

Anscombe, Isabelle. *A Woman's Touch: Women in Design from 1860 to the Present Day*. New York: Elizabeth Sifton/Viking, 1984.

Apter, Emily. "Cabinet Secrets: Fetishism, Prostitution, and the Fin de Siècle Interior." *Assemblage* 9 (1989): 6–19.

Ardis, Ann L. *New Women, New Novels: Feminism and Early Modernism*. New Brunswick, NJ: Rutgers University Press, 1990.

Arendt, Hannah. *The Hannah Arendt Reader*. Ed. Peter Baehr. New York: Penguin, 2000.

Armstrong, Nancy. *Desire and Domestic Fiction: A Political History of the Novel*. New York: Oxford University Press, 1989.

Bachelard, Gaston. *The Poetics of Space*. 1958. Reprint, Boston: Beacon, 1994.

Banfield, Ann. *The Phantom Table: Woolf, Fry, Russell and the Epistemology of Modernism*. Cambridge: Cambridge University Press, 2000.

Bazin, Nancy Topping. *Virginia Woolf and the Androgynous Vision*. New Brunswick, NJ: Rutgers University Press, 1973.

Bell, Quentin. *Virginia Woolf*. San Diego: Harcourt Brace, 1972.

Bell, Vanessa. *Sketches in Pen and Ink*. Ed. Lia Giachero. London: Hogarth, 1997.

Bendix, Deanna Marohn. *Diabolical Designs: Paintings, Interiors, and Exhibitions of James McNeill Whistler*. Washington, DC: Smithsonian Institution Press, 1995.

Benjamin, Walter. "Paris, Capital of the Nineteenth Century." In *Reflections: Essays, Aphorisms, Autobiographical Writing*, ed. Peter Demetz and trans. Edmund Jephcott, 146–62. New York: Schocken, 1986.

Bennett, Arnold. *The Pretty Lady*. London: Cassell, 1918.

Benstock, Shari. *Women of the Left Bank: Paris, 1900–1940*. Austin: University of Texas Press, 1986.

Bloom, Ursula. *Sixty Years of Home*. London: Hurst and Blackett, 1960.

Borelius, Birgit. *Oscar Wilde, Whistler and Colours*. Lund, Swed.: Gleerup, 1968.

Bowen, Elizabeth. *Bowen's Court*. London: Longmans and Green, 1942.

Bowlby, Rachel. *Still Crazy After All These Years: Women, Writing and Psychoanalysis*. London: Routledge, 1992.

Branca, Patricia. *Silent Sisterhood: Middle-Class Women in the Victorian Home*. London: Croom Helm, 1975.

Briggs, R. A. *The Essentials of a Country House*. London: B. T. Batsford, 1911.

Broughton, Trev Lynn. *Men of Letters, Writing Lives: Masculinity and Literary Auto/Biography in the Late Victorian Period*. London: Routledge, 1999.

Brown, Bill. "The Secret Life of Things (Virginia Woolf and the Matter of Modernism)." *Modernism/Modernity* 6, no. 2 (1999): 1–28.

——. *A Sense of Things: The Object Matter of American Literature*. Chicago: University of Chicago Press, 2003.

Brown, Julia Prewitt. *Cosmopolitan Criticism: Oscar Wilde's Philosophy of Art*. Charlottesville: University Press of Virginia, 1997.

Bullen, J. B., ed. *Post-Impressionists in England: The Critical Reception*. London: Routledge, 1988.

Butts, Mary. *The Crystal Cabinet: My Childhood at Salterns*. 1937. Reprint, Boston: Beacon, 1988.

Castle, Terry. *The Apparitional Lesbian: Female Homosexuality and Modern Culture*. New York: Columbia University Press, 1993.

Caws, Mary Ann. *The Metapoetics of the Passage*. Hanover, NH: University Press of New England, 1981.

——. *Reading Frames in Modern Fiction*. Princeton, NJ: Princeton University Press, 1985.

——. *Women of Bloomsbury: Virginia, Vanessa, and Carrington*. New York: Routledge, 1990.

Chandler, Marilyn. *Dwelling in the Text: Houses in American Fiction*. Berkeley: University of California Press, 1991.

Chartier, Roger. "The Practical Impact of Writing." *A History of Private Life*. Vol. 3, *Passions of the Renaissance*. Trans. Arthur Goldhammer. Cambridge: Harvard University Press, 1989. 111–59.

Chase, Karen, and Michael Levenson. *The Spectacle of Intimacy: A Public Life for the Victorian Family*. Princeton, NJ: Princeton University Press, 2000.

Cherry, Bridget, and Nikolaus Pevsner. *The Buildings of England, London 3: North West*. London: Penguin, 1991.

Cohen, Monica. *Professional Domesticity in the Victorian Novel: Women, Work, and Home*. Cambridge: Cambridge University Press, 1998.

Cohen, William A. "Trollope's Trollop." *Novel* 28 (spring 1995): 235–56.

Colette. *My Mother's House and Sido*. Trans. Una Vicenzo Troubridge and Enid McLeod. New York: Farrar, Straus and Giroux, 1953.

Collins, Judith. *The Omega Workshops*. Chicago: University of Chicago Press, 1984.

Colomina, Beatriz, ed. *Sexuality and Space*. New York: Princeton Architectural Press, 1992.

Cork, Richard. *Art Beyond the Gallery in Early-Twentieth-Century England*. New Haven, CT: Yale University Press, 1985.

Crary, Jonathan. *Suspensions of Perception: Attention, Spectacle, and Modern Culture*. Cambridge: MIT Press, 2001.

Curry, David Park. "Total Control: Whistler at an Exhibition." In *Studies in the History of Art*, vol. 19, *James McNeill Whistler: A Reexamination*, ed. Ruth E. Fine, 67–84. Hanover, NH: University Press of New England, 1987.

Dahl, Christopher C. "Virginia Woolf's Moments of Being and the Autobiographical Tradition in the Stephen Family." *Journal of Modern Literature* 10, no. 2 (1983): 175–96.

Dal Co, Francesco. *Figures of Architecture and Thought: German Architecture and Thought 1880–1920*. New York: Rizzoli, 1990.

Danahay, Martin A. *A Community of One: Masculine Autobiography and Autonomy in Nineteenth-Century Britain*. Albany: State University of New York Press, 1993.

Davidoff, Leonore. "The Rationalisation of Housework." In *Sexual Divisions Revisited*, ed. Diana Leonard and Sheila Allen. 59–94. New York: St. Martin's, 1991.

——. "The Family in Britain." In *The Cambridge Social History of Britain, 1750–1950*. Vol. 2, *People and Their Environment*, ed. F. M. L. Thompson, 71–130. Cambridge: Cambridge University Press, 1990.

Davidoff, Leonore, and Catherine Hall. *Family Fortunes: Men and Women of the English Middle Class, 1750–1850*. Chicago: University of Chicago Press, 1987.

DeKoven, Marianne. *Rich and Strange: Gender, History, Modernism*. Princeton, NJ: Princeton University Press, 1991.

Derrida, Jacques. *The Truth in Painting*. Trans. Geoff Bennington and Ian McLeod. Chicago: University of Chicago Press, 1987.

DeSalvo, Louise. *Virginia Woolf: The Impact of Childhood Sexual Abuse on Her Life and Work*. New York: Ballantine, 1989.

Dick, Susan, ed. *The Complete Shorter Fiction of Virginia Woolf*. 2nd ed. San Diego: Harvest Books, 1989.

Dillon, Steve. "Victorian Interior," *MLQ* 62, no. 2 (2001): 83–115.

Douglas, Mary. *Purity and Danger: An Analysis of the Concepts of Pollution and Taboo*. 2nd ed. London: Routledge, 1966.

Dowling, David. *Virginia Woolf: Mapping Streams of Consciousness*. Boston: Twayne, 1991.

Doyle, Arthur Conan. "A Scandal in Bohemia." In *The Adventures of Sherlock Holmes*, ed. Richard Lancelyn Green. New York: Oxford University Press, 1993.

Dunlop, Ian. *The Shock of the New: Seven Historic Exhibitions of Modern Art*. London: Weidenfeld and Nicolson, 1972.

Dunn, Jane. *A Very Close Conspiracy: Vanessa Bell and Virginia Woolf*. London: J. Cape, 1990.

Eastlake, Charles L. *Hints on Household Taste*. 3rd ed. London: Longmans, Green, 1872.

Edis, Robert W. *Decoration and Furniture of Town Houses*. London: C. Kegan Paul, 1881.

Eliot, George. *Daniel Deronda*. 1876. Reprint, Harmondsworth, UK: Penguin, 1986.

Ellman, Richard. *Oscar Wilde*. New York: Vintage, 1987.

Evans, Robin. "Figures, Doors, and Passages." *Architectural Design* 48, no. 4 (1978): 267–78.

Eysteinsson, Astradur. *The Concept of Modernism*. Ithaca, NY: Cornell University Press, 1990.

Ezell, Margaret J. M. *Writing Women's Literary History*. Baltimore: Johns Hopkins University Press, 1993.

Feldman, Jessica. *Victorian Modernism: Pragmatism and the Varieties of Aesthetic Experience*. Cambridge: Cambridge University Press, 2002.

Felski, Rita. *The Gender of Modernity*. Cambridge: Harvard University Press, 1995.

Fisher, Jane. " 'Silent as the Grave': Painting, Narrative, and the Reader in *Night and Day* and *To the Lighthouse*." In *The Multiple Muses of Virginia Woolf*, ed. Diane F. Gillespie, 90–109. Columbia: University of Missouri Press, 1993.

Flint, Kate. *The Woman Reader, 1837–1914*. Oxford: Clarendon, 1993.

Forster, E. M. "Confidential Journal, 1909–1967." Vol. 4/4 (24 November 1911). King's College Archives, Cambridge University.

——. *Howards End*. 1910. New York: Norton, 1998.

——. "Three Generations." E. M. Forster Papers. King's College Archives, Cambridge University.

Foster, Thomas. *Transformations of Domesticity in Modern Women's Writing: Homelessness at Home*. New York: Palgrave Macmillan, 2002.

Frank, Ellen Eve. *Literary Architecture, Essays Toward a Tradition: Walter Pater, Gerard Manley Hopkins, Marcel Proust, Henry James*. Berkeley: University of California Press, 1983.

Franklin, Jill. *The Gentleman's Country House and Its Plan, 1835–1914*. London: Routledge and Kegan Paul, 1981.

Friedman, Alice T. *Women and the Making of the Modern House: A Social and Architectural History*. New York: Harry N. Abrams, 1998.

Fry, Roger. *Vision and Design*. Ed. J. B. Bullen. Mineola, NY: Dover, 1998.

Fryer, Judith. *Felicitous Space: The Imaginative Structures of Edith Wharton and Willa Cather*. Chapel Hill: University of North Carolina Press, 1986.

Fuss, Diana. "Interior Chambers: The Emily Dickinson Homestead." *differences* 10, no. 3 (1998): 1–46.

Gagnier, Regenia. *Subjectivities: A History of Self-Representation in Britain, 1832–1920*. New York: Oxford University Press, 1991.

Gardiner, Judith Kegan. "Good Morning, Midnight: Good Night, Modernism." *Boundary 2* 11 (1983): 233–51.

Gere, Charlotte. *The House Beautiful: Oscar Wilde and the Aesthetic Interior*. Hampshire: Lund Humphries in association with the Geffrye Museum, 2000.

Giedion, Siegfried. *Mechanization Takes Command: A Contribution to Anonymous History*. New York: Norton, 1969.

——. *Space, Time, and Architecture: The Growth of a New Tradition*. 5th rev. ed. Cambridge: Harvard University Press, 1982.

Gilbert, Sandra M., and Susan Gubar. *No Man's Land: The Place of the Woman Writer in the Twentieth Century*. Vol. 1, *The War of the Words*. New Haven, CT: Yale University Press, 1988.

——. *No Man's Land: The Place of the Woman Writer in the Twentieth Century*. Vol. 2, *Sexchanges*. New Haven, CT: Yale University Press, 1989.

——. *No Man's Land: The Place of the Woman Writer in the Twentieth Century*. Vol. 3, *Letters from the Front*. New Haven, CT: Yale University Press, 1989.

Gill, Richard. *Happy Rural Seat: The English Country House and the Literary Imagination.* New Haven, CT: Yale University Press, 1972.

Gill, Winifred. Letter to Duncan Grant. June 1966. "Memoir of the Omega." Unpublished manuscript. Tate Gallery Archives, London.

Gillespie, Diane Filby. *The Sisters' Arts: The Writing and Painting of Virginia Woolf and Vanessa Bell.* Syracuse, NY: Syracuse University Press, 1988.

Girouard, Mark. *Life in the English Country House.* New Haven, CT: Yale University Press, 1978.

——. *The Victorian Country House.* Rev. ed. New Haven, CT: Yale University Press, 1979.

Gissing, George. *The Odd Women.* 1893. Reprint, New York: Norton, 1977.

Gleber, Anke. *The Art of Taking a Walk: Flanerie, Literature, and Film in Weimar Culture.* Princeton, NJ: Princeton University Press, 1999.

Gloag, John. *Victorian Comfort.* New York: St. Martin's, 1973.

Gloag, John, and Leslie Mansfield. *The House We Ought to Live In.* London: Duckworth, 1923.

Goldman, Jane. *The Feminist Aesthetics of Virginia Woolf: Modernism, Post-Impressionism, and the Politics of the Visual.* Cambridge: Cambridge University Press, 1998.

Gordon-Staples, L. "On Painting and Decorative Painting." *Colour Magazine*, June 1916, 187–88.

Grand, Sarah. *The Heavenly Twins.* 1893. Reprint, Ann Arbor: University of Michigan Press, 1992.

Hackel, Heidi Brayman. "The 'Great Variety' of Readers and Early Modern Reading Practices." In *A Companion to Shakespeare*, ed. David Scott Kastan, 139–57. Oxford: Blackwell, 1999.

Halberstam, Judith. *Female Masculinity.* Durham: Duke University Press, 1998.

Hall, Radclyffe. *The Well of Loneliness.* 1928. Reprint, New York: Anchor, 1990.

Harbron, Dudley. *The Conscious Stone: The Life of Edward William Godwin.* London: Latimer House, 1949.

Hardy, Thomas. *A Laodicean.* 1881. Reprint, New York: Oxford, 1981.

Harrington, Harry. "The Central Line Down the Middle." *Contemporary Literature* 21 (1980): 363–83.

Harrison, Elizabeth Jane, and Shirley Peterson, eds. *Unmanning Modernism: Gendered Re-Readings.* Knoxville: University of Tennessee Press, 1997.

Hayden, Dolores. *The Grand Domestic Revolution: A History of Feminist Designs for American Homes, Neighborhoods, and Cities.* Cambridge: MIT Press, 1981.

Hepworth, Mike. "Privacy, Security and Respectability: The Ideal Victorian Home." In *Ideal Homes? Social Change and Domestic Life*, ed. Tony Chapman and Jenny Hockey, 17–29. London: Routledge, 1999.

Heydenryk, Henry. *The Art and History of Frames.* New York: James H. Heineman, 1963.

Holland, Vyvyan. *Son of Oscar Wilde.* London: Rupert Hart-Davies, 1954.

Horowitz, Ira M. "Whistler's Frames." *Art Journal* 39, no. 2 (1979–80): 124.

Huxley, Aldous. *Crome Yellow.* 1921. Reprint, Chicago: Dalkey Archive Press, 2001.

Hyde, Montgomery. *Cases That Changed the Law.* London: William Heinemann, 1951.

——. "Oscar Wilde and His Architect." *Architectural Review* 109 (March 1951): 175–76.

Irwin, Raymond. *The Heritage of the English Library.* New York: Hafner, 1964.

Jacobus, Mary. *Reading Women: Essays in Feminist Criticism.* New York: Columbia University Press, 1986.

Jameson, Fredric. *Fables of Aggression, Wyndham Lewis, the Modernist as Fascist.* Berkeley: University of California Press, 1979.

Kamuf, Peggy. "Penelope at Work: Interruptions in *A Room of One's Own,*" *Novel: A Forum on Fiction* 16, no. 1 (1982): 3–18.

Katz, Tamar. *Impressionist Subjects: Gender, Interiority, and Modernist Fiction in England.* Urbana: University of Illinois Press, 2000.

Kern, Stephen. *The Culture of Time and Space, 1880–1918.* Cambridge: Harvard University Press, 1983.

Kernahan, Coulson. *In Good Company.* 1917. Reprint, Freeport, NY: Books for Libraries, 1968.

Kerr, Robert. *The Gentleman's House.* 1871. Rev. ed. New York: Johnson Reprint, 1972.

Kestner, Joseph A. *Sherlock's Men: Masculinity, Conan Doyle, and Cultural History.* Aldershot, UK: Ashgate, 1997.

Konody, P. G. "Post Impressionism in the Home." *Observer,* 14 December 1913, 8.

Lacan, Jacques. *The Seminar of Jacques Lacan.* Book 2: *The Ego in Freud's Theory and in the Technique of Psychoanalysis, 1954–1955,* trans. Sylvana Tomaselli. New York: Norton, 1988.

Lambourne, Lionel. *The Aesthetic Movement.* London: Phaidon, 1996.

Langbauer, Laurie. "The City, the Everyday, and Boredom: The Case of Sherlock Holmes." *differences* 5, no. 3 (1993): 80–120.

Langland, Elizabeth. "Gesturing Toward and Open Space: Gender, Form, and Language in E. M. Foster's *Howards End.*" In *Out of Bounds: Male Writers and Gender(ed) Criticism,* ed. Laura Claridge and Elizabeth Langland, 252–67. Amherst: University of Massachusetts Press, 1990.

———. *Nobody's Angels: Middle-Class Women and Domestic Ideology in Victorian Culture.* Ithaca, NY: Cornell University Press, 1995.

Lanser, Susan Sniader. *Fictions of Authority: Women Writers and Narrative Voice.* Ithaca, NY: Cornell University Press, 1992.

Laporte, Dominique. *History of Shit.* Trans. Nadia Benhabib and Rodolphe el-Khoury. Cambridge: MIT Press, 2000.

Ledger, Sally. *The New Woman: Fiction and Feminism at the Fin de Siècle.* Manchester: Manchester University Press, 1997.

Lee, Hermione. *Virginia Woolf.* New York: Knopf, 1997.

Lessing, Doris. *The Grass Is Singing.* 1950. Reprint, New York: Plume, 1978.

Lupton, Ellen, and J. Abbott Miller. *The Bathroom, the Kitchen, and the Aesthetics of Waste: A Process of Elimination.* New York: Princeton Architectural Press, 1992.

MacCarthy, Fiona. *British Design since 1880.* London: Lund Humphries, 1982.

Maleuvre, Didier. *Museum Memories: History, Technology, Art.* Stanford: Stanford University Press, 1999.

Malik, Charu. "To Express the Subject of Friendship: Masculine Desire and Colonialism in *A Passage to India.*" In *Queer Forster,* ed. Robert K. Martin and George Piggford, 221–36. Chicago: University of Chicago Press, 1997.

Mao, Douglas. *Solid Objects: Modernism and the Test of Production.* Princeton, NJ: Princeton University Press, 1998.

Marcus, Jane. "Sapphistory: The Woolf and the Well." In *Lesbian Texts and Contexts:*

Radical Revision, ed. Karla Jay, Joanne Glasgow, and Catharine R. Stimpson, 164–79. New York: New York University Press, 1990.

———. *Virginia Woolf and the Languages of Patriarchy*. Bloomington: Indiana University Press, 1987.

Marcus, Sharon. *Apartment Stories: City and Home in Nineteenth-Century Paris and London*. Berkeley: University of California Press, 1999.

Marshall, John, and Ian Willox. *The Victorian House*. London: Sidgwick and Jackson, 1986.

Martin, Robert K. " 'It Must Have Been the Umbrella': Forster's Queer Begetting." In *Queer Forster*, ed. Robert K. Martin and George Piggford, 255–73. Chicago: University of Chicago Press, 1997.

Mathey, J. "The Letters of James McNeill Whistler to George A. Lucas." *Art Bulletin* 49 (1967): 247–57.

May, Keith. "The Symbol of Painting in Virginia Woolf's *To the Lighthouse*." *Research in English Literature* 8 (1967): 91–98.

McClintock, Anne. *Imperial Leather: Race, Gender, and Sexuality in the Colonial Contest*. New York: Routledge, 1995.

McLeod, Mary. "Undressing Architecture: Fashion, Gender, and Modernity." In *Architecture In Fashion*, ed. Deborah Fausch et al., 38–123. New York: Princeton Architectural Press, 1994.

Mendgen, Eva. Introduction. *In Perfect Harmony: Picture and Frame, 1850–1920*, ed. Eva Mendgen and trans. Rachel Esner. Amsterdam: Van Gogh Museum, 1995.

Meyer, Esther Da Costa. "La Donna è Mobile: Agoraphobia, Women and Urban Space." In *The Sex of Architecture*, ed. Diana Agrest, Patricia Conway, and Leslie Kanes Weisman, 141–56. New York: Harry N. Abrams, 1996.

Michaelson, Patricia Howell. *Speaking Volumes: Women, Reading, and Speech in the Age of Austen*. Stanford: Stanford University Press, 2002.

Miles, Eustace. *The Ideal Home and Its Problems*. London: Methuen, 1911.

Miller, C. Ruth. *Virginia Woolf: The Frames of Art and Life*. Basingstoke, UK: Macmillan, 1988.

Miller, D. A. *The Novel and the Police*. Berkeley: University of California Press, 1988.

Miller, Jane Elridge. *Rebel Women*. London: Virago, 1994.

Miller, Tyrus. *Late Modernism: Politics, Fiction, and the Arts between the World Wars*. Berkeley: University of California Press, 1999.

Millgate, Michael. *Thomas Hardy: His Career as a Novelist*. New York: Random House, 1971.

Munhall, Edgar. *Whistler and Montesquiou: The Butterfly and the Bat*. New York: Frick Collection; Paris, Flammarion, 1995.

Munt, Sally R. *Heroic Desire: Lesbian Identity and Cultural Space*. New York: New York University Press, 1998.

Muthesius, Stefan. *The English Terraced House*. New Haven, CT: Yale University Press, 1982.

Myers, Kenneth John. *Mr. Whistler's Gallery: Pictures at an 1884 Exhibition*. London: Freer Gallery of Art and Scala; Washington, DC: Smithsonian Institution, 2003.

Nava, Mica. "Modernity Disavowed: Women, the City, and the Department Store." In

Modern Times: Reflections on a Century of English Modernity, ed. Mica Nava and Alan O'Shea, 38–76. London: Routledge, 1996.

Newton, Esther. "The Mythic Mannish Lesbian: Radclyffe Hall and the New Woman." *Signs* 9, no. 4 (1984): 557–75.

Nicholson, Virginia. *Among the Bohemians: Experiments in Living, 1900–1939.* London: Viking, 2002.

Nightingale, Florence. *Notes on Nursing for Labouring Classes.* London: Harrison, 1860.

Nord, Deborah Epstein. *Walking the Victorian Streets: Women, Representation, and the City.* Ithaca, NY: Cornell University Press, 1995.

Nunokawa, Jeff. "The Importance of Being Bored: The Dividends of Ennui in *The Picture of Dorian Gray*." In *Novel-Gazing: Queer Readings in Fiction*, ed. Eve Kosofsky Sedgwick, 151–66. Durham: Duke University Press, 1997.

O'Brien, Kevin. *Oscar Wilde in Canada: An Apostle for the Arts.* Toronto: Personal Library, 1982.

Orlin, Lena Cowen. *Private Matters and Public Culture in Post-Reformation England.* Ithaca, NY: Cornell University Press, 1994.

Ortega y Gasset, José. "Meditations on the Frame." Trans. Andrea L. Bell. In *The Art of the Edge: European Frames 1300–1900*, ed. Richard Brettell and Steven Starling, 21–25. Chicago: Art Institute of Chicago, 1986.

Pardailhé-Galabrun, Annik. *The Birth of Intimacy.* Trans. Jocelyn Phelps. Philadelphia: University of Pennsylvania Press, 1991.

Parsons, Deborah. *Women and the City: Streetwalking in the Metropolis.* Oxford: Oxford University Press, 2000.

Pater, Walter. "The Child in the House." *Macmillan's.* London: Macmillan, 1878. Rpt. in *Miscellaneous Studies*, 1895.

Pearson, Jacqueline. *Women's Reading in Britain, 1750–1835: A Dangerous Recreation.* Cambridge: Cambridge University Press, 1999.

Pennell, E. R., and J. Pennell. *The Life of James McNeill Whistler.* 2 vols. Philadelphia: J. Lippincott, 1909.

Pevsner, Nikolaus. *The Building of England: Worcestershire.* London: Penguin, 1968.

Poe, Edgar Allan. "The Purloined Letter." In *The Short Fiction of Edgar Allan Poe*, ed. Stuart Levine and Susan Levine, 225–35. Urbana: University of Illinois Press, 1976.

Pollock, Griselda. "Modernity and the Spaces of Femininity." *Vision and Difference: Femininity, Feminism, and Histories of Art.* London: Routledge, 1988. 50–90.

Poovey, Mary. *Uneven Developments: The Ideological Work of Gender in Mid-Victorian England.* Chicago: University of Chicago Press, 1988.

Prosser, Jay. *Second Skins: The Body Narratives of Transsexuality.* New York: Columbia University Press, 1998.

Prost, Antoine, and Gérard Vincent, eds. *A History of Private Life.* Vol. 5, *Riddles of Identity in Modern Times.* Trans. Arthur Goldhammer. Cambridge: Belknap Press of Harvard University Press, 1991.

Proust, Marcel. *Remembrance of Things Past: The Past Recaptured.* Trans. Andreas Mayor. New York: Random House, 1981.

Radford, Jean. "An Inverted Romance: *The Well of Loneliness* and Sexual Ideology." In *The Progress of Romance: The Politics of Popular Fiction*, ed. Jean Radford, 97–112. London: Routledge and Kegan Paul, 1986.

Ranum, Orest. "The Refuges of Intimacy." In *A History of Private Life*. Vol. 3, *Passions of the Renaissance*, ed. Roger Chartier and trans. Arthur Goldhammer, 111–59. Cambridge: Harvard University Press, 1989.

Raven, James. "From Promotion to Proscription: Arrangements for Reading and Eighteenth-Century Libraries." In *The Practice and Representation of Reading in England*, ed. James Raven, Helen Small, and Naomi Tadmor, 175–201. Cambridge: Cambridge University Press, 1996.

Reading Wilde. Exhibition Catalog. Fales Library, New York University. New York: New York University Press, 1995.

Reed, Christopher, ed. *Not at Home: The Suppression of Domesticity in Modern Art and Architecture*. London: Thames and Hudson, 1996.

——, ed. *A Roger Fry Reader*. Chicago: University of Chicago Press, 1996.

——. "Through Formalism: Feminism and Virginia Woolf's Relation to Bloomsbury Aesthetics." *Twentieth Century Literature* 38 (1992): 20-43.

Rhys, Jean. *Good Morning, Midnight*. 1939. Reprint, London: Penguin, 1969.

Roberts, Lynn. "Nineteenth Century English Picture Frames. I: The Pre-Raphaelites." *International Journal of Museum Management and Curatorship* 4 (1985): 155–72.

Robins, Anna Gruetzner. *Modern Art in Britain, 1910–1914*. London: Merrell Holberton in association with the Barbican Art Gallery, 1997.

Rosenbaum, S. P. *Aspects of Bloomsbury: Studies in Modern English Literary and Intellectual History*. London: Macmillan, 1998.

——. *Victorian Bloomsbury: The Early Literary History of the Bloomsbury Group*, vol. 1. New York: St. Martin's Press, 1987.

Ross, Robert, ed. *Collected Works of Oscar Wilde*. Vols. 6, 8, 14. London: Routledge/Thoemmes Press, 1993.

Rothschild, Joan, and Victoria Rosner. "Feminism and Design: Review Essay." In *Design and Feminism: Revisioning Spaces, Places, and Everyday Things*, ed. Rothschild et al., 7–33. New Brunswick, NJ: Rutgers University Press, 1999.

Ruehl, Sonja. "Inverts and Experts: Radclyffe Hall and the Lesbian Identity." In *Feminist Criticism and Social Change: Sex, Class, and Race in Literature and Culture*, ed. Judith Newton and Deborah Rosenfelt, 165–80. New York: Methuen, 1985.

Ruskin, John. *The Genius of John Ruskin*. Ed. John D. Rosenberg. Boston: Routledge and Kegan Paul, 1979.

Sackville-West, Vita. *Knole and the Sackvilles*. London: W. Heinemann, 1923.

Schaffer, Talia. *The Forgotten Female Aesthetes: Literary Culture in Late-Victorian England*. Charlottesville: University Press of Virginia, 2000.

Schapiro, Meyer. "On Some Problems in the Semiotics of Visual Art: Field and Vehicle in Image-Signs." *Semiotica* 1, no. 3 (1969): 223–42.

Schnapp, Jeffrey. "Crash (Speed as Engine of Individuation)." *Modernism/Modernity* 6, no. 1 (1999): 1–49.

Schwartz, Frederic J. *The Werkbund: Design Theory and Mass Culture before the First World War*. New Haven, CT: Yale University Press, 1996.

Scott, Bonnie Kime. *Refiguring Modernism*. Vol. 1, *The Women of 1928*. Bloomington: Indiana University Press, 1995.

——, ed. *The Gender of Modernism*. Bloomington: Indiana University Press, 1990.

Scott, Geoffrey. *The Architecture of Humanism: A Study in the History of Taste.* 2nd ed. Gloucester, UK: Peter Smith, 1965.

Scott, Gilbert. *Remarks on Secular and Domestic Architecture, Present and Futures.* London: J. Murray, 1857.

Sedgwick, Eve Kosofsky. *Epistemology of the Closet.* Berkeley: University of California Press, 1990.

Sheppard, F. H. W., ed. *The Survey of London.* Vol. 38, *The Museums Area of South Kensington and Westminster.* London: Athlone Press and University of London, 1975.

Shone, Richard. *The Art of Bloomsbury: Roger Fry, Vanessa Bell and Duncan Grant.* London: Tate Gallery, 1999.

——. *Bloomsbury Portraits: Vanessa Bell, Duncan Grant and Their Circle.* Rev. ed. London: Phaidon, 1993.

Showalter, Elaine. *A Literature of Their Own: British Women Novelists from Brontë to Lessing.* Princeton, NJ: Princeton University Press, 1977.

——. *Sexual Anarchy: Gender and Culture at the Fin-de-Siècle.* New York: Viking, 1990.

Simmel, Georg. "The Metropolis and Mental Life." *The Sociology of Georg Simmel.* Ed. Kurt Wolff, 409–24. New York: Free Press, 1964.

Simon, Jacob. *The Art of the Picture Frame: Artists, Patrons and the Framing of Portraits in Britain.* London: National Portrait Gallery, 1996.

Sinfield, Alan. *The Wilde Century: Effeminacy, Oscar Wilde and the Queer Moment.* London: Cassell, 1994.

Smith, Warren Hunting. *Architecture in English Fiction.* New Haven, CT: Yale University Press, 1934.

Snaith, Anna. *Virginia Woolf: Public and Private Negotiations.* Hampshire: Palgrave Macmillan, 2000.

Soros, Susan Weber. *The Secular Furniture of E. W. Godwin.* New York: Bard Graduate Center and Yale University Press, 1999.

——, ed. *E. W. Godwin, Aesthetic Movement Architect and Designer.* New York: Bard Graduate Center and Yale University Press, 1999.

Spalding, Frances. *Duncan Grant.* London: Pimlico, 1998.

——. *Vanessa Bell.* New Haven, CT: Ticknor and Fields, 1983.

Squier, Susan Merrill. "Tradition and Revision: The Classic City Novel and Virginia Woolf's *Night and Day.*" In *Women Writers and the City: Essays in Feminist Literary Criticism,* ed. Susan Merrill Squier, 114–33. Knoxville: University of Tennessee Press, 1984.

Stansky, Peter. *On or About 1910: Early Bloomsbury and Its Intimate World.* Cambridge: Harvard University Press, 1996.

Stephen, Leslie. *The Mausoleum Book.* 1895. Oxford: Oxford University Press, 1977.

Stevenson, J .J. *House Architecture.* Vol. 2, *House-Planning.* London: Macmillan, 1880.

Stewart, Alan. *Close Readers: Humanism and Sodomy in Early Modern England.* Princeton, NJ: Princeton University Press, 1997.

Stone, Lawrence. *The Family, Sex, and Marriage in England, 1500–1800.* New York: Harper, 1979.

Strachey, Lytton. *Eminent Victorians.* Harmondsworth, UK: Penguin, 1948.

——. Letter to Duncan Grant. 6 June 1907. British Library Archives.

——. *Lytton Strachey by Himself.* Ed. Michael Holroyd. New York: Holt, Rinehart, and Winston, 1917.

Thirkell, Angela. *Three Houses.* London: Oxford University Press, 1931.

Thornton, Peter. *Authentic Decor: The Domestic Interior, 1620–1920.* London: Weidenfeld and Nicolson, 1984.

Thorpe, Nigel, ed. *Whistler on Art: Selected Letters and Writings of James McNeill Whistler.* Washington, DC: Smithsonian Institution Press, 1994.

Tickner, Lisa. *Modern Life and Modern Subjects: British Art in the Early Twentieth Century.* New Haven, CT: Yale University Press, 2000.

Tosh, John. *A Man's Place: Masculinity and the Middle-Class Home in Victorian England.* New Haven, CT: Yale University Press, 1999.

Tristram, Philippa. *Living Space in Fact and Fiction.* London: Routledge, 1989.

Twitchell, James B. *Forbidden Partners: The Incest Taboo in Modern Culture.* New York: Columbia University Press, 1987.

Urbach, Henry. "Closets, Clothes, disClosure." In *Desiring Practices: Architecture, Gender and the Interdisciplinary,* ed. Katerina Rüedi, Sarah Wigglesworth, and Duncan McCorquodale, 246–63. London: Black Dog, 1996.

Vidler, Anthony. *The Architectural Uncanny.* Cambridge: MIT Press, 1992.

——. "Bodies in Space/Subjects in the City." *Differences* 5, no. 3 (1993): 31–51.

——. *Warped Space: Art, Architecture, and Anxiety in Modern Culture.* Cambridge: MIT Press, 2000.

Vincent, Gérard. "A History of Secrets?" In *A History of Private Life,* vol. 5, *Riddles of Identity in Modern Times,* ed. Antoine Prost and Gérard Vincent and trans. Arthur Goldhammer. Cambridge: Belknap Press of Harvard University Press, 1991.

Walker, Lynne. "Home and Away: The Feminist Remapping of Public and Private Space in Victorian London." In *New Frontiers of Space, Bodies, and Gender,* ed. Rosa Ainley, 65–75. London: Routledge, 1998.

Walkowitz, Judith. *City of Dreadful Delight: Narratives of Sexual Danger in Late-Victorian London.* Chicago: University of Chicago Press, 1992.

Walshe, Christina. "Post-Impressionism and Suffrage." *Daily Herald,* 25 March 1913.

Watney, Simon. *English Post-Impressionism.* London: Studio Vista, 1980.

Watt, William. *Art Furniture From Designs by E. W. Godwin, F. S. A., and Others.* London: B. T. Batsford, 1877.

Weisman, Leslie Kanes. *Discrimination by Design: A Feminist Critique of the Man-Made Environment.* Urbana: University of Illinois Press, 1992.

Weston, Richard. *Modernism.* London: Phaidon Press, 1996.

Whistler, James McNeill. "To Waldo Story, 5 February 1883. 'Arrangement in White and Yellow' at the Fine Art Society." In *Whistler on Art: Selected Letters and Writings of James McNeill Whistler,* ed. Nigel Thorpe. Washington, DC: Smithsonian Institution Press, 1994.

Wilde, Oscar. *The Complete Letters of Oscar Wilde.* Ed. Merlin Holland and Rupert Hart-Davies. London: Fourth Estate, 2000.

——. *The Letters of Oscar Wilde.* Ed. Rupert Hart-Davies. New York: Harcourt, Brace and World, 1962.

——. *The Collected Works of Oscar Wilde,* vol. 6, *The Importance of Being Earnest.* Ed. Robert Ross. London: Routledge/Thoemmes Press, 1993.

——. *The Collected Works of Oscar Wilde,* vol. 8, *Intentions, The Soul of Man Under Socialism.* Ed. Robert Ross. London: Routledge/Thoemmes Press, 1993.

———. *The Collected Works of Oscar Wilde*, vol. 14, *Miscellanies*. Ed. Robert Ross. London: Routledge/Thoemmes Press, 1993.

———. *The Picture of Dorian Gray*. Ed. Donard L. Lawler. New York: Norton, 1988.

———. "The Soul of Man Under Socialism." In *The Collected Works of Oscar Wilde*, vol. 3, ed. Robert Ross. London: Routledge/Thoemmes Press, 1993.

Williams, Raymond. Culture and Society, 1780–1950. New York: Harper, 1958.

Wilson, Elizabeth. "The Invisible Flâneur." *New Left Review* 191 (January/February 1992): 90–110.

———. *The Sphinx in the City: Urban Life, the Control of Disorder, and Women*. Berkeley: University of California Press, 1991.

Woodward, Kathleen. *Jipping Street: Childhood in a London Slum*. New York: Harper, 1928.

Wolff, Janet. *Feminine Sentences: Essays on Women and Culture*. Berkeley: University of California Press, 1990.

———. "The Invisible Flâneuse: Women and the Literature of Modernity." *Theory, Culture and Society* 2, no. 3 (1985): 37–46.

Woolf, Virginia. *A Room of One's Own*. 1928. Reprint, New York: Harcourt Brace and World, 1945.

———. "The Art of Biography." *The Death of the Moth and Other Essays*. San Diego: Harvest/ Harcourt Brace Jovanovich, 1970. 188–89.

———. *Collected Essays*. Vol. 1. New York: Harcourt, Brace, 1925.

———. *Diary*. Vol. 1. Ed. Anne Olivier Bell. San Diego: Harcourt Brace Jovanovich, 1980.

———. *Diary*. Vol. 3. Ed. Anne Olivier Bell. San Diego: Harcourt Brace Jovanovich, 1980.

———. *Letters*. Vol. 3. Ed. Nigel Nicolson and Joanne Trautmann. New York: Harcourt Brace Jovanovich, 1977.

———. "Modern Fiction." *The Common Reader*. Ed. Andrew McNeillie. San Diego: Harcourt Brace Jovanovich, 1984. 146–54.

———. *Moments of Being*. Ed. Jeanne Schulkind. 2nd rev. ed. San Diego: Harcourt Brace Jovanovich, 1985.

———. *Mrs. Dalloway*. 1925. Reprint, San Diego: Harvest/ Harcourt Brace Jovanovich, 1997.

———. "The New Biography." *Granite and Rainbow*. New York: Harcourt Brace, 1958.

———. *Night and Day*. 1919. Reprint, New York: Harcourt Brace Jovanovich, 1948.

———. *Roger Fry*. San Diego: Harvest/ Harcourt Brace Jovanovich, 1940.

———. "Street Haunting: A London Adventure." *Collected Essays*, vol. 4. New York: Harcourt Brace and World, 1967. 155–66.

———. *Three Guineas*. 1938. Reprint, San Diego: Harvest/HBJ, 1966.

———. *To the Lighthouse*. 1927. Reprint, San Diego: Harvest/HBJ, 1955.

"Would You Let a Child Play in This Nursery?" *Daily Sketch*, 20 December 1913, 9.

Index

Page numbers in italics refer to illustrations.